QUEER OZ

Children's Literature Association Series

QUEER OZ

L. FRANK BAUM'S TRANS TALES
AND OTHER ASTOUNDING
ADVENTURES IN SEX AND GENDER

TISON PUGH

University Press of Mississippi / Jackson

The University Press of Mississippi is the scholarly publishing agency of the Mississippi Institutions of Higher Learning: Alcorn State University, Delta State University, Jackson State University, Mississippi State University, Mississippi University for Women, Mississippi Valley State University, University of Mississippi, and University of Southern Mississippi.

www.upress.state.ms.us

The University Press of Mississippi is a member of the Association of University Presses.

Any discriminatory or derogatory language or hate speech regarding race, ethnicity, religion, sex, sexual orentation, gender, class, national origin, age, or disability that has been retained or appears in elided form is in no way an endorsement of the use of such language outside a scholarly context.

Copyright © 2023 by University Press of Mississippi
All rights reserved

First printing 2023
∞

Library of Congress Cataloging-in-Publication Data

Names: Pugh, Tison, author.
Title: Queer Oz : L. Frank Baum's trans tales and other astounding adventures in sex and gender / Tison Pugh.
Other titles: Children's Literature Association series.
Description: Jackson : University Press of Mississippi, 2023. | Series: Children's literature association series | Includes bibliographical references and index.
Identifiers: LCCN 2022060187 (print) | LCCN 2022060188 (ebook) | ISBN 9781496845313 (hardback) | ISBN 9781496845320 (trade paperback) | ISBN 9781496845337 (epub) | ISBN 9781496845344 (epub) | ISBN 9781496845351 (pdf) | ISBN 9781496845368 (pdf)
Subjects: LCSH: Baum, L. Frank (Lyman Frank), 1856–1919—Criticism and interpretation. | Queer theory. | Homosexuality in literature. | Gender identity in literature. | Sexual orientation in literature. | Transgender people in literature. | Fantasy fiction, American—History and criticism. | Children's stories, American—History and criticism.
Classification: LCC PS3503.A923 Z84 2023 (print) | LCC PS3503.A923 (ebook) | DDC 813/.4—dc23/eng/20230127
LC record available at https://lccn.loc.gov/2022060187
LC ebook record available at https://lccn.loc.gov/2022060188

British Library Cataloging-in-Publication Data available

CONTENTS

Abbreviated Titles of Baum's Works
- IX -

Acknowledgments
- XI -

Introduction: A Primer on L. Frank Baum's Queer Lexicon
- 3 -

Chapter 1. L. Frank Baum's "Progressive Fairies" and the Queerness of Children's Literature
- 17 -

Chapter 2. Trans Tales of Oz and Elsewhere
- 34 -

Chapter 3. Queer Eroticisms in Oz and Elsewhere
- 66 -

Chapter 4. The Queer Creatures of Oz and Elsewhere Eat One Another
- 90 -

Chapter 5. John R. Neill: Illustrator (and Author) of L. Frank Baum's Queer Oz and Elsewhere
- 110 -

Chapter 6. Cultural Projection, Homosocial Adventuring, and the Queer Conclusions of Floyd Akers's Boy Fortune Hunters Series
- 133 -

Chapter 7. Gender, Genres, and the Queer Family Romance of
Edith Van Dyne's Aunt Jane's Nieces Series
- 159 -

Conclusion: Queer Ethics and Baum's Prejudices
- 186 -

Notes
- 193 -

Works Cited
- 205 -

Index
- 217 -

This book is dedicated to
SUSAN ARONSTEIN
and
KENT DRUMMOND,
my fellow wanderers
in Queer Oz,
and to
LAURIE FINKE
and
MARTIN B. SHICHTMAN,
my foster parents in
the Middle Ages.

ABBREVIATED TITLES OF BAUM'S WORKS

American Fairy Tales	*American*
Annabel: A Novel for Young Folks	*Annabel*
Aunt Jane's Nieces	*Nieces*
Aunt Jane's Nieces Abroad	*Abroad*
Aunt Jane's Nieces and Uncle John	*Uncle*
Aunt Jane's Nieces at Millville	*Millville*
Aunt Jane's Nieces at Work	*Work*
Aunt Jane's Nieces in Society	*Society*
Aunt Jane's Nieces in the Red Cross	*Cross*
Aunt Jane's Nieces on the Ranch	*Ranch*
Aunt Jane's Nieces on Vacation	*Vacation*
Aunt Jane's Nieces Out West	*West*
The Boy Fortune Hunters in Alaska	*Alaska*
The Boy Fortune Hunters in China	*China*
The Boy Fortune Hunters in Egypt	*Egypt*
The Boy Fortune Hunters in Panama	*Panama*
The Boy Fortune Hunters in the South Seas	*South Seas*
The Boy Fortune Hunters in Yucatan	*Yucatan*
By the Candelabra's Glare: Some Verse	*Glare*
The Daring Twins: A Story for Young Folk	*Twins*
Daughters of Destiny	*Daughters*
Dorothy and the Wizard in Oz	*Dorothy*
Dot and Tot of Merryland	*Merryland*
The Emerald City of Oz	*Emerald*
The Enchanted Island of Yew	*Yew*
The Fate of a Crown	*Fate*
The Flying Girl	*Flying*
The Flying Girl and Her Chum	*Chum*
Glinda of Oz	*Glinda*
John Dough and the Cherub	*Dough*

The Last Egyptian: A Romance of the Nile	Egyptian
The Life and Adventures of Santa Claus	Santa
Little Wizard Stories of Oz	Little
The Lost Princess of Oz	Lost
The Magic of Oz	Magic
The Marvelous Land of Oz	Marvelous
Mary Louise	Mary
Mary Louise Adopts a Soldier	Soldier
Mary Louise and the Liberty Girls	Liberty
Mary Louise in the Country	Country
Mary Louise Solves a Mystery	Mystery
The Master Key: An Electrical Fairy Tale	Key
Mother Goose in Prose	Goose
Our Landlady	Landlady
Ozma of Oz	Ozma
The Patchwork Girl of Oz	Patchwork
Phoebe Daring	Phoebe
Policeman Bluejay	Bluejay
Queen Zixi of Ix, or The Story of the Magic Cloak	Zixi
Queer Visitors from the Marvelous Land of Oz	Visitors
Rinkitink in Oz	Rinkitink
The Road to Oz	Road
The Scarecrow of Oz	Scarecrow
The Sea Fairies	Sea
Sky Island	Sky
The Songs of Father Goose	Songs
The Surprising Adventures of the Magical Monarch of Mo and His People	Mo
Tamawaca Folks: A Summer Comedy	Tamawaca
Tik-Tok of Oz	Tik-Tok
The Tin Woodman of Oz	Woodman
The Woggle-Bug Book	Woggle-Bug
The Wonderful Wizard of Oz	Wonderful

All italics, punctuation, and spellings in quotations of Baum's fiction are his own. Due to the many editions of the Oz books, citations refer to chapters rather than to page numbers, except for books without chapters, such as *Our Landlady* and *The Woggle-Bug Book*.

ACKNOWLEDGMENTS

I am grateful to the editors and publishers of *Marvels & Tales* and *The Lion and the Unicorn* for permission to republish essays, in substantially revised form, that first appeared in their pages. Chapter 4 was originally published as "'Are We Cannibals, Let Me Ask? Or Are We Faithful Friends?': Food, Interspecies Cannibalism, and the Limits of Utopia in L. Frank Baum's *Oz* Books," *The Lion and the Unicorn* 32, no. 3 (2008): 324–43. Chapter 5 was originally published as "John R. Neill: Illustrator (and Author) of L. Frank Baum's Queer Oz," *Marvels & Tales* 29, no. 1 (2015): 64–86.

QUEER OZ

Introduction

A PRIMER ON
L. FRANK BAUM'S QUEER LEXICON

Let's indulge in a moment of freewheeling and anachronistic queer speculation. Although you surely consider yourself above giving credence to any stereotypes about queer people, perhaps your gaydar would lightly ping if you met a man who traveled with a musical theater company in his youth and returned to this passion later in life. When you discovered that he dabbled in the field of interior design and wrote a how-to manual on the art of window dressing, perhaps it would chime a bit more persistently. If you then learned that this man penned multiple series of novels, including some under female pseudonyms, in which he often eschewed heteronormative conclusions of man and woman united in eternal love, and if you continued reading his works and pondered the staggering number of gender reversals, trans characters, homosocial couples, and other such queer tropes, surely your gaydar would now, honking loudly, assist you in reaching a definitive conclusion. To quote an apropos moment from the film *Clueless*, you would likely determine that your new friend is "a disco-dancing, Oscar-Wilde-reading, Streisand-ticket-holding friend of Dorothy."[1]

But to counterargue these speculative points, the man in question is L. Frank Baum, which necessitates that we recalibrate our gaydars from the early twenty-first century to the turn of the twentieth century, a far different environment for queer people than today's and one in which today's expectations cannot be transported seamlessly to the past. Developing this counterargument, some of Baum's occupations—business owner, newspaper editor—do not fall under longstanding queer stereotypes, and he was by all accounts a happily married man and the devoted father of four sons. But to counterargue this counterargument, some queer tropes, while neither transcultural nor transhistorical, nonetheless appear to be quite enduring, with the theatrical world long providing a refuge for queer people, as even the most cursory examination of William Shakespeare's plays and the seventeenth-century dramatic milieu evinces. Moreover, many queer men married women in the days before (and even after) gay liberation. And so on the question of whether L. Frank Baum was a gay, trans, or otherwise queer man, I must now cease such idle speculation—gaydar does not offer a foolproof tool for literary criticism, and only a fool would apply it too liberally—and simply remain agnostic. On the question of whether L. Frank Baum was and remains an author of extraordinarily queer fictions, I stand firmly convinced. At the very least, in an initial insight that guides the remainder of this volume, he used and created a queer slang lexicon that evinces his knowledge of sexuality's complexity, which is then suggestive that one should examine his works for the queer themes both hidden in their subterranean depths and readily apparent on their surfaces.

BAUM'S QUEER LEXICON IN OZ AND ELSEWHERE

To gauge the full complexity of his fictional worlds, it is essential to note that, while Baum is remembered today primarily for his Oz series, his fantasy fiction extends well beyond this fairyland's borders to include such works as *John Dough and the Cherub*, *Queen Zixi of Ix*, *The Magical Monarch of Mo*, *American Fairy Tales*, and *The Master Key: An Electrical Fairy Tale*, among others. He also published a juvenile fiction series featuring the Daring family—*The Daring Twins: A Story for Young Folk* and *Phoebe Daring*—under his own name, while also employing a host of pseudonyms. For adult audiences, he penned the torrid adventures *The Fate of a Crown* and *Daughters of Destiny* as Schuyler Staunton, and the social comedy *Tamawaca Folks: A Summer Comedy* as John Estes Cook. *The Last Egyptian: A Romance of the Nile* was published anonymously. He also produced a staggering number of children's and juvenile book series under pseudonyms: the six Boy Fortune Hunters novels by Floyd Akers; the ten Aunt Jane's Nieces novels, five Mary Louise novels, and two Flying Girl novels by Edith Van Dyne; and three books for younger readers—*The Twinkle Tales*, *Policeman Bluejay*, and *Twinkle and Chubbins: Their Astonishing Adventures in Nature-Fairyland*—by Laura Bancroft. As Suzanne Metcalf he penned the stand-alone title *Annabel: A Novel for Young Folks*.

Throughout his many novels set in Oz and elsewhere, Baum delights in punning, homophones, and other forms of wordplay, which provides a preliminary clue to his queer lexicon. For example, in *The Life and Adventures of Santa Claus*, the Master Woodman of the World is named Ak, with other characters addressing him respectfully as "O Ak"; these three letters combine to form "oak" (*Santa*, ch. 3 of "Youth," cf. ch. 1 of "Old Age"). The tyrant Kwytoffle in *The Enchanted Island of Yew* is as "quite awful" as his name suggests, and lest any young reader miss the wordplay in the name of the isle of Phreex, a chapter in *John Dough and the Cherub* titled "The Freaks of Phreex" gives a clear clue. *Ozma of Oz* features Princess Langwidere, and a more languid, or "languider," princess could hardly be imagined as she daily preens before her mirrors; her uncle, King Evoldo, sells his wife and children to the Nome King, an evil act by an evildoer. Many, many additional examples of such innocent wordplay could be added to this discussion, but other specimens hint that Baum encoded more ribald fare. Baum knew sufficient French to name the queen of the mermaids Aquareine ("water queen") in *The Sea Fairies* and to assign Madame Leontine, who is "quite short and quite fat," the surname "Grogrande" (*Dough*, ch. 1); thus, he very likely realized that his Baron Merd from *The Enchanted Island of Yew* sounds suspiciously like *merde*, or shit. Traces of sexual vocabulary appear in *The Life and Adventures of Santa Claus* in the character Nuter, "the sweetest-tempered Ryl ever known," (*Santa*, ch. 2 of "Old Age"), with this name approximating "neuter" in its pronunciation.[2] *The Songs of Father Goose* includes "Cootchie Coulou," a short song of a "girl of Hindoo" (*Songs*, 75), and his tale of "Humpty Dumpty" from *Mother Goose in Prose* includes the character "Coutchie Coulou," a brown egg who runs away with Humpty Dumpty only to be crushed under a horse's hoof ("Humpty Dumpty," *Goose*). Given Baum's interest in filmmaking and the many references to Thomas Edison in his fiction (e.g., *Key*, chs. 2 and 4; *West*, ch. 3; *Patchwork*, ch. 7)—it seems probable that he knew of the inventor's 1896 short film *Fatima's Coochee Coochee Dance* and its depiction of belly dancing. It is also likely that he observed this style of dance during the Chicago World's Fair of 1893.

Alongside these rather mild specimens of suggestive punning and allusions, other passages showcase Baum's evocatively queer wordplay. Beginning with his works for adult audiences, Schuyler Staunton's *The Fate of a Crown* features characters named "Lesba" and "Figgot"—which sound provocatively like "lesbian" and "faggot"—and so it is either a truly extraordinary, linguistically stunning coincidence that both these character names appear in a single novel or a clear sign that Baum encoded queer allusions, references, and inside jokes throughout his fiction. In a particularly enigmatic passage found in *Mary Louise in the Country*, one of the juvenile fictions of Edith Van Dyne, the undercover detective O'Gorman registers at a local hotel under the name "Lysander Antonius Sinclair, B.N." By compressing the initials of this rococo name with its spurious degree, readers find L.A.S.B.N., an abbreviation that would be pronounced similarly to "lesbian." "I wonder what the 'B.N.' stands for," wonders one of the hotel employees, with this unanswered question suggesting the spuriousness of the degree but the likelihood of wordplay (*Country*, ch. 21). A male character, O'Gorman/Sinclair is by definition not a lesbian, yet it is then curious that his gender performance registers as queer in his clothes and movements. He is "dressed in a dandified fashion, with tall silk hat, a gold-headed cane and yellow kid gloves," and he walks with "nervous, mincing steps" (*Country*, ch. 23). The *Oxford English Dictionary* defines the verb *mince* as "to walk with short steps and an affected preciseness or daintiness; to walk or move in an affected or effeminate manner."[3] These attributes combine to form the stereotype of the fussy queen, and in another passage the narrator states that O'Gorman/Sinclair "came mincing along from an opposite direction and entered the hotel. He went to his room but soon came down and in a querulous voice demanded his omelet" (*Country*, ch. 23). As with "Lesba" and "Figgot" in *The Fate of a Crown*, the doubled coincidence of a queerly inflected character sporting a name with the initials L.A.S.B.N. suggests, in fact, that this is not a coincidence.

Featuring more rugged versions of queer masculinity than that of Lysander Antonius Sinclair, B.N., Baum's Boy Fortune Hunter series includes in its predominantly male cast of characters Captain Gay, Dr. Gaylord, Dick Steele, and Dick Leavenworth. Two "gay" characters and two "dick" characters stretch one's credulity in simple coincidence, especially with one of these "dicks" hard as steel and the other "dick" signifying its capacity for "rising well." *The Boy Fortune Hunters in Alaska* begins with sailor Ned Britton rescued after his ship founders; he recalls his desperate attempts to survive until finally "makin' at last Andros Isle, where a fisherman pulled me ashore more dead 'n alive" (*Alaska*, ch. 1). Andros Isle is one of the Bahamas, yet its Greek roots in *andro*, meaning *male*, *man*, and *masculine*, hint at a homosocial paradise. Of all the colors of the rainbow, Baum paints the ruler of Bear Center as the Lavender Bear (*Lost*, ch. 15), a shade whose queer connotations trace to the late nineteenth century. *Green's Dictionary of Slang* defines *lavender* as "a euphemism for homosexual and anything referring to homosexuality," with the earliest documented use in 1870.[4] Sometimes a cigar is just a cigar, and sometimes lavender is just a shade of purple; at other times, a cigar represents a penis, and lavender marks a queer. And sometimes in a fairyland one finds a character named Diksey Horner, a name that approximates a tail-end spoonerism of horny dick.[5] If this too should be discounted as simply as a coincidence, then the naysayers must contend with the fact that this character, more than any other of Baum's characters throughout his corpus of dozens and dozens of books, appears especially amorous: "'What's up, Chief?' asked Diksey, winking nineteen times at the nineteen girls, who demurely cast down their eyes because their father was looking" (*Patchwork*, ch. 23). Such is the ambiguity of textual interpretation.

Despite these apparently coded references to sexuality and queerness in Baum's fiction, care must be exercised in interpreting whispered allusions during the period of the early twentieth century, particularly given the ambiguity of queer slang. For example, the *Oxford English Dictionary* attests that the denotation of *lesbian* as a "woman who engages in sexual activity with other women" dates to 1732, which gives credence to a reference to lesbianism in Lesba's name and the initials of Lysander Antonius Sinclair, B.N.[6] Also, the *Oxford English Dictionary* dates the slang meaning of *dick* as *penis* to 1890, even as *Green's Dictionary of Slang* documents this usage decades earlier to 1836; in either instance, it is therefore quite plausible that Baum knew the sexual connotations of this word.[7] On the other hand, the *Oxford English Dictionary*-corroborated denotation of *faggot* as a "homosexual man, sometimes *spec.* one considered to be effeminate" is dated to 1913, but *The Fate of a Crown* was published in 1905.[8] As invaluable a resource as the *Oxford English Dictionary* is, however, it can rarely capture the precise moment when the meaning of a slang word gels into common usage, for by definition slang words loiter in an oral underworld long before seeing the light of day in a duly approved printed source. *Green's Dictionary of Slang* traces the queer history of *faggot* decades, and possibly centuries, earlier: "More feasible is the descent from the 18C use of *faggot* as a pej[orative] for a woman ... (thus playing on homosexual effeminacy), esp. in the derog[atory] form of a 'baggage,' which stems from the faggots that one had to haul to the fire. The abbr[eviation] *fag* may be linked independently to the British public school use *fag*, a junior boy performing menial tasks and poss[ibly] conducting homosexual affairs with the seniors."[9] If Baum knew queer slang and incorporated it into his fiction, the very ambiguity of these words granted him the ability to use them without his readers' parents condemning their salacious denotations.

These linguistic conditions are also evident in, if not exacerbated by, the word *gay*, and thus contribute to the ambiguity concerning any encoded meanings in Captain Gay and Dr. Gaylord's names. The *Oxford English Dictionary* defines *gay* as meaning "of a person. homosexual" but dates this usage to 1929—ten years after Baum's death—as it also hedges with the following caveat: "A number of quotations have been suggested as early attestations of this sense. . . . It is likely that, although there may be innuendo in some cases, these have been interpreted anachronistically in the light either of the context, or of knowledge about an author's sexuality."[10] *Green's Dictionary of Slang* dates the usage of *gay* to refer to homosexuality several years earlier to 1922, in the following passage: "Unless they change the laws, they'll never keep it from being gay. / I had the time, the time of my life, / I found a guy who had another guy for his wife. / Well, where else, but in Chicago."[11] This song locates Chicago as a queer metropolis, and, as discussed briefly in this volume's first chapter, Baum lived there for several years. Furthermore, *gay* also bears the earlier sexual, but not precisely queer, denotation of "persons . . . dedicated to social pleasures; dissolute, promiscuous; frivolous, hedonistic. Also (esp. in *to go gay*): uninhibited; wild, crazy; flamboyant"; this denotation dates to 1597 and was current in Baum's era as well, as in the decade known as the "Gay '90s."[12] One can clearly see this usage in Baum's *The Last Egyptian*, in which he describes Charles Consinor, ninth Earl of Roane, as having led a "gay and dissipated life" (*Egyptian*, ch. 9). In addition to the gay conundrum of Captain Gay and Dr. Gaylord, the Boy Fortune Hunter books include the enigmatically named Nor Ghai—the young Chinese woman with whom protagonist Sam Steele flirts until he clearly states the platonic nature of his intentions. Is this name pronounced as "nor gay"? A female/male couple more queerly named than Gayelette and her husband Quelala can hardly be imagined (*Wonderful*, ch. 14)—or for a single man, Judge Toodles (*Tamawaca*, ch. 7).

Offering a particularly perplexing example of Baum's queer lexicon, *The Enchanted Island of Yew*, published in 1903, features the "Ki-Ki," who are portrayed as "two young men, [with] golden hair combed over their brows and 'banged' straight across; and their eyes were blue and mild in expression, and their cheeks pink and soft" (*Yew*, ch. 14). As Prince Marvel explains of the Ki-Ki and the other inhabitants of this mysterious setting: "in the Land of Twi no person is complete or perfect without its other half, and it seems to take two of you to make one man—or one maid" (*Yew*, ch. 16). The Ki-Ki are thus two young and attractive men linked together for life. The *Oxford English Dictionary* overlooks the word *kiki* entirely, whereas *Green's Dictionary of Slang* defines it as "a homosexual who is equally happy in active or passive sex roles" but dates this usage to 1935.[13] It strains credulity to believe that this word languished in a linguistic underworld for over three decades before its usage could be attested, yet it is equally strange that among all of Baum's magical and unexpected creatures, among his Kalidahs, Mangaboos, Scoodlers, Skeezers, Gillikins, Quadlings, Growleywogs, Winkies, and Pinkies and so many more, the Ki-Ki are two handsome men united for eternity and that this word simply coincides with a later slang term for a versatile gay man. Perhaps a queer man remembered this passage from childhood and introduced it into queer culture as he sought his perfect match, his perfect kiki? Or maybe it really is just a coincidence, and along these lines it should be noted that one of the antagonists of *The Magic of Oz* bears the name Kiki yet without displaying similar hints of queerness. Other intriguing names appear throughout Baum's fictions, raising similar questions: does the character name Omby Amby in *The Emerald City of Oz* suggest the rather queer adjective *namby-pamby*? Mere speculation does not belong in the toolkit of literary criticism, but sometimes informed speculation and wonder are the only tools at hand.

As a final example of this queer lexicon, let us consider the word *queer* itself, which Baum uses energetically throughout his many fictions and for which, in most instances, readers can readily substitute *odd* or *eccentric*. Indeed, as Michelle Ann Abate and Kenneth Kidd document, the word *queer* was used promiscuously throughout children's literature of the late nineteenth and early twentieth centuries: "In children's titles [from this era], the term *queer* appears not infrequently and has a range of associations, among them the strange, the fantastic, the animal, and the aristocratic." They cite myriad titles demonstrating the connection between queerness and children's literature—Harriet Beecher Stowe's *Queer Little People* (1867), E. H. Knatchbull-Hugessen's *Queer Folk: Seven Stories* (1874), Olive Thorne Miller's *Queer Pets at Marcy's* (1880), and Palmer Cox's *Queer People with Wings and String and Their Kweer Kapers* (1895), among others. Abate and Kidd then note that "by the early twentieth century . . . such usage tapered off as *queer* became more pejorative and more closely associated with same-sex attraction and gender-bending behavior."[14]

Baum's affinity for the word *queer* is evident throughout his corpus. Within the opening pages of his iconic work *The Wonderful Wizard of Oz*, readers are deluged with queerness, as Dorothy meets the Munchkins, "the queerest people she had ever seen" (*Wonderful*, ch. 2). She then finds the Scarecrow, who has a "queer, painted face" (*Wonderful*, ch. 3). The four travelers to the Emerald City—Dorothy, the Scarecrow, the Tin Woodman, and the Cowardly Lion—comprise a "queer party" (*Wonderful*, ch. 8), and even Oz itself is queer: "So [Dorothy] told [the Scarecrow] all about Kansas, and how gray everything was there, and how the cyclone had carried her to this queer Land of Oz" (*Wonderful*, ch. 4). At one point during their travels throughout Oz, Dorothy and her friends encounter a young girl who observes, "You have some queer friends, Dorothy," to which the heroine replies, "The queerness doesn't matter, so long as they're friends" (*Road*, ch. 17). In a similar vein, Uncle Henry is one of the series' least marvelous characters because he bears no magical abilities, and considering this point he declares that he and Aunt Em are unlikely citizens in a fairyland: "'Pears to me, Dorothy, we won't make bang-up fairies" (*Emerald*, ch. 5).[15] Nonetheless, he quickly realizes that one must appreciate people as they are in Oz: "This is a queer country, and we may as well take people as we find them" (*Emerald*, ch. 12). In one of Baum's juvenile fictions set in the United States, rural resident Bub uses the word to characterize his mistrust of city folk—"They's someth'n' queer 'bout them, too; but I guess all the folks is queer that comes here from the city" (*Mary*, ch. 22)—but any presumption that Bub assumes all city dwellers are LGBTQ+ veers wildly from Baum's likely meaning. In another example, Kiki and Ruggedo, the antagonists of *The Magic of Oz*, consider mixing the shapes of several animals into a new hybrid creature. Kiki initially resists the idea, asking "Won't that make a queer combination?" to which Ruggedo tersely replies, "The queerer the better" (*Magic*, ch. 7). These examples of Baum's use of the word *queer* do not refer to homosexuality or other enactments of sexual queerness, but they nonetheless create a fictional world in which diversity and uniqueness are esteemed over sameness and uniformity. They also highlight the fundamentally queer drive of children's literature in that it so frequently rejects the banal for the unique. "The queerer, the better" could serve as a slogan for children's literature that lionizes a topsy-turvy and carnivalesque social order. More so, as much as Baum appears to be using *queer* as a synonym for *odd* and *eccentric* in these instances, The *Oxford English Dictionary* dates the meaning of *queer* as "a homosexual; esp. a homosexual man" to 1894, and so the word could never be fully divorced from its increasingly sexual connotations.[16]

The question of a queer lexicon in children's fiction is further complicated by the presumed innocence of the genre, as two side-by-side allusions in *The Emerald City of Oz* demonstrate. During her travels Dorothy visits the town of Bunnybury, and few would dispute the notion that Lewis Carroll's *Alice's Adventures in Wonderland* inspired this scene. In Bunnybury Dorothy encounters a village of rabbits—reminiscent of Alice's encounter with the White Rabbit—and she must shrink down to an appropriate size to enter their land (*Emerald* 201), as did Alice during her explorations of Wonderland. In the front matter of this book, illustrator John R. Neill depicts Dorothy sitting down to tea with a rabbit, which connects this scene to the similar, if more madcap, tea party in Carroll's book. But would readers likewise agree that in depicting Dorothy's journey to Bunnybury, Baum alludes to Oscar Wilde's *The Importance of Being Earnest* and Algernon Moncrieff's imaginary invalid friend Bunbury, whom he cites to avoid unwelcome social obligations? Bunbury's queerness in Wilde's play has been thoroughly excavated: Algernon's ruse allows him to escape the expected duties of kinship and thus to indulge in undetailed activities away from his family's prying eyes, but does the word's undercurrents of anal desire—to bury in the bun—register in Baum's fiction?[17] Furthermore, even if Wilde's Bunbury lodged in the back of Baum's mind, it need not carry in Oz the queer connotations from the play. It is worth remembering, however, that Baum participated in the theatrical world for many years of his life, and thus one would expect theatrical influences on his fiction, and more so, that the theater has long been a site of queer expression. For example, chapter 20 of *The Boy Fortune Hunters in China* is titled "Three Little Maids from School," which clearly alludes to the similarly titled song from Gilbert and Sullivan's *The Mikado*. Given his theatrical experiences, Baum's allusions to Wilde provide further evidence for discerning a cloaked subtext in his fiction.

In a curious and flawed collapse of their fictions and their lives, some authors of children's literature, such as Beatrix Potter and J. M. Barrie, are themselves assumed in the popular imaginary to have been asexual or presexual—as if their interest in children's culture coincided with arrested psychosexual development and thus that their fictions could not carry a trace of mature subtexts. Baum's fictions prove otherwise. With Lesba, Figgot, L.A.S.B.N., "Gay" characters, "Dick" characters, even a "Kiki" and an "Omby Amby," and with *queer* abounding and a Bunbury allusion, Baum was either fully conversant in queer vocabulary or coincidentally prefigured a striking range of queer words. And although Baum in his Edith Van Dyne persona cautions against slang—"ladies do not use [slang words] ... because they soil the purity of our language" (*Country*, ch. 6), slang words, particularly those that would almost certainly be overlooked by their readers, offer authors a means to insert subversive humor and queer subtexts into their fiction. Whereas the above examples exist in linguistic ambiguity but hint strongly that Baum knew of queer slang, in another instance Baum quite possibly created a queer idiom for which he ironically does not receive credit. The phrase "friend of Dorothy" became a shibboleth for many in the mid-twentieth-century US queer community, but *Green's Dictionary of Slang* credits this locution not to Baum's fictions but to Victor Fleming's 1939 film and to Judy Garland's iconic performance as Dorothy. The phrase is defined simply as "a homosexual" and linked to "Dorothy, the character played by Judy Garland (1922–69), an icon for much of the gay world, in the film *The Wizard of Oz* (1939)."[18] Oddly, though, the phrase "friend of Dorothy" is never spoken in the film but appears repeatedly in Baum's books. Tip refers to the Scarecrow as "Another friend of Dorothy's" (*Marvelous*, ch. 3), and the Cowardly Lion states, "Any friend of Dorothy ... must be our friend, as well" (*Dorothy*, ch. 16). Aunt Em asks the Cowardly Lion, "Are you Dorothy's friend?" and the Cowardly Lion replies that, "Had I not known you were Dorothy's friends" (*Emerald*, ch. 7), he would likely have eaten her and Uncle

Henry. The idiom is repeated in Baum's works but absent in the film, which indicates—inconclusively but suggestively—that Baum inadvertently created a gay catchphrase for his queer readers.[19]

Moving forward from this obscured vocabulary that presents challenging questions regarding Baum's recognition and creation of a queer lexicon, the ensuing pages of *Queer Oz: L. Frank Baum's Trans Tales and Other Astounding Adventures in Sex and Gender* explore these and similar queer tensions throughout Baum's corpus, those published both under his own name and under his many pseudonyms. The first chapter, "L. Frank Baum's 'Progressive Fairies' and the Queerness of Children's Literature," provides a short biography of Baum and a historical context for reading his works. Baum viewed his fictions as representing progressive values, but progressivism, as a political ideology of the early twentieth century, was subject to several inconsistencies and ethical lapses, notably in its endorsement of racist policies and practices. Baum's works thus require contextualization both for the historical era of their production and for their negotiations of the genre of children's literature, a field subject to numerous paradoxical conditions in the tension between adult authors and child readers. Scholars of children's literature have increasingly grappled with questions of queer representation in the field, theorizing the intersection of carnivalesque tropes and nonnormative identities based on gender, sexuality, and race, among other such considerations, all of which are pertinent to Baum's corpus.

Building from this contextual foundation of Baum's biography and preferred genre, the second chapter, "Trans Tales of Oz and Elsewhere," assesses his recurrent depictions of trans identities, in which either by magical enchantment or by personal ingenuity, characters change from male to female or from female to male. Additional characters throughout Baum's corpus are painted with what we might term "trans touches," in unexpectedly transgender features noted in an otherwise apparently cisgender character. Escalating Baum's trans themes, some characters thought to be one sex are magically revealed to be another or magically change themselves into another, or avoid the male/female binary altogether, as evident in such fantasy works as *The Marvelous Land of Oz*, *The Enchanted Island of Yew*, *Queen Zixi of Ix*, and *John Dough and the Cherub*. In two of his pseudonymously penned novels—Schuyler Staunton's *The Fate of a Crown* and Edith Van Dyne's *Aunt Jane's Nieces Abroad*—Baum leaves fantasy behind but maintains gender play as a key pathway for transgressive characters to pursue their personal objectives in environments inhospitable to women's agency. As Judith Butler explains of the intersection of gender and ideology,

"The very criterion by which we judge a person to be a gendered being, a criterion that posits coherent gender as a presumption of humanness . . . justly or unjustly . . . governs the recognizability of the human."[20] Gender traps countless individuals into preordained narrative and life plots, but in these quasi-realistic yet still farfetched tales, trans characters revolt against the banal pleasantries expected of women in the fin-de-siècle era, opting instead for the excitement afforded to men who fight gallantly to quell a rebellion or who kidnap American tourists for fun, adventure, and profit.

The following chapter, "Queer Eroticisms in Oz and Elsewhere," begins by investigating the antinormative varieties of masculinity throughout Baum's fictions, including girl-haters, dandies, mollycoddles, and more. From these foundations the analysis turns to the rejection of heteroerotic couples in favor of same-sex friendships throughout Baum's Oz novels, most notably in the strongly homosocial and pointedly antiheteroerotic amatory adventures of the Scarecrow and the Tin Woodman, with the latter resorting to extreme measures to avoid reuniting with his long-lost fiancée. Absences are notoriously difficult to investigate—one cannot examine what one cannot see—yet the very "presence" of absences alerts readers to themes and plotlines that an author chooses to obscure. Such is the case with Baum's fantasyland eroticisms, in which readers must first consider the absence of heteroeroticism to then focus on the muted presence of homoeroticisms and other expressions of desire. This chapter concludes with a brief miscellany of queer and otherwise unexpected identities and desires in Baum's fantasy novels, including split men, fetishists, a masochist, and the enigmatic Shaggy Man, whose Love Magnet makes all people, including a magical craftsman and an ardent gardener, declare their eternal devotions.

The fourth chapter, "The Queer Creatures of Oz and Elsewhere Eat One Another," pursues the unexpected consequences of queerness in establishing the boundaries of Baum's fairy-tale utopias and the characters therein. Even if readers interpret Baum's use of the word *queer* solely for its denotations as the odd, eccentric, and unusual, divorcing it from matters of gender and sexuality, the normative order of his fairylands frequently collapses under the pressures of their topsy-turvy sense of the quotidian. Each creature is queerly unique, or uniquely queer, yet this collective uniqueness, ostensibly a sign of Oz's utopian setting, succumbs to myriad narrative pressures necessitating some measure of tension and conflict. This dynamic is noticeable, both comically and grotesquely, in Baum's frequent turn to consumption and cannibalism as a theme in his fantasy fictions. The shockingly thin line between one's friend and one's food establishes that normativity cannot function in this world, and thus that all creatures cannot uphold any coherent sense of normative identity. Simply put, in a land where everyone is queer, anything can happen—or be eaten.

Moving from texts to pictures, the fifth chapter, "John R. Neill: Illustrator (and Author) of L. Frank Baum's Queer Oz and Elsewhere," examines the illustrator's eroticized depictions of Baum's Oz and other fantasylands. Except for the first book in the series, *The Wonderful Wizard of Oz*, Neill illustrated all of Baum's Oz books, and as Baum's stories showcase a queer and magical wonderland, one that continually flouts cultural constructions of gender and sexual normativity, so too do Neill's illustrations capture its transgressive and marvelous aspects. The vast majority of Neill's drawings faithfully depict, without any hints of erotic undertones, the fantastic quests of Dorothy, the Scarecrow, the Tin Woodman, and Oz's other adventurers, yet other pictures encode vaginal, phallic, and sexual imagery into their accounts of the narrative action, thus troubling the assumed innocence of children's literature. Furthermore, Neill frequently draws the close friendship between the Scarecrow and the Tin Woodman, which Baum describes as a long-term relationship resembling a marriage, with visual double entendre suggesting the erotic aspects of their union. Following Baum's death, Neill wrote four books in the Oz series—*The Wonder City of Oz* (1940), *The Scalawagons of Oz* (1941), *Lucky Bucky in Oz* (1942), and *The Runaway in Oz* (1995, published posthumously); these books adhere to Baum's queer legacy, both narratively and pictorially, while reconceiving some of its erotic foundations.

Titled "Cultural Projection, Homosocial Adventuring, and the Queer Conclusions of Floyd Akers's Boy Fortune Hunters Series," the sixth chapter of this volume explores Baum's six novels featuring young hero Sam Steele and his imperialist adventures across the globe. In Alaska, Panama, Egypt, China, Yucatan, and the South Seas, Sam and his friends vanquish foes and win fortunes, and in a familiar process of Western othering, the boys cast their adversaries in unfavorable terms, in contrast to the narrative praise afforded to the white heroes. This prevalent pattern of denigrating the Other is simultaneously complicated by Sam's attraction to the handsome Indigenous men he encounters. Indeed, he often extols their beauty in rapturous terms, with such scenes counterbalanced by his boyish denigration of women and heteroerotic attraction. In protecting the homosocial foundations of his series, Baum depicts the boys' distaste for heteroerotic attachments, and each of the six novels' conclusions illustrates the thematic challenge of overwriting romance in favor of boy friends united in their pursuit of treasure and their queer commitment to one another.

The final chapter, "Gender, Genres, and the Queer Family Romance of Edith Van Dyne's Aunt Jane's Nieces Series," tackles the adventures of the eponymous heroines—Patsy, Beth, and Louise—and investigates the ways in which Baum, in the years prior to women's enfranchisement, envisions his Progressive Era protagonists as simultaneously liberated from and conditioned to prevailing antifeminist codes. These novels partake of three primary genres—fairy tale, detective novel, and romance—and Baum reframes each of these narrative traditions for young girls of a new generation, all the while remaining hidebound to their conservative features. The series' fairy-tale elements favor a man's fortune over a woman's agency, and its tropes from detective fiction discount the necessity of Patsy, Beth, and Louise to solve the crimes through their keen perceptiveness and intellectual insights. In reformulating romance as an affair for the characters' extended family, these novels illustrate the ways in which heteroerotic attractions threaten the nieces' newfound happiness with one another and with their Uncle John. Narrative penalties are thus meted out to any niece whose interest might be piqued by an attractive young man, negating the desirability of romance in favor of an ultimately queer union with one's extended family.

In the volume's conclusion, titled "Queer Ethics and Baum's Prejudices," the discussion addresses the benefits and liabilities of considering Baum's fictions of foundational significance to the field of queer children's literature. With so many queer and trans themes throughout his works, with his consistent rejection of heteroerotic desire in favor of homosocial friendships and other visions of love and kinship, Baum created a world where queer desires fall within the realm of the normative, yet today's readers cannot overlook his derogatory views of a range of nonwhite and other marginalized peoples, including Hispanics, Blacks, Indigenous Americans, Jews, and Asians. For the most part, these attitudes are apparent in his fantasy works through the uniform whiteness of his human characters, but not in deprecatory assessments of people of color, whose absence registers his lack of interest in creating a diverse fairyland. Further complicating Baum's racial politics, although for Oz he can create new peoples wholly from his imagination, these figures carry traces of racist ideologies in their depiction. More so, in his non-Oz works, casual flashes of cruel language mar his otherwise engaging stories. While readers can ascribe these instances of prejudice to the era in which he wrote, they also call for a deeper understanding of a queer ethics of reading, one that queries the ways in which queerness can propagate alternate ideologies to heteronormativity that nonetheless bolster regimes of whiteness.

Despite these troubling issues, it is clear that Baum's Oz novels have resonated with many LGBTQ+ readers for decades since their publication, with their antinormative themes key to their appeal.[21] Long before Lady Gaga's queer anthem "Born This Way," in which she sings, "God makes no mistakes / I'm on the right track, baby, / I was born this way,"[22] Baum expressed similar themes in his fiction, in which characters accept themselves despite the prejudices of the wider culture. The Cowardly Lion assesses his cowardice and matter-of-factly concludes, "I suppose I was born that way" (*Wonderful*, ch. 6). When the adventurers encounter the Chiss, an overgrown porcupine who shoots his quills into the Patchwork Girl's body, he refuses to halt his attacks: "it is my nature to throw quills, and every animal must do what Nature intends it to do" (*Patchwork*, ch. 12). The Shaggy Man's words resonate with queer meaning—"I think our longings are natural, and if we act as nature prompts us we can't go far wrong" (*Tik-Tok*, ch. 22)—and the Cowardly Lion sounds a paean to individuality and uniqueness: "To be individual, my friends, to be different from others, is the only way to become distinguished from the common herd. Let us be glad, therefore, that we differ from one another in form and in disposition" (*Lost*, ch. 10). While denying any special pride in herself, Dorothy wholly affirms herself: "I've never been 'specially proud of myself, but I'd rather be the way I was born than anything else in the whole world" (*Magic*, ch. 13). The Scarecrow convinces Jack Pumpkinhead, who fears that his ragtag body invites ridicule, to appreciate his uniqueness: "That proves you are unusual . . . and I am convinced that the only people worthy of consideration in this world are the unusual ones. For the common folks are like the leaves of a tree, and live and die unnoticed" (*Marvelous*, ch. 16). Finally, although Baum's omniscient narrator of the Oz series rarely speaks directly to readers, this voice asserts an interest in queerness that is assumed to belong to readers as well: "It was a queerly assorted company, indeed, for there are more quaint and unusual characters in Oz than in all the rest of the world, and Ozma was more interested in unusual people than in ordinary ones—just as you and I are" (*Magic*, ch. 22). You and I like such a queerly assorted company, the narrator asserts, inviting readers to join in the resistance against quotidian conformity. And sharing in this spirit, I invite you to turn the page, for more queer sights to come but also for a clear eye on the concomitant limitations of Baum's queer fictions.

Chapter 1

L. FRANK BAUM'S "PROGRESSIVE FAIRIES" AND THE QUEERNESS OF CHILDREN'S LITERATURE

As the introductory discussion of his queer lexicon establishes, Baum interweaves a range of transgressive and nonnormative erotic possibilities into his fictions, both for juvenile and adult audiences. In so doing, he simultaneously advances a progressive worldview aligned with women's enfranchisement and other forward-looking measures, although this progressivism is undercut by strikingly regressive views of nonwhite peoples; moreover, he addresses these themes while challenging the parameters and meaning of children's literature as a nascent genre. These conflicting tendencies—of advocating themes of openness and acceptance while perpetuating troubling stereotypes, of writing within the constraints of a commercially remunerative subfield of publishing while pushing carnivalesque themes to their utmost—define his career and legacy, both positively and negatively. The striking paradoxes of Baum's fiction require that his works be contextualized within their historical milieu while acknowledging that his antiquated and discriminatory views influence their continued reception in the present, with the objective of more clearly discerning his resonant use of queer themes to challenge prevailing regimes of gender, desire, and sexuality in the United States of America.

 To better situate the queerness of Baum's literature and its cultural context, a brief biographical sketch of the author will set the stage. His parents' seventh child, Lyman Frank Baum was born on May 15, 1856, near Syracuse, New York, to a wealthy family.[1] He suffered from a defective heart as a child and was privately educated until enrolling at the Peekskill Military Academy but left after two years to recommence his education at home. To encourage his son's literary predilections, Baum's father bought him a small printing press, and the family produced their *Rose Lawn Home Journal* throughout the early 1870s. Baum initially pursued his theatrical interests under the stage name George Brooks and in 1878 enjoyed his first success, appearing in

Bronson Howard's *The Banker's Daughter*. During this period he also wrote several plays: *The Macrummins*, *Matches*, and *The Maid of Arran*. In 1881 he met Maud Gage, daughter of prominent feminist Matilda Joslyn Gage; the couple married on November 9, 1882, and over the ensuing years, the Baums welcomed four children: Frank Joslyn, Robert Stanton, Harry Neal, and Kenneth Gage. In 1888 the young family moved to Aberdeen, South Dakota, where Baum opened Baum's Bazaar; it closed in 1890. He then edited the *Aberdeen Saturday Pioneer*, for which he wrote his *Our Landlady* columns. In 1891 the family relocated to Chicago, where he worked for the *Evening Post* and established a trade journal for window dressers, *The Show Window*. Baum's first children's book, *Mother Goose in Prose*, appeared in 1897, with several more produced in rapid succession, including *Father Goose: His Book*, *The Army Alphabet*, and *The Navy Alphabet*. His poetry collection, *By the Candelabra's Glare: Some Verse*, was privately published to little notice. Then, with the publication of *The Wonderful Wizard of Oz* in 1900, his writing career exploded, and dozens and dozens of works appeared over the next two decades, including those written under the pseudonyms of Schuyler Staunton, Suzanne Metcalf, John Estes Cook, Edith Van Dyne, Floyd Akers, and Laura Bancroft. He died on May 6, 1919.

As evident from these pseudonyms and their respective series, Baum perceived subdivisions in the children's literature market: the Laura Bancroft works were envisioned for younger readers of both sexes, the Edith Van Dyne and Suzanne Metcalf works for girl readers, and the Floyd Akers works for boy readers. Baum's pseudonyms, however, are not merely blank placeholders for the author himself; on the contrary, these names were devised to communicate to readers the personalities and backgrounds of their fictive authors. For example, a contract with his publisher records Baum's commitment to "deliver to The Reilly & Britton Company on or before November 15, 1905 six complete children's stories of about 4500 words each, written by him under the pen name of 'Laura Bancroft,' or some female appellation of equally dignified comprehensiveness" (*Bluejay* viii), with these words hinting at the type of woman dreamed up for this female persona. Literary history documents the widespread practice of women adopting male or androgynous pseudonyms—Emily, Charlotte, and Anne Brontë as Ellis, Currer, and Acton Bell; Joanne Rowling as J. K. Rowling—and Baum refers to this practice in his Aunt Jane's Nieces series when Patsy proposes that the cousins publish a local newspaper while cloaking their identities: "You see, by using our initials only, no one will ever suspect we are girls" (*Vacation*, ch. 5). Baum inverted this formula by selecting the female pseudonyms of Edith Van Dyne, Laura Bancroft, and Suzanne Metcalf, even though, as critics such as Mary Cadogan and Patricia Craig rightly caution, "the classification of a book according to the sex of its author or its protagonists can only have a limiting, a cutting-off, effect."[2] Despite this caveat, Baum's prodigious productivity necessitated these many pseudonyms because his publishers worried that parents would hesitate to purchase so many books by the same author for their children. In their advertising materials the publishers could nonetheless point out similarities between the pseudonymous works and those works appearing under Baum's name, as in an advertisement for *The Twinkle Tales* proclaiming, "Several critics who have read *The Twinkle Tales* favorably compare Miss Bancroft's stories to Mr. Baum's works" (*Bluejay* back matter).[3]

Following the breakout success of *The Wonderful Wizard of Oz* in 1900, Baum recognized the commercial potential of creating multiple fiction series, particularly as the contemporary bookselling market demonstrated the financial payoffs of replicating successful formulas. As Paul Deane explains of this commercial genre, "'fiction series' refers to books written by one author (either an actual person using his or her own name or a pseudonym, or a syndicate, such as that of Edward Stratemeyer, producing books under the name of a single non-existent author), involving the same major characters—heroes, friends, parents, villains—in a successive series of actions, scenes, and situations, each complete in itself but continuing the adventures of the major characters"[4] This formula applies to each of Baum's major series—Oz, the Boy Fortune Hunters, Aunt Jane's Nieces, Mary Louise—as well as to his minor and underdeveloped series (the Daring Twins, the Flying Girl), in which he plays a variation on standard narrative themes: Dorothy or another adventurer encountering the odd creatures and unexpected dangers of Oz; Sam Steele and his fellow fortune hunters traveling the world while eluding deadly adversaries and pursuing untold riches; Aunt Jane's nieces and Mary Louise endeavoring to resolve a local problem or solve a perplexing mystery; and so on. Indeed, virtually all of Baum's fiction, particularly the Oz stories, can be read as variations of the quest narrative.[5] Baum profited handsomely from his multiple series, yet he expressed frustration with them as well, most notably in his effort to conclude the Oz books. Similar to Arthur Conan Doyle, who famously killed Sherlock Holmes only to resurrect him in response to readers' demands, Baum depicted Glinda's magical effort to isolate Oz from the rest of the world in *The Emerald City of Oz*, as Dorothy sends a final note to Baum in his role as Oz's "Royal Historian": "*You will never hear anything more about Oz, because we are now cut off forever from all the rest of the world. But Toto and I will always love you and all the other children who love us*" (*Emerald*, ch. 30). A lull of three years followed until Baum responded to his fans' pleas for the continuation of the Oz books; he published *The Patchwork Girl of Oz* in 1913, and a new Oz book was published annually until 1920, with his final installment *Glinda of Oz*.[6]

BAUM'S PROGRESSIVE FICTIONS

Both in his series and in his stand-alone titles, Baum envisioned himself as a progressive voice in children's fiction, as evident in his forewords. He describes *The Wonderful Wizard of Oz*, and by extension the entire series, as "a modernized fairy tale, in which the wonderment and joy are retained and the heartaches and nightmares are left out"; he explains that he will eliminate "the stereotyped genie, dwarf, and fairy . . . together with all the horrible and blood-curdling incidents designed by their authors to point a fearsome moral to each tale" (*Wonderful*, "Introduction").[7] In *American Fairy Tales*, he stresses the modernity and forward-thinking themes of his efforts: "So I am obliged to offer our wide-awake youngsters modern tales about modern fairies, and while my humble efforts must not be compared with the classic stories of my masters, they at least bear the stamp of our own times and depict the progressive fairies of to-day" (*American*, "Author's Note"). Sounding a similar theme, he proclaims in the foreword of *The Master Key: An Electrical Fairy Tale* that it is "a fairy tale founded upon the wonders of electricity and written for children of this generation" (*Key*, "Who Knows?"). Such declarations are striking, for the very timelessness of fairy tales—their "once upon a time" beginnings, their oral transmission over centuries—has long been viewed as key to their charm, yet Baum revises their long-standing foundations to build their appeal for a new and modern generation. His stories typically achieve their "happily ever after" endings yet by evading, rather than embracing, the standard narrative framework of heteroerotic romance, as he also introduces modern machinery and other innovative tropes reflective of his historical moment.[8]

To ponder these issues further, Baum's phrase "progressive fairies" potentially signals his intention to align his narratives with current political issues, for his prolific output coincided with the rise of the Progressive Era in the United States. This far-reaching movement aspired to restructure US society on many levels; Alonzo Hamby summarizes its multiple and overlapping aims: "Above all, the progressives saw themselves as fighters for democracy ('the people') locked in combat with 'the interests' (primarily concentrated corporate and financial power), as crusaders with a moral mission, and as battlers for social justice in relations between the classes. Most shared a vision of citizenship built around the ideal of a common social interest that transcended the goals of economic interest groups; they wanted a larger role for the state in advancing that common interest."[9] While not speaking of progressivism's connection to fairy tales, Michael McGerr nevertheless links the movement to utopianism, a key subtheme of fantastic literature: "Progressivism, the creed of a crusading middle class, offered the promise of utopianism," he argues; its advocates sought to achieve this vision through its "stunningly broad agenda that ranged well beyond the control of big business, the amelioration of poverty, and the purification of politics to embrace the transformation of gender relations, the regeneration of the home, the disciplining of leisure and pleasure."[10]

Many of Baum's biographers align him with progressive political causes. Katharine M. Rogers avows that "Baum's Oz reflects the thinking of progressive contemporaries who were appalled by the misery produced by exploitative big business, industrialization and wide class distinctions."[11] In an amusing incident illustrating Baum's support of progressive economics and his distaste for monopolistic capitalism taken from his fiction, the young adventurer Trot, while journeying underseas, insults an octopus upon making its acquaintance: "Why, ev'rybody knows that octopuses are jus' wicked an' deceitful.... Up on the earth, where I live, they call the Stannerd Oil Company an octopus, an' the Coal Trust an octopus." Mistaken for a rapacious corporation, the distraught octopus defends the innocence of her species: "Just because we have several long arms, and take whatever we can reach, they accuse us of being like—like—oh, I cannot say it! It is too shameful—too humiliating!" (*Sea Fairies*, ch. 9). John D. Rockefeller, founder of Standard Oil, likely never felt the sting of Baum's satire, yet Trot's words align Baum with a progressive worldview suspicious of such concentrated wealth and power. Baum's *The Daring Twins* features another such antimonopolistic moment, when Mr. Ferguson, the Darings' family lawyer, explains that the children's honest and honorable father lost his fortune by spurning the invitation to join a beet-sugar cartel: "He refused, believing such a trust unjust and morally unlawful" (*Twins*, ch. 2). In a famous but debunked reading of *The Wonderful Wizard of Oz* as a populist allegory, Henry Littlefield linked the Scarecrow to farmers and the Tin Woodman to industrial workers, traveling with the Cowardly Lion (representing William Jennings Bryan) to the Emerald City (Washington, DC) to confront the Wizard (President William McKinley)—although he conceded that the "analogies outlined" in his essay "are admittedly theoretical."[12] His theory nonetheless testifies to an interpretive tendency to align Baum's fictions with progressivism, even when unmerited.

While in the main Baum's fictions support a progressive worldview, it is also true that various moments of his fiction appear notably elitist, even snobbish, and not merely in the focus on the queens and kings in his fairy tales. When Will, the plucky protagonist of *Annabel*, plans to seek employment in the local steelworks, his mentor Dr. Meigs envisions a more auspicious future for the boy: "You're going to be more than a mere laboring man when you grow up, Will Carden, and I don't mean to let you get into those beastly mills" (*Annabel*, ch. 4). In *Mary Louise Solves a Mystery*, Mary Louise is puzzled that her friend Alora's father could be so rude and uncultured, but by the novel's end she has proved him an imposter and identified Alora's true father: "Mary Louise came back, leading by the hand a tall, handsome gentleman who bore in every feature, in every movement, the mark of good birth, culture, and refinement" (*Mystery*, ch. 25). Few phrases carry as much social snobbery as "the mark of good birth," with this novel deploying it to celebrate the victory of an aristocratic man over his (admittedly nefarious) "social inferior." Moreover, some of Baum's proposals in his fiction appear not merely regressive in their politics but nearly fascist, such as in a frightening passage prefiguring the internment of Japanese Americans during World War II. Girl detective Josie O'Gorman, seeking to identify a local saboteur, advocates mass imprisonment for German and Austrian Americans during World War I: "A lot of these Germans and Austrians are liberty-loving Americans, loyal and true, but we must round up the innocent many, in order to squelch the guilty few" (*Liberty*, ch. 10). No one rebuts her viewpoint.

Baum's thematic consideration of women's rights is marked by similar paradox and contradiction, and so determining a consistent viewpoint remains elusive. For the most part, he heartily endorses women's suffrage, arguing that Americans "must do away with sex prejudice and render equal distinction and reward to brains and ability, no matter whether found in man or woman" (*Landlady*, 42). Sairy Ann Bilkins, the eponymous boardinghouse proprietor of his *Our Landlady* columns, pinpoints the chief objection to the women's vote: "It's the conceit o' men as is the biggest stumblin' block ter universal sufferin' o' women!" (*Landlady*, 43). Baum's "progressive" fairy tales and other fictions, however, both endorse and undercut women's equality. Following their marvelous journey to the ocean's depths in *The Sea Fairies*, Trot and Cap'n Bill fly to the heavens in *Sky Island*, where they encounter the Pinkies, a people who have achieved perfect equity between the sexes: "In this country the women seemed fully as important as the men, and instead of being coddled and petted, they performed their share of the work, both in public and private affairs, and were expected to fight in the wars exactly as men did" (*Sky*, ch. 15). On other occasions, however, women's full participation in the civic sphere is presented more ambiguously, such as in a particularly vexed passage in *Phoebe Daring*. Cousin Judith, who serves as the adoptive mother of the Daring children, rejects women's emancipation and the suffragettes: "The women of Riverdale haven't organized the army militant, I'm glad to say; for I've an idea I would never join it." In response, her cousin, the state governor, argues, "You're wrong.... The women of the world will dominate politics, some day, and you mustn't be too old-fashioned in your notions to join the procession of progress" (*Phoebe*, ch. 12). At the very least, a sharp irony arises in a man explaining to a woman—"mansplaining," in today's parlance—that she should support her own enfranchisement. Edith Van Dyne's Flying Girl books showcase a new vision of female daring and bravery in aviator Orissa Kane, with this passage capturing their gendered contradictions: "Most girls would have been bewildered by the technicalities and passed the drawings with a glance; but Orissa understood how important to them all this venture was destined to be, so she sat down and studied the designs minutely, making her brother explain anything she found the least puzzling" (*Flying*, ch. 2). Orissa stands as the exception to female bewilderment, yet even she relies on her brother to explain aviation's finer points. Baum and many other early twentieth-century progressivists expressed such revolutionary beliefs that were nonetheless undercut by regressive viewpoints, a fact strikingly evident in the movement's treatment of race.

PROGRESSIVE POLITICS AND RACIST THEMES IN BAUM'S FICTION

The chief ethical failure of US progressivism arose in its embrace of blatantly racist policies, evident in, as McGerr notes, the movement's efforts for the "establishment of segregation."[13] President Woodrow Wilson and his circle embodied this moral flaw in contemporary progressivism, advocating a range of forward-thinking proposals while defending and endorsing flagrantly racist policies, such as in the purging of Black employees from the federal government.[14] Troubling instances from Baum's corpus illustrate the racist limits of his progressive worldview, as notoriously evident in his editorial in the *Aberdeen Saturday Pioneer* of January 3, 1891, that called for the genocide of Indigenous Americans: "The *Pioneer* has before declared that our only safety depends upon the total extermination of the Indians. Having wronged them for centuries we had better, in order to protect our civilization, follow it up by one more wrong and wipe these untamed and untamable creatures from the face of the earth."[15] Some readers have defended Baum's intentions with this essay, viewing it as a satire that demands white Americans to confront their own savagery against Native populations. Reneau H. Reneau advocates this viewpoint: "Baum was obviously disgusted by the betrayal and slaughter of the Indian peoples, and used a deliberate technique to shake his readers into the recognition of what the white man was really doing."[16] On the other hand, readers such as Robert W. Venables cannot discern a satiric impulse in his words, despite their efforts on his behalf. "I've tried to read his editorials as satire or parody. . . . They aren't. . . . [T]heir core message is genocide," he concludes, as he then ponders the paradox of genocidal instincts in an otherwise genial person: "Like so many humans who are capable of uttering and doing the unthinkable, L. Frank Baum was in many respects a sensitive and loving man."[17] At best, Baum's essay fails as satire, for if readers cannot discern whether it targets its white readers or their Indigenous American neighbors, it mounts a confused argument. Jonathan Swift's "A Modest Proposal" offers an apt comparison: if some readers of this masterwork become convinced that Swift is advocating the cannibalism of Irish babies rather than the right of Irish self-determination and the need for national unity, they misread Swift's irony as his sincerity, and thus miss his point altogether. In contrast, Baum's editorial admits both readings, although any sympathetic readings of his intentions must chafe against the grain of his words.

Furthermore, most of Baum's references to Indigenous Americans in his fictions depict them with familiar stereotypes as slyly furtive and murderously aggressive. In his *Our Landlady* newspaper columns, Baum's Sairy Ann Bilkins refers to Native Americans as "red demons" (*Landlady*, 145) and for Thanksgiving expresses her gratitude that "the Injins haven't tommyhawked us yet" (*Landlady*, 141). Slurs against Indigenous Americans appear in his works for young children, such as his retelling of "The Woman Who Lived in a Shoe," in which the woman's many grandchildren "all painted their faces, to look as Indians do when they are on the warpath" (*Goose*). An Italian bandit in the United States—a problematic stereotype in itself—mentions, "I have been told these Americans are painted Indians, who are bloodthirsty and terrible" (*American*, "The Box of Robbers"). In his fiction for boys, Indigenous Americans are used metaphorically to suggest slyness and duplicity, such as in the phrase "stealthy as . . . an Indian" (*Egypt*, ch. 1), a sentiment similarly expressed as "With all the caution of the American savage, these Turks approached the tree" (*Key*, ch. 13).

Baum's anti-Semitism further exemplifies his prejudices and the ways in which they seep into his fiction. Although Jews rarely appear in Baum's writings, and although his fantasy novels are mostly unconcerned with issues of religious identity and do not encode a christological allegory (such as in

C. S. Lewis's *Chronicles of Narnia*), the rare occasions of Jewish presence are larded with long-standing stereotypes, as particularly evident with the character David the Jew in *Daughters of Destiny*, one of Baum's Schuyler Staunton novels. The very fact that he is referred to as "David the Jew"—as in the title of chapter 11, "Capture of David the Jew"—marks him as defined by his difference from the novel's white, Christian protagonists. The plot unfolds in Baluchistan, a fictional nation located in an ambiguous zone between Europe and Asia, as American capitalists seeking to secure railroad rights require the assistance of a local resident amidst their bewildering new surroundings. Baum typecasts David as an avaricious Jew, whom Colonel Moore hires by appealing to his greed: "This is real wealth, David—good yellow gold. And it shall all be yours, with an equal sum added to it, if you consent to serve us faithfully" (*Daughters*, ch. 11). Allison Moore, the colonel's son, senses David's double-dealing—"You're making money, fast, you dirty pig of a Jew" (*Daughters*, ch. 17)—and his lover Maie concurs: "Gold is his only master" (*Daughters*, ch. 12). Aunt Lucy sees through David's obsequious ploys and recognizes his intelligence, yet stereotypes twist even positive features into negative ones: "He's playing possum. You mark my words, that Jew's no fool. If he was, he wouldn't be a Jew" (*Daughters*, ch. 11). In this antisemitic realm, David profits from his role of unscrupulous double-dealer—"De easiest t'ing in de vorlt to sell . . . iss secrets!," he proclaims (*Daughters*, ch. 17)—with his heavily accented speech further marking him as the Other in this land, even more so than the Americans who have only recently arrived. When he betrays the secret of Allison and Maie's forbidden romance, the two are murdered, yet Maie obtains revenge from beyond the grave by arranging for a scorpion to be delivered to him. In *Aunt Jane's Nieces Out West*, set during Hollywood's foundational years, Mr. Goldstein represents an early instance of the stereotype of the Jewish film producer more concerned with costs than kindness. (In complementary contrast to the villainous David and grasping Mr. Goldstein, Abe Kauffman of *Mary Louise and the Liberty Girls* is presumed to be a conspirator against the United States by girl detective Josie O'Gorman, yet in line with Baum's consistent portrayal of girl detectives failing to solve the mysteries before them, she accuses him with insufficient evidence and fails to identify the true culprit—the local school superintendent.)

Concomitant with the ways in which the queerness of much of children's literature has been obscured by authorial coding and cultural presumptions of heterosexual normativity, so too have many racist elements of children's literature been overlooked by authorial coding and cultural presumptions of normative whiteness, particularly when cloaked under an author's otherwise progressive sensibilities. Toni Morrison powerfully denounces the "willed scholarly indifference" to depictions of race in American literature,[18] and Ebony Elizabeth Thomas pillories the "imagination gap" that continues to this day in the field of children's literature and its long history of foregrounding whiteness and marginalizing characters of color.[19] Robin Bernstein examines how "the idea of childhood innocence and the bodies of living children have historically mystified racial ideology by hiding it in plain sight,"[20] and Philip Nel explicates in *Was the Cat in the Hat Black? The Hidden Racism of Children's Literature and the Need for Diverse Books* the ways in which Dr. Seuss's books "reveal [his] racial unconscious, indicating how his imagination resuscitated and revised early twentieth-century stereotypes."[21] All of these ideas powerfully circulate around Baum's fictions and their reception both in the past and today: that his problematic depictions of race and ethnicity have been overlooked by the scholarly community; that his "imagination gap" is evident in the foregrounding of whiteness as an unquestioned norm of civilization, even in his fairylands; that his treatments of race are nonetheless evident as they "hide in plain sight"; and that his novels expose his racial unconscious and his repackaging of troubling contemporary tropes.

At first glance, it might appear that Baum's fantasy worlds mostly evade racial issues, for few readers would likely take offense at such antagonists and strange beings as angry Nomes, Goozzle Goblins, and Scoodlers. Nonetheless, the volumes tacitly valorize the blanket whiteness of their human protagonists, and Baum depicts many of his fantastic creatures as belonging to races, thus introducing an allegory of racial distinctions in books that, on their surface, avoid such topics. In *The Wonderful Wizard of Oz*, mention is made of "a race of queer men who do not like strangers to cross their country" (ch. 18); in *The Marvelous Land of Oz*, the Woggle-Bug states, "Jackdaws are the greatest enemies of my race" (ch. 18); and in *Ozma of Oz*, the narrator records Dorothy's encounter with Wheelers in racial tones, in which she "first caught sight of the first individual of a race that was destined to cause her a lot of trouble" (ch. 3). Race thus serves as an organizing and taxonomical principle among the various beings of Oz, and it merges with contemporary racism with Baum's Tottenhots—with obvious wordplay on the Hottentots, the Dutch term for the Khoikhoi people of South Africa—who are derived from biased visions of Black Africans: "Their skins were dusky and their hair stood straight up, like wires, and was brilliant scarlet in color. Their bodies were bare except for skins fastened around their waists and they wore bracelets on their ankles and wrists, and necklaces, and great pendant earrings" (*Patchwork*, ch. 19). More so, Baum's Tottenhots are conceived as a less evolved form of humanity, as evident when Glinda transforms the goat Bilbil into the human Prince Bobo: "Glinda was not discouraged, however, but by a powerful spell transformed the ostrich into a tottenhot—which is a lower form of man. Then the tottenhot was transformed into a mifket" and then into a prince (*Rinkitink*, ch. 22). Racist themes intrude into the fantasy land of Merryland when one candy-man character laments the laziness of his "colored servants": "One of our greatest troubles is that we cannot depend upon our colored servants, who are chocolate. Chocolates can seldom be depended on, you know" (*Merryland*, ch. 8). *The Magical Monarch of Mo* includes "a monstrous Gigaboo," with the narrator asserting that "scientists say these creatures are by nature destructive, and love to ruin everything they come across" (*Mo*, ch. 8).[22] In a short story set in Africa, Baum refers to "the oily odor of black people" (*American*, "The Laughing Hippopotamus"), and when, in *The Enchanted Island of Yew*, Prince Marvel must confront Terribus's wrestler, a "tall blackamoor," the Prince recoils: "I beg your Majesty will not compel me to touch him . . . for his skin is greasy, and will soil my hands" (*Yew*, ch. 9).

Further underscoring the racist undercurrents of Baum's progressivism, Black characters appear in Baum's nonfantasy novels primarily in the role of domestic servants who insist on refusing payment for their services, which construes them as willingly enslaved. Aunt Hyacinth in the Daring Twins series and Aunt Sally in the Mary Louise series are depicted in the "mammy" tradition (*Phoebe*, ch. 11; *Liberty*, ch. 2; *Soldier*, ch. 8). The epithet "aunt" suggests that these characters are envisioned as beloved family members, in a likely well-intended gesture that quickly devolves into caricatures who speak in an exaggerated dialect and proclaim their distaste for their salaries. Aunt Hyacinth protests, "Ol' Marse allus done pay me mo' wages 'n I could earn, nohow. I ke' sayin' I didn' want no money; but he insis', childe; dat ol' Marse Wallace insis' I take all he guv me" (*Twins*, ch. 6). In the Mary Louise novels, the narrator introduces Aunt Sally and Uncle Eben with similarly regressive tropes: "Their servants consisted of an aged pair of negroes named 'Aunt Sally' and 'Uncle Eben,' who considered themselves family possessions and were devoted to 'de ole mar'se an' young missy'" (*Liberty*, ch. 6). Baum includes a scene in which Mary Louise takes offense at racism, when the storekeeper Mr. Jerrems wonders why she is purchasing dinner plates: "Thought ther' was plenty o' dishes in that place. . . . But p'r'aps ye don't want the black folks t' eat off'n the same things ye do yerselves." In response to Mr. Jerrems's bigotry, as the narrator reports, "Mary Louise ignored this speech and selected the dishes she wanted" (*Country*, ch. 4). Hardly a fierce advocate of racial equality, Mary Louise leaves Mr. Jerrem's bigotry unchallenged, with Baum overlooking how this scene undercuts the moral authority his heroine otherwise embodies.

Baum frequently uses the N-word, particularly in his adventure novels (e.g., notably *The Boy Fortune Hunters in Alaska*, and also *Egypt*, ch. 1), yet it appears in his fantasy fiction, too. It is particularly jarring to hear this ugly word in the mouths of child characters, such as when young Allerton Randolph explains to his sister the source of their parent's marital discord: "It's true, Doris. Father detests [their mother's religiosity] with all his heart, and says our mother has ruined his home for a lot of naked n-----s in Africa" (*Twins*, ch. 3). Baum saw no contradiction in including this ugly word in his Edith Van Dyne books, despite the genteel implications of this aristocratic pseudonym. Although the Mary Louise series was advertised as "wholesome without being tiresome, and full of action without being sensational" (*Mary*, "To Young Readers,"), it includes the word on several occasions (*Mary*, ch. 5; *Country*, chs. 1 and 8; *Soldier*, ch. 16), as does the Aunt Jane's Nieces series (*Millville*, ch. 19). Baum's characters also apply the N-word to a range of nonwhite cultures and ethnicities, including Arabs, Begas, and Egyptians (e.g., *Egypt*, ch. 15; *Egyptian*, chs. 16 and 19).

More so, in Baum's quasi-realist fiction for children and adults, disturbing stereotypes are frequently launched at a range of human ethnic groups and racial minorities. As the flawed concept of "the Orient" and "the Oriental" showcases the ways in which Western culture overlooks racial and ethnic differences across the vast stretch of Asia in favor of a universalized Other, Baum's characters Bryonia and Nux in the Boy Fortune Hunter series highlight the plasticity of race yet the endurability of racist tropes. These men are described alternatively as Black, as Southeast Asians (specifically, as Malaysians and as Filipinos), and as Pacific Islanders. Series protagonist Sam Steele first says that Bryonia and Nux "were natives of some small island of the Sulu archipelago, and their history was a strange one" (*Alaska*, ch. 5); the Sulu archipelago is located in the Pacific Ocean, in the southwestern Philippines. Contradictions accrue: "Although these men were dark-skinned they were not negroes, but belonged to a branch of the Malay race. Their hair was straight, their noses well formed and their eyes very expressive and intelligent. The English they had picked up from the crew, however, was spoken with an accent not unlike that peculiar to the African negroes, but with a softer and more sibilant tone" (*Alaska*, ch. 5). Sam later qualifies his earlier statement of the men's ethnicity and declares, "It was the language of their own island of Tayakoo, for these were not properly Sulus but natives belonging to a distinct tribe of South Sea Islanders which owed allegiance to no other ruler than their own" (*Panama*, ch. 8). Later, Sam says that Nux and Bryonia "were gigantic blacks; not negroes of the African type, but straight-haired ebony fellows who were natives of some island in these very seas where we were now sailing" (*South Seas*, ch. 4). These contrasting assertions concerning Nux and Bryonia's homeland expose Baum's lack of concern for geographical detail, and additional comments take these men farther afield from their roots. Uncle Naboth likens Nux and Bryonia to Native Americans—"They're civilized Injuns, now, an' their life on shipboard is luxury compared to what they used to have" (*South Seas*, ch. 4)—and Sam connects them to Africans: "I have often thought the desert Moors the nearest approach to them of any people I have ever seen" (*South Seas*, ch. 4). This hodgepodge of racial and ethnic descriptors for Bryonia and Nux underscores Baum's desire to depict them as distinct from his white characters, all the while exposing, if inadvertently, the ways in which race is a cultural and imaginative construction reflective of individual decisions rather than somatic truths.

As the racist elements of Baum's fiction (of which many more examples will be examined throughout this volume) undercut his otherwise progressive viewpoints, they also point to the historical moment of their creation, when such bigotry was insufficiently challenged—and indeed, often reinforced—by the nation's white power structures. To contextualize the racist tropes of Baum's fiction is not to exculpate the author or his works, but such a historical backdrop is likewise essential for understanding his provocative treatment of queer themes. For, as Siobhan Somerville so richly documents, race and sexuality were interrelated in their ideological construction during this era: "nascent models of sexual inversion and homosexuality in the 'expert' discourse of sexology were entwined in various ways with the logic of American scientific racism."[23] These discourses of sexology, and their concomitant treatments of race, appear in a range of surprising ways in Baum's fictions, despite the presumed strictures of children's literature as a genre.

L. FRANK BAUM AND THE QUEERNESS OF CHILDREN'S LITERATURE

Given such a prodigious output across a spectrum of genres, and for a range of readers of various ages, and under a variety of masculine and feminine personas, Baum could hardly have avoided the topic of human sexuality, which surfaces oddly—and to use one of his preferred words, *queerly*—in a range of surprising circumstances. Baum's young adult years in the late nineteenth century coincided with the rise of sexology in the Western world, as a cascade of studies heightened awareness of the complexity of human sexuality, including such trailblazing works as Jacques-Joseph de Tours's *Des aberrations du sens genesique* (1880), Valentin Magnan's *Des anomalies, des aberrations, et des perversions sexuelles* (1885), Julien Chevalier's *De l'inversion de l'instinct sexuel au point de vue medico-legal* (1885), Paolo Mantegazza's *Gli amori degli uomini* (1886), Richard von Krafft-Ebing's *Psychopathia Sexualis* (1886), Benjamin Ball's *La folie erotique* (1888), and Albert Moll's *Die Contraire Sexualempfindung* (1891). Havelock Ellis began publishing his multivolume *Studies in the Psychology of Sex* in 1897; the final volume appeared in 1928. Sigmund Freud published his first work, *On Aphasia*, in 1891; *Three Essays on the Theory of Sexuality* appeared in 1905, and considerably more studies were distributed until his death in 1939. As Scott Herring observes of these works and others of their ilk, "words and phrases such as *inversion, fetishism* (or *fetichism*), *sadism, masochism, eroto-mania, psychical hermaphroditism, congenital sexual inversion,* and *homosexuality* proliferate," with this "sexological argot quickly filter[ing] into European and American middle-class societies."[24]

The lion's share of these works addresses adult sexuality, yet several texts adumbrate children's sexuality as well, even if elliptically, and children's sexuality was treated in the juvenile fiction of the day, even if only more elliptically. Eric Tribunella's recuperative and archival work on Edward Prime-Stevenson's *Left to Themselves: Being the Ordeal of Philip and Gerald* (1891) brings to light the ways in which queer themes of "Uranian adolescence" surfaced in children's fiction published a decade prior to Baum's novels, and Tribunella rightly cautions, "Children and depictions of children usually do not conform to expectations of normative, heterosexual, dyadic, genital relations, and the sexual categories that are operative in adult culture typically do not apply to children and can even obscure the desires, pleasures, and possibilities of childhood."[25] Moreover, Baum's fiction has "long been associated with psychoanalytic culture," as Kenneth Kidd documents, as he details the range of theorists and practitioners decoding the novels' meanings and applying their findings to the field.[26] Derritt Mason posits that many texts of children's and young adolescent culture depict a range of "latent queernesses that provide powerful opportunities for reading in all kinds of creative, nonnormative ways."[27] As the pages of this volume illustrate, a surprising number of such queernesses finds their ways into Baum's fictional works, despite his status as a preeminent author of children's literature.

Because early twentieth-century children's literature written by Baum and other authors revels in contradictions and paradoxes, in the carnivalesque and the comic, and in upside-down worlds where children's moral authority often outweighs that of the adults, readers should overlook its apple-cheeked veneer of plucky innocence and ponder its deeper investments in questioning the culture from which it arose.[28] Steven Bruhm and Natasha Hurley argue that, in creating a piece of children's literature, authors inculcate children into an ideological system: "If writing is an act of world making, writing about the child is doubly so: not only do writers control the terms of the worlds they present, they also invent, over and over again, the very idea of inventing humanity, of training it and watching it evolve."[29] Children's narratives frequently envision topsy-turvy settings where readerly expectations are tweaked, and Alison Lurie perceives a subversive quality in the genre, because these stories "recommended—even celebrated—daydreaming, disobedience, answering back, running away from home, and concealing one's private thoughts and feelings from unsympathetic grown-ups. They overturned adult pretensions and made fun of adult institutions."[30] At the same time, subversive features of children's literature are often tamed by the narrative's end when a return to ideological and cultural normalcy is effected. Much children's literature thus appears congruent with theoretical conceptions of the carnivalesque, an overturning of social structures and decorum that stimulates momentary release from the status quo yet ultimately reinforces the status quo.[31] Umberto Eco acknowledges that the return to normalcy after a carnivalesque eruption tames any momentary offences of their revolutionary potential: "comedy and carnival are not instances of real transgressions: on the contrary, they represent paramount examples of law reinforcement."[32] Even in overtly queer children's literature, Roberta Seelinger Trites identifies a tension in which "homosexuality seems at once enunciated and repressed," an apt assessment of the ways in which children's literature breaks some taboos in its carnivalesque revels while upholding others.[33] No matter how much explosive fun has been unleashed in children's literature, its target audience of young readers is smart enough to realize that, even after enjoying *The Cat in the Hat*, they are still expected to clean their rooms.

But who are these young readers? Children's literature and the field of children's literature studies continually confront the mystery of the so-called child at their heart. In her classic study *The Case of Peter Pan, or the Impossibility of Children's Fiction*, Jacqueline Rose exposed the contradictions constitutive of the genre, in that "children's fiction sets up a world in which the adult comes first (author, maker, giver) and the child comes after (reader, product, receiver), but where neither of them enter the space in between."[34] Further studies by such scholars as Karin Lesnik-Oberstein, Perry Nodelman, and Michelle Ann Abate have enhanced our understanding of the crosscurrents between children and adults involved in the construction and consumption of children's literature, pointing out the inherent paradox of the genre and the conflicted status of "the child" in cultural discussions.[35] Adding to these contradictions, the child is a phantom construction, subject to shifting cultural mores and demands, with a range of ideological issues centered on the protection and promotion of childhood, as well as the exclusions that inevitably crop up alongside these protected and ostensibly fragile young humans.[36] Robin Bernstein powerfully explicates children's active role in creating meaning through literature and play,[37] and Marah Gubar delineates the utility of kinship-model theories, proposing that "though the categories of 'child' and 'adult' neatly carve up the human community into two separate classes of people," theories of kinship "try to counteract that tendency by stressing the gradual, erratic, and variable nature of the developmental process."[38] Finally, to posit a theoretical construction of childhood requires, to some degree or another, positing a theoretical construction of adulthood, and scholars have similarly grappled with defining this key term.[39]

Complicating matters further, while children are recognized as gendered beings—for trans children, sometimes coercively so—they are much less frequently recognized as beings with sexual orientations. As a consequence, children's literature studies has succeeded marvelously in uncovering the gendered contours of the field, in such trailblazing studies as Kimberley Reynolds's *Girls Only? Gender and Popular Children's Fiction in Britain, 1880–1910*, Roberta Seelinger Trites's *Waking Sleeping Beauty: Feminist Voices in Children's Novels*, Beverly Lyon Clark's *Regendering the School Story: Sassy Sissies and Tattling Tomboys*, and Kenneth Kidd's *Making American Boys: Boyology and the Feral Tale*. Queerness remains more elliptical, more ephemeral to trace, because the question of children's sexuality is largely overlooked in the narrative action of many works yet spectrally appears only under closer examination. Many child characters are simply depicted as presexual or asexual, but it should not be overlooked that the presumed asexuality of children is itself an ideological construction. Kathryn Bond Stockton outlines the paradox of describing children's sexuality: "Children, as children, cannot be 'gay'—our culture, at least officially, presumes—a category deemed too adult since it is sexual. And yet, to forbid a child this designation uncovers contradictions in the public discourse on childhood sexual orientation: the general cultural and political tendency to officially treat *all* children as straight, while continuing to deem them asexual."[40] Children's literature thus sets up oppositional expectations: given its ostensible innocence, one should not expect queer children or themes within its pages, but given its carnivalesque tendencies, one should expect virtually anything within its pages, including the odd moments of queerness that inevitably arise.

Within such topsy-turvy settings, standard social constructions of gender and sexuality are frequently turned upside down as well, and as Kenneth Kidd observes, "many classics of Anglo-American children's literature are fundamentally homosocial, or concerned with same-sex friendships and family bonds. In retrospect, some of these classics seem decidedly queer."[41] In another study, Kidd details how the queerness of children's literature can be found in its many homosocial narratives and in the form of "singular or eccentric kids" who reject heteronormative imperatives; he trenchantly summarizes, "If children's literature has heteronormative tendencies, which it assuredly does, it also homes all sorts of queerness."[42] In this light, children's literature questions the cultural ideal of childhood innocence by confronting readers with unexpected, deviant, and truly marvelous reimaginings of human and nonhuman sexuality. In the carnivalesque playground of Oz and his many other fictional settings, Baum enjoys a comic freedom to invert traditional social codes and to allow gendered freedoms to flourish, no matter the sex of his various characters. Baum's creation of a carnivalesque fantasyland extends beyond the realm of asexuality and erotic innocence, for queerness—as oddness yet also as the sexually antinormative, both within the historical parameters of the texts' creation and in the interpretive praxes of today's readers—permeates the land as one of its defining virtues. In this light, issues of sexuality and sexual desire cannot be cordoned off from the novel's celebration of queerness, for the topsy-turvy world of children's literature respects few truths as sacrosanct in its boundless play with normality.

In the following pages and chapters, I toggle back and forth among Baum's fantasy fictions, his gently realist juvenile fiction series, and even his books for adult audiences, the better to illuminate the scope of his work, its overarching interest in queerness, and the ways in which queer themes in one branch of his fictions enlighten similar themes elsewhere. The stunning paradoxes of Baum's fictions—progressive themes coupled with overt racism, the carnivalesque freedoms of children's literature simultaneously subverting and constrained by presiding ideologies of gender and sexuality—demand scrutiny for their ability to anticipate a queer future still coming into focus and their concomitant rearguard actions defending whiteness. Writing during a time of increased interest and study of human sexuality, and sufficiently aware of America's queer subculture to subtly speak in its lexicon, Baum creates in his fictions various trans and queer fantasies that transcend and are trapped by the cultural milieu from which they spring.

Chapter 2

TRANS TALES OF OZ AND ELSEWHERE

> We pride ourselves . . . on having a greater variety of queer personages than any other kingdom in existence.
> —THE KINGLET OF THE ISLE OF PHREEX (*DOUGH*, CH. 5)

Seeing is not believing in the fictions of L. Frank Baum, for by clothes, magic, and other means he camouflages the gender and sex of various characters and reveals not only the performativity of gender but the inscrutability of bodily morphology in communicating gender. Characters including Billina the hen, the generals of Oz's female armies, and Tony Seaver of Edith Van Dyne's *Mary Louise Solves a Mystery* derail the binary genders of masculinity and femininity in their names and actions; such gender transgressions are at times marked on bodies as well, primarily those of Baum's male characters who evince surprisingly feminine physical traits. Moreover, several apparently male characters in Baum's fantasy fictions are revealed to be female, most famously Tip in the Oz series, who as an infant was transformed into a boy by the witch Mombi and then revealed to all—including herself—to be the lovely Empress Ozma of Oz. Baum's fantasy novels also feature such gender-transgressive characters as Prince Marvel of *The Enchanted Island of Yew* (a female fairy transformed into a male mortal), and a minor figure in *Queen Zixi of Ix* (a fisherman's daughter who longs to be a man). These characters likewise prove the flimsiness of the boundary between female and male. Perhaps best understood through the more modern conceptions of intersex or genderqueer, Chick the Cherub in *John Dough and the Cherub* demolishes binaries of gendered and sex difference altogether. In his non-fantasy works for adult and girl readers, Baum features Valcour in Schuyler Staunton's lurid romance *The Fate of a Crown* and Tato in Edith Van Dyne's *Aunt Jane's Nieces Abroad*. Both of these characters live as males despite being culturally perceived and ideologically framed as female, and the conclusions of their respective novels foreshadow their continued resistance to gendered norms, no matter the coercive force of marriage or femininity. Through the trans elements of these characters, Baum queries the likelihood of clothing and corporeal semiotics communicating accurately and instead takes advantage of their inherent uncertainty. Whether as an intriguing plot twist or as a profound musing on the mutability of gender, sex, and sexuality, Baum's trans tales confront readers with the instability of the human body as a defined and steady signifier. Given the challenges of applying modern theories of transgender identity to literature written over a hundred years ago, it is useful to consider the ways in which Baum applies what we might term *trans touches* in his novels, thus better to contextualize his continued interest in trans topics that often resist definitive interpretations of trans identities.

Stretching collectively over the last several decades, feminist, queer, and trans theories have attuned readers to the inherent contradictions of genders, desires, and bodies. These perspectives jointly investigate the ways in which cultures employ long-standing norms of gender, sexuality, and identity to define themselves while depriving certain members of the full dignity of their lives, and thus they expose the coercive force of these norms and imagine new ways of being. Succinctly framed, feminist theories query the presumptions and oversights of patriarchal ideologies, especially their privileging of masculine identities over feminine ones. Queer theories challenge the biases and bigotries of heteronormative cultures, puncturing myths of sexual normativity and highlighting the diverse range of sexual desires and expressions. Trans theories probe the simplistic assumptions undergirding cisgendered networks, tracing the variability of gender in its multiple enactments and its unsteady relationship to sexual morphology. Feminist, queer, and trans theories overlap productively in many regards, with their intersections pinpointing the inequities exacted upon women, queer, and trans people as broadly and ecumenically defined. As Heather Love opines, queer and trans theories discern and challenge the borders delimiting the normative from the nonnormative: "Etymologically, both *trans* and *queer* refer to crossing, and in that sense both terms invoke mobility as well as its limits."[1] In particular, trans theorists have exposed the oversights that accompanied the invaluable earlier work of gender and queer theorists. Yolanda Martínez-San Miguel and Sarah Tobias delineate the problematic foundational axioms of much queer theory as well as of wider normative cultures: "Trans activism therefore reveals that understandings of 'homo, hetero, and bi' are all predicated on congruent conceptions of what it means to be a woman or a man. By problematizing these conceptions, trans activists challenge the necessity for trans people to define themselves against hetero/homo norms."[2] Susan Stryker and Paisley Currah, discussing the variability of trans theories, acknowledge that "the term *transgender*, then, carries its own antinomies: Does it help make or undermine gender identities and expressions? Is it a way of being gendered or a way of doing gender? Is it an identification or a method? A promise or a threat?"[3] Concluding this brief overview of gender, queer, and trans theories, it should be noted that each perspective resists attempts to distill it into a singular framework and that each can instead be deployed from a wide range of converging viewpoints.

As relevant to studies of children's literature, trans theories have encouraged scholars to rethink the parameters of the field. As Derritt Mason poignantly asks, "Can we see *trans* as an invitation—or provocation—to think 'across, through, over, beyond, and outside of' existing paradigms of gender *and/in* children's literature scholarship?"[4] Both children's literature and the discipline of children's literature studies have historically overlooked trans issues and trans children within its overlapping corpora, but as Julian Gill-Peterson argues, any such oversight requires a determination not to perceive what is otherwise apparent: "Not meant to exist at all in the present tense of their childhoods, the ghostliness of trans children over the past one hundred years takes unique residence in the medical archive, hiding in plain sight, invisible to the inverse degree of being pervasively present, yet always slightly out of reach, even as they come into discourse."[5] With this statement Gill-Peterson focuses on narratives available in medical archives to recover lost stories of trans children, and the archive of children's literature provides a complementary space for considering ways in which fictional characters of the past are constructed as unique reflections of trans identities and trans desires.

Of course, any trans theory applied to Baum's fictions risks anachronism and misalignment, for his characters do not represent trans people as ones incorrectly assigned a gender at birth who, upon realizing their misgendering by others, assert their authentic selves.[6] On the contrary, some of Baum's trans characters find their true gender revealed to them magically, as with Ozma of Oz, whereas others whimsically adopt a new gender and sex, as with Prince Marvel of *The Enchanted Island of Yew*. Other characters inhabit an indeterminate zone between cross-dressing as a means of pursuing their personal objectives and transgenderism as a core aspect of their identity, in which readers are given little insight into their (the characters') motivations for assuming the trappings of another sex. More than simply questioning the semiotic denotations of clothing and bodily morphology, more than merely a magical feature of his fantasy worlds, Baum's trans story lines reveal the tyranny of gendered protocols and the freedoms to be found in rejecting them. Jody Norton perceives a "liberatory role that children's literature . . . can play in creating interpretive strategies, curricular revisions, and pedagogical interventions that will contribute substantially to the amelioration of the condition of cultural, institutional, and political neglect through which transchildren have been denied their reality, and their worth"—an objective to which many of Baum's many stories can contribute.[7] Although the carnivalesque freedoms of children's literature frequently posit the return to order at the story's end, many of Baum's trans characters derail any presumption that gender play can be contained by the story's end, that the trans touches of his stories will cease provocatively "touching" readers once the final page is turned.

BAUM'S GENDERED FANTASIES AND CHARACTERS ON THE TRANS BORDER

Throughout Baum's fictions, characters challenge the presumed borders between the masculine and feminine spheres, and some of these characters display gendered characteristics, both affective and physiological, correlated with the other gender—what we might term as trans touches in otherwise cisgendered characters. One might expect these conditions in Oz and Baum's other fairylands, where their carnivalesque conditions facilitate the depiction of women, men, and sexuality as fundamentally different from the gendered paradigms of the early twentieth-century United States, but these shifting gender dynamics are also apparent in many of Baum's pseudonymous fictions, which occur in a recognizable version of his contemporary world. Certainly, Oz is a utopia for women, where they are largely freed from traditional gender roles.[8] Even in the texts not featuring her in the lead role, Dorothy is never forgotten, and her fame throughout Oz establishes her as the primary focus of the series. J. L. Bell describes her as a conquering hero,[9] and Joel Chaston observes that she rejects her home life in Kansas that threatens to domesticate her.[10] Moreover, Dorothy regenders the standard parameters of Joseph Campbell's monomyth, as Edward W. Hudlin notes: "The fact that Dorothy is an orphan whose parentage and origins are obscure and mysterious is essential to the further development of the story, as it prepares the reader for Dorothy's future apotheosis."[11] Assuming the masculine narrative position of a questing hero, Dorothy queers the quest narrative from its heteronormative generic foundations because, in the interplay of gender and genre, regendering the hero often destabilizes the narrative expectations of a given genre. As Susan Crane explains, "Gender and genre can make claims to transhistorical permanence when they ground their claims in nature in the former case and art in the latter, but both categories prove to be subject to negotiation as they are mobilized in particular identities and works."[12] The individual titles of the Oz series all follow the mythic structure of departure, initiation, and return, yet they do so by focusing on a mixed gender community rather than on the individualist quest of a lone male, even in the adventures featuring a male character in the lead role (e.g., Ojo in *The Patchwork Girl of Oz*, Inga in *Rinkitink in Oz*).

This is not to say that the Oz books construct a protofeminist utopia entirely free from regressive attributes in regard to gender and sexuality. Many elements of the series undermine cisgendered normativity, yet many other elements reinforce gendered stereotypes. Such statements as "all girls are fond of finery" (*Woodman*, ch. 3) paint women as consumerist fashion plates, and similar gendered stereotypes appear frequently in the texts.[13] At the same time that such declarations construct women with regressively feminine characteristics, typically feminine stereotypes can also be applied to men: if it is true that "all girls are fond of finery" in Oz, so too are many of the men portrayed as indulging in excessively stylish clothing and accessories, such as those who wear a multitude of colored ribbons in their hair (e.g., *Dorothy*, ch. 10; *Road*, ch. 3; *Tik-Tok*, ch. 5). This tension between traditional and topsy-turvy gender roles recurs when the men of the Emerald City undertake the domestic responsibilities abandoned by their rebellious wives. One exhausted man thanks the Scarecrow for reinstituting order to the land:

> "I'm glad you have decided to come back and restore order, for doing housework and minding the children is wearing out the strength of every man in the Emerald City."
> "Hm!" said the Scarecrow, thoughtfully. "If it is such hard work as you say, how did the women manage it so easily?"
> "I really do not know" replied the man, with a deep sigh. "Perhaps the women are made of cast-iron." (*Marvelous*, ch. 15)

Here readers see the reinstitution of the status quo after a period of carnivalesque chaos, in which men will once again be men and women will once again be women, yet the passage also illustrates the toughness of women who can easily handle household tasks that men find exhausting. The descriptor "cast-iron women" metaphorically represents the difficulty of pinning down the depictions of gender in Oz and Baum's other tales, which are frequently in tension between first-wave feminism and traditional sexism yet nonetheless highlight the potential of women to act with strength and determination.[14]

Because the sexed body of a character bears a fluctuating correspondence to personal identity in Oz, and because stereotypes of femininity and masculinity can be applied to persons regardless of sex, it is not surprising that gender roles are frequently overturned in this queer land. Traditionally male activities are often performed by women, notably in the many female armies that march about the country.[15] Such gender inversions of a traditionally male military occur commonly in Oz. In the following dialogue between Ozma and the revolutionary Jinjur, this usurper to the throne declares that she has already succeeded in toppling masculine authority in her household:

> "Where is your husband?" asked Ozma.
> "He is in the house, nursing a black eye," replied Jinjur, calmly. "The foolish man would insist upon milking the red cow when I wanted him to milk the white one; but he will know better next time, I am sure." (*Ozma*, ch. 20)

Rebellious women are a recurring concern in Oz, and Ann Soforth's rebellion is linked to her rejection of female chores ("'I won't, cried Ann; 'I won't sweep the floor. It is beneath my dignity'" [*Tik-Tok*, ch. 1]); instead, she raises an army to seize authority from Ozma. Unfortunately, her army is composed of milquetoast men who have been previously conquered by their wives:

> "Jo," said Ann, "I am going to conquer the world, and you must join my Army."
> "Excuse me, please," said Jo Cone. "I am a bad fighter. My good wife conquered me years ago, for she can fight better than I. Take her, Your Majesty, instead of me, and I'll bless you for the favor."
> "This must be an army of men—fierce, ferocious warriors," declared Ann, looking sternly upon the mild little man. (*Tik-Tok*, ch. 1)

The humorous paradoxes in this passage—a female general enlisting a timid male soldier who proposes the conscription of his more powerful wife—upend traditional constructions of masculinity and femininity. The primary gender role valorized in this passage is that armies should be made of men, but this concept is itself undone by the fact that Ann commands her reluctant troops.

The regendering of armies in Oz ridicules pretensions of masculine authority in battle and simultaneously satirizes women who would replace men in these armies. Although Baum derides aggressive women as rebellious leaders—and it must be remembered that Jinjur's army is defeated when her female soldiers flee the sudden appearance of mice (*Marvelous*, ch. 15)—he consistently depicts women as more successful soldiers than men, and female troops appear better capable of serving militarily than male troops in many of the Oz books. Ozma's male army comprises twenty-six officers and one private, and they are all cowards: "But when it came to the twenty-six officers and the private, their knees were so weak that they could not walk a step" (*Ozma*, ch. 10). Again, the tension between subverting and reinforcing traditional gender roles obscures definitive conclusions, but the respect some characters express for female soldiers demonstrates that such armies should not be dismissed as unthreatening: "'Girls are the fiercest soldiers of all,' declared the Frogman. 'They are more brave than men, and they have better nerves. That is probably why the magician uses them for soldiers and has sent them to oppose us'" (*Lost*, ch. 21). Female armies humorously contribute to the carnivalesque social structures of Oz, but the respect accorded these warriors cannot be entirely erased due to the comic elements of their depiction.

The queer land of Oz delights in inversions of gender roles and upsets the ideological impact of gender in constructions of normativity, and even when these comic rebellions are quelled and the status quo is reinstated, it is evident that gender roles and sexual morphism mean little in this queer utopia. The subversions of gender evident in these passages illuminate the ways in which many characters reconceive its cultural force, and these themes are amplified in the many flashes of characters exhibiting small yet telltale hints of trans/queer identities. These are mostly grace notes of characterization yet they collectively contribute to the trans/queer themes percolating throughout Baum's fiction. In *Tik-Tok of Oz* the men of Oogaboo are all named Jo—Jo Apple, Jo Bunn, Jo Cone, and so on—despite that *Jo* more often represents an abbreviated form of Josephine, not Joseph (*Tik-Tok*, ch. 1). In *Rinkitink in Oz* Baum promises in his foreword, in contrast to the many Oz novels featuring female leads, that "Here is a story with a boy hero, and a boy of whom you have never before heard" (*Rinkitink*, "Introducing the Story"), but this boy's name is Inga—a decidedly feminine name. The talking chicken Billina, with her aggressive personality and forthright demeanor, prefers to be called Bill:

> "So Bill I've always been called, and Bill is my name."
> "But it's all wrong, you know," declared Dorothy, earnestly; "and, if you don't mind, I shall call you 'Billina.' Putting the 'eena' on the end makes it a girl's name, you see."
> "Oh, I don't mind it in the least," returned the yellow hen. "It doesn't matter at all what you call me, so long as I know the name means *me*."
> (*Ozma*, ch. 2)

Although this encounter may be read as Dorothy's policing of gendered identities, Billina's reaction—that gendered names do not affect her sense of personal identity—demonstrates that she remains recalcitrant in disrupting gender roles. Escalating this theme, Baum's chicken cares little about the sex of her brood and names all of her hatchlings in honor of Dorothy, regardless of their sex at birth. When she realizes that "two turned out to be horrid roosters" (*Emerald*, ch. 7), she changes their names from Dorothy to Daniel, but these young cocks spent their formative period incorrectly identified in regard to their morphological sex, with "Dorothy" now, in modern parlance, their deadname. Such hints of trans identities extend into Baum's gently realistic fictions, such as in *Mary Louise Solves a Mystery*, in which the indomitable Mrs. Antoinette Seaver rejects gender norms in notable ways, such as when the narrator states, "'Tony' Seaver, as she was generally called in those days, combined culture and refinement with a thorough knowledge of mining" (*Mystery*, ch. 1). A woman of high society and dirty mines, Tony Seaver also rejects the typical spelling of her nickname: the name Antoinette is usually shortened to Toni, whereas Anthony is usually shortened to Tony, in respect to both names' spellings. Commenting on Tony's spouse Jason Jones, the narrator states that "his fame rested on his being 'Tony Seaver's husband'" (*Mystery*, ch. 1), with the spelling of her name creating a queer undercurrent to their heteroerotic marriage.

In moving from the gendered ambiguity of his characters' names to their physical characteristics, it is apparent that Baum undermines the fiction of gender seamlessly unified with bodily morphology by introducing male characters with feminine features, physical characteristics, or personalities, especially those playing the role of antagonists. These characters further dismantle any presumptions of gendered stability in Baum's fictions. Zog, the wicked sea magician of *The Sea Fairies*, mixes masculine monstrosity and aspects of feminine morphology. "Zog's face was that of a man, except that the tops of his ears were pointed like horns . . . his mouth and nose were not only perfect in shape, but quite handsome," the narrator explains, and then balances this depiction by emphasizing the creature's feminine traits: "The best features of which Zog could boast were his arms and hands, the latter being as well formed, as delicate and white as those of a well-bred woman. When he spoke, his voice sounded sweet and clear, and its tones were very gentle" (*Sea Fairies*, ch. 13). Ahmed, one of the contenders for the throne of Baluchistan in Schuyler Staunton's *Daughters of Destiny*, is envisioned as "a big and burly fellow, it was true, but he seemed as gentle as a woman. Evidently a monastery training did not stimulate virility of mind" (*Daughters*, ch. 10). When embarrassed, some male characters physiologically react as if they were women. In *The Last Egyptian* protagonist Gerald Winston "blushed like a girl" when Lola Everingham tells him that Aneth Consinor loves him (*Egyptian*, ch. 18), and in *The Flying Girl and Her Chum*, "[H. Chesterton Radley-Todd] blushed like a girl, but declared he would be perfectly safe" (*Chum*, ch. 21).

Baum describes several male characters as having women's eyes. The social comedy *Tamawaca Folks* includes in its cast of characters the entrepreneur Wilder, depicted as "a stocky built, middle sized man, with round features chubby and merry" who bears "soft brown eyes that ought to have been set in a woman's face" (*Tamawaca*, ch. 3). *Aunt Jane's Nieces Out West* features Captain Carg, who sports similarly feminine features: "As for his eyes, which instantly attracted attention, they were brown and gentle as a girl's but had that retrospective expression that suggests far-away thoughts or an utter lack of interest in one's surroundings" (*West*, ch. 22). Men typically have deeper voices than women, but Baum upsets this expectation with the Major, the antagonist of *The Boy Fortune Hunters in Alaska*. Protagonist Sam Steele first describes him as "a personage so remarkable that he instantly riveted our attention. His height was enormous—at least six feet and three inches—and his chest was broad and deep as that of ancient Hercules"; Sam further stresses, "No stage pirate, no bandit of Southern Europe, was ever half so formidable in appearance as this terrible personage." It is then surprising, as Sam notes, to hear this man speak: "I gave a start. The voice of the huge bandit was as gentle and soft as that of a woman" (*Alaska*, ch. 7). In California, Aunt Jane's nieces meet Bulwer Runyon, who speaks in a "shrill, high-pitched tenor voice [such] that the sound was positively startling, coming from so massive a chest" (*Ranch*, ch. 6); indeed, in a moment of duress, Runyon's "voice reach[ed] high C in his excitement" (*Ranch*, ch. 8). In a short story about magic bonbons and the chaos they cause, Mr. Bostwick, described succinctly as "a big man," begins "to sing in a shrill, tremolo soprano voice" after eating one (*American*, "The Magic Bonbons"), and a similar event occurs in *The Enchanted Island of Yew*: "Then the king [Terribus] spoke, his voice sounding so sweet and agreeable that it almost shocked Nerle, who had expected to hear a roar like that from a wild beast" (*Yew*, ch. 8).

Although these male characters with physically feminine characteristics blur the borders between male and female and some approach what we might term today a genderqueer identity, many readers would rightfully hesitate to label them as trans. As readers move further along Baum's spectrum of gender, they see that, in a fairy kingdom such as Oz, several magical creatures can transform their sexed bodies—and they do so, for no apparent reason other than their desire to do so. The monstrous Phanfasm shifts into a range of forms and shapes, including that of a woman: "The First and Foremost [of the Phanfasms] slowly raised his arms, and in a twinkling his hairy skin fell from him and he appeared before the astonished Nome as a beautiful woman, clothed in a flowing gown of pink gauze" (*Emerald*, ch. 11). In another such example, the antagonist Kiki, while arguing with an immense yellow leopard named Gugu, transforms the beast "into a fat Gillikin woman, and [he] laughed aloud to see how the woman pranced with rage" (*Magic*, ch. 12). The Wizard of Oz, who is actually an "old man, with a bald head and a wrinkled face" (*Wonderful*, ch. 15), appears to Dorothy and her fellow travelers in a variety of forms, including a Terrible Beast and a Ball of Fire, but also as "a most lovely lady. She was dressed in green silk gauze and wore upon her flowing green locks a crown of jewels. Growing from her shoulders were wings, gorgeous in color and so light that they fluttered if the slightest breath of air reached them" (*Wonderful*, ch. 11). In this example, the Wizard's assumption of a woman's persona serves as part of his theatrical efforts to deceive and frighten Dorothy and her friends, while nonetheless thematizing the transience of gender.

For the most part, the narrators of these stories mention the gender disruptive, gender queer, and trans aspects of their characters and then proceed with their tales. The masculine spelling of Tony Seaver's name, or the Major's high-pitched voice, do not play significant roles in the remainders of the narratives. Also, it should not be overlooked that Baum stages some gender transgressions for simple laughs, such as in one of his *American Fairy Tales*, in which the protagonist inadvertently causes time to stand still and then exchanges the clothing of a man and a woman: "So [Jim] took off the policeman's cap and brass-buttoned coat and put them on Miss Scrapple, while the lady's feathered and ribboned hat he placed jauntily upon the policeman's head" (*American*, "The Capture of Father Time"). These and other such moments nonetheless matter significantly in the creation of Baum's fantasies and other fictional worlds, for they lay the groundwork for more probing explorations of gender performance and trans characters.

TRANS FANTASY TALES

As the characters addressed in the previous section may be described as having trans touches to their portrayals, other characters veer closer to trans identities. In both cases, the impermanence of gendered identities and sexual morphism in Oz and Baum's other fantasy lands, in that one's gender as well as one's sexed body can metamorphose in a moment, fundamentally subverts the ideological power of gender and sexuality to discipline subjects into traditional gender roles. With Ozma of Oz, Prince Marvel of *The Enchanted Island of Yew*, the multiple trans story lines of *Queen Zixi of Ix*, and Chick the Cherub of *John Dough and the Cherub*, Baum considers the thematic repercussions of characters fracturing the binary of male and female and pursuing their unique sense of gendered identity.

After Dorothy, the most prominent character in Baum's Oz series is the fairy princess Ozma, who ascends to the throne in the second book of the series, *The Marvelous Land of Oz*, with her reign positioning Oz as a trans utopia. Ozma was raised as a boy named Tip, a shortened form of Tippetarius, before learning her true identity as a fairy queen. Baum describes Tip in contrasting terms, first stating that he "grew as strong and rugged as a boy may be" (*Marvelous*, ch. 1) but later qualifying this assessment and stressing that Tip is "small and rather delicate in appearance" (*Marvelous*, ch. 4). More attention is paid to Tip's adventures than to his sex as the story unfolds until the surprising revelation that the witch Mombi transformed an infant girl into this young boy. Tip initially resists retransitioning from boy to girl—"Why, I'm no Princess Ozma—I'm not a girl! . . . I don't want to be a girl!"—but she eventually accepts her female identity and regal duty to rule as a queen instead of as a king: "Ozma made the loveliest Queen the Emerald City had ever known; and, although she was so young and inexperienced, she ruled her people with wisdom and justice" (*Marvelous*, ch. 23). The name Tip connotes phallic images, and this boy must be reframed semiotically and physically to assume her position as queen of the utopian land, with a new name positioning her as the mother of Oz: *Oz + ma*.

Tip's transition to Ozma is greeted supportively by the majority of Ozites, few of whom find her history worthy of additional comment or concern. The Tin Woodman, the Scarecrow, and the Woggle-Bug assure Tip that their relationships will continue as before—"we will all remain your faithful friends just the same" (*Marvelous*, ch. 23); only Jack Pumpkinhead frets over the consequences of the transition. Despite their difference in species, Tip and Jack Pumpkinhead view their relationship in father/son terms, for the former built the latter that was then brought to life. Upon learning his creation story, Jack Pumpkinhead first identified Tip in paternal terms—"you must be my creator—my parent—my father!"—to which Tip agreed: "'Or your inventor,' replied the boy with a laugh. 'Yes, my son; I really believe I am'" (*Marvelous*, ch. 3). Realizing that the boy Tip is actually the fairy princess Ozma, Jack Pumpkinhead must reconceptualize his family: "'But—see here!' said Jack Pumpkinhead, with a gasp: 'if you become a girl, you can't be my dear father any more!'" (*Marvelous*, ch. 23). Any hesitations over his father's transition into his mother are resolved, or at least attenuated, when in a later novel Jack Pumpkinhead refers to Ozma with the gender-neutral term "parent" (*Road*, ch. 16). After Tip transitions to Ozma, she says, "speaking the words with sweet diffidence," "I hope none of you will care less for me than you did before. I'm just the same Tip, you know; only—only—" As Ozma's words falter, Jack Pumpkin inserts, "Only you're different!" with the narrator assessing that all of the Ozites "thought it was the wisest speech he had ever made" (*Marvelous*, ch. 23). The Ozites see the same person now with her true gender and sex, in a daringly nonchalant rejection of any gender panic and trauma.

Throughout the remainder of the Oz books, Ozma's years as Tip are mentioned only once, when Dorothy divulges this information to her companion and second cousin Zebadiah. She explains that Ozma "brought [the Sawhorse] to life with a witch-powder, when she was a boy." Still unaccustomed to the surprises one finds in fairylands, Zeb inquires, "Was Ozma once a boy?" and Dorothy confirms Ozma's transition: "Yes; a wicked witch enchanted her, so she could not rule her kingdom. But she's a girl now, and the sweetest, loveliest girl in all the world" (*Dorothy*, ch. 14). Upon meeting Ozma, Zeb is awed by her beauty: "Here [Zeb] found Dorothy seated beside a young girl so marvelously beautiful that the boy stopped suddenly with a gasp of admiration" (*Dorothy*, ch. 15). As discussed in the following chapter, Baum frequently refrains from portraying heteroerotic attraction, and so this moment is notable not merely for Zeb's admiration of Ozma's beauty but for his utter embrace of her trans identity. Apparently pansexual in his orientation, or at least not transphobic, Zeb appreciates Ozma for the attractive girl she is now and is wholly unconcerned with the boy she was before.

Ozma's magical transition demonstrates the ease with which genders and sexes are swapped in Oz, and additional examples of such transitions abound in Baum's fantasy fictions. In *The Enchanted Island of Yew*, Baum creates another utopia where "the people of the [island] were happy and prosperous. No grass was greener, no forests more cool and delightful, no skies more sunny, no sea more blue and rippling than theirs" (*Yew*, ch. 2). Such an oasis of perfection threatens both to bore its inhabitants and to quell any narrative tension, and so Baum turns to gender transition to enliven this land of otherwise blissful ennui. The narrative action begins as Baron Merd's daughter Seseley and her friends Berna and Helda meet a fairy fatigued by the island's endless banality: "I am so utterly tired of a fairy life that I would do anything to change it" (*Yew*, ch. 3). Helda advises that all creatures should accept their lot in life and not seek to change—"I must say . . . that you are foolish to wish to become anything different from what you are"—but then reverses herself and suggests that the fairy adopt a new sex. "If you want variety, you should become a boy. . . . The life of a boy is one round of excitement," she proposes, to which the fairy excitedly agrees, "Then make me a boy!" (*Yew*, ch. 4).

The fairy's eager embrace of a masculine identity sparks a slight controversy over the meaning of gender and sex, for Seseley realizes that she is unsure of this magical creature's gendered identity. Within this world in which sex can be reconstructed instantly, this brief moment of gender panic establishes the ways in which some characters attempt to confirm their perceptions of another's identity. "Why—you're a *girl* fairy, aren't you?" she inquires; the fairy replies both affirmatively yet cryptically: "'Well—yes; I suppose I am,' answered the beautiful creature, smiling; 'but as you are going to change me anyway, I may as well become a boy as a girl.'" Seseley then questions the ethics of such a transition—"But would it be right?"—to which the fairy replies enthusiastically, "Why not? . . . I can see nothing wrong in being a boy. Make me a tall, slender youth, with waving brown hair and dark eyes. Then I shall be as unlike my own self as possible, and the adventure will be all the more interesting. Yes; I like the idea of being a boy very much indeed" (*Yew*, ch. 4).[16] Following the fairy's transformation, he asserts the unity of his identity: "'Yes, indeed,' said he, smiling; 'and I am really a fairy now, being but changed in outward form.'" Baum then depicts Seseley attempting to learn more about the fairy's previous identity, inquiring of his former appellation in a scene that anticipates deadnaming—"What were you called as a fairy?"—to which he asserts his desire for an identity liberated from his past: "'That does not matter in the least,' he answered, hastily. 'I must have an entirely new name'" (*Yew*, ch. 4). Readers might not have realized the female fairy did not divulge her name until this point of the narrative when it is stressed, and so his refusal to disclose his prior feminine name underscores the profound meaning of the change of both his morphology and his appellation. With his new name, gender, sex, and identity as Prince Marvel, this fairy's adventures can now begin.

As much as gender and sex transitions are key to the plot of *The Enchanted Island of Yew*, Baum distinguishes between Prince Marvel's masculine exterior and his feminine interior, such as when the hero and his companion Nerle discuss punishing thieves by hanging them on trees. "Well, there are trees handy," Prince Marvel states, with the narrator recording that "his girlish heart insisted on making him shiver in spite of his resolve to be manly and stern" (*Yew*, ch. 5). This moment underscores the limitations of the male/female binary in assessing Baum's characters, for Prince Marvel is here conceived as a creature of a visually masculine exterior yet of an inherently feminine interior. Throughout his adventures Prince Marvel defeats numerous adversaries with his masculinity unquestioned, yet by the novel's end, he resolves to revert to his original form: "I am no one but myself; and, really, I believe I shall now be content to exist for a few hundred years in my natural form. I have quite enjoyed my year as a mortal; but after all there are, I find, some advantages in being a fairy" (*Yew*, ch. 26). From female fairy to male mortal and then back again, the being once known as Prince Marvel now evinces stereotypically feminine characteristics such as wearing "gossamer robes of rose and pearl color" (*Yew*, ch. 26). Whereas Seseley earlier attempted to confirm the fairy's gender but only received an ambiguous reply, this ending reinstates the gender binary, positing the carnivalesque nature of some of Baum's trans identities, in which the rejection of daily routines and identities can be jettisoned for a period of play and pleasure but not forever. At the same time, the title of the novel—*The Enchanted Island of Yew*—homophonically conveys the idea that yew/you, the reader, can be the site of such magical transformations. With this possibility at hand, any young fairies and trans children among Baum's readers might be inspired not to curtail the freedoms of embracing a different gender from the one presumed to belong to them but to extend them onward into the future.

In *Queen Zixi of Ix*, Baum introduces three trans storylines, two of which contribute to the novel's sense of whimsical fancy by depicting gender's impermanence and performativity and the third building its overarching theme that one must accept what one cannot change. In the first of these plotlines, readers encounter the female fairy Ereol, who is "very lovely in appearance, and with her fluffy golden hair and clear blue eyes was marvelously fair to look upon" (*Zixi*, ch. 1). Ereol joins the other fairies in weaving a magical cloak to be bestowed upon a mortal in need, and when Fluff, an orphaned girl traveling with her brother Bud and cranky Aunt Rivette, feels "that she had never been more unhappy than at that moment" and weeps "as if her little heart would break," she is surprised to find a "tall and handsome youth standing before her." The narrator reports, "It was none other than Ereol, who had assumed this form for her appearance among mortals" (*Zixi*, ch. 3; see figures 2.1 and 2.2). Baum does not explain Ereol's reason for appearing in masculine form, and so this moment accentuates the relative banality of such transitions in a fairyland, in which one's gender and sex can be changed as easily as one's clothing. The name Ereol suggestively approximates *areola*, an appropriately genderless signifier of the pigmented circle around human nipples, both male and female.

In the second trans storyline of *Queen Zixi of Ix*, each of the king's five advisors—Tallydab, Tellydeb, Tillydib, Tollydob, and Tullydub—drapes himself in Fluff's resplendent and magical cloak, despite its feminine

"Yes, your Majesty, I am late."

Figures 2.1 and 2.2. Ereol is a female fairy who appears to Fluff in male form. Baum offers little explanation for the change in genders (Zixi, ch. 1 and ch. 3).

appearance as a "pretty" garment featuring "every hue of the rainbow" (*Zixi*, ch. 9 and ch. 1). As the surly dog Ruffles succinctly assesses, "It's a girl's cloak" (*Zixi*, ch. 10). Clothing plays a key role in the expression of trans desires and identities,[17] and as the king's advisors don the magic cloak, some of these scenes resonate with the experiences of trans people dressing for the first time in clothes properly gendered for them: "So Tellydeb picked up the cloak and laid it over his arm; then he admired the bright hues that ran through the fabric, and presently his curiosity got the better of him; he decided to try it on and see how he would look in it" (*Zixi*, ch. 10). Other than his curiosity, the story leaves Tellydeb's motivation for trying on the magic cloak tantalizingly unexplained, and thus the only apparent answer is his desire to see himself in feminine attire. Tallydab similarly enjoys donning such feminine finery, asking Ruffles—"How do I look in it, Ruffles? . . . How do I look in such gorgeous apparel?"—but the dog dashes Tallydab's evident pleasure in cross-dressing. "You look perfectly ridiculous," he barks, and soon adds, "It's . . . not fit for a wrinkled old man like you" (*Zixi*, ch. 10). Ironically, a male dog named Ruffles, which is itself suggestive of femininely gendered clothing, polices Tallydab's trans desires.

In the novel's third trans storyline, Queen Zixi encounters an alligator who cannot climb a tree, an owl who cannot swim, and a young girl who cannot be a man. Each of these characters yearns for an unattainable objective, which corresponds to Zixi's own unmet desire: although to all the world she appears young and beautiful, the truth of her 683 years and its unyielding effect on her former beauty is reflected in every mirror she sees. The dialogue between Zixi and the young girl stresses the depth of the latter's heartfelt but impossible aspiration:

> In one end of the boat crouched a little girl, the ferryman's daughter, and she sobbed continually, so that the sound of the child's grief finally attracted Zixi's attention.
> "Why do you sob?" questioned the queen.
> "Because I want to be a man," replied the child, trying to stifle her sobs.
> "Why do you want to be a man?" asked Zixi, curiously.
> "Because I'm a little girl," was the reply.
> This made Zixi angry.
> "You're a little fool!" she exclaimed loudly.
> "There are other fools in the world," said the child, and renewed her sobs. (*Zixi*, ch. 15)

As with so many instances in Baum's fiction, it is worthwhile to consider the limitations of viewing this young girl as a trans character: she does not insist that she is male and seek to have this identity confirmed as much as she desires the transformation from one sex to another. The child's replies nonetheless capture the experience of many trans people, who are told they are not who they are. Zixi's sharp response, denigrating the girl's heartfelt wish as foolish, wins the girl's implicit rejoinder that many people's desires could be considered foolish but are consequently no less real.

Following her failed efforts to steal Fluff's magic cloak, and thus to achieve her objective of appearing forever young in mirrors, Zixi again meets the alligator, owl, and the ferryman's daughter. "Do you not still wish to be a man?" Zixi inquires, to which the "little maid" replies: "No, indeed! . . . For I have discovered all men must work very hard to support their wives and children, and to buy them food and raiment. So I have changed my mind about becoming a man, especially as that would be impossible" (*Zixi*, ch. 21). Her trans desire to be a man notwithstanding, this little girl can only foresee a normative future for herself in this role and therefore rejects her earlier dream. The alligator who hoped to climb trees agrees on the futility of some desires: "Isn't it fortunate we cannot have everything we are stupid enough to wish for?" (*Zixi*, ch. 21). From these encounters, Zixi learns to accept her fate and concludes: "We are all alike—the alligator, the owl, the girl, and the powerful Queen of Ix. We long for what we cannot have, yet desire it not so much because it would benefit us, as because it is beyond our reach. If I call the others fools, I must also call myself a fool for wishing to see the reflection of a beautiful girl in my mirror when I know it is impossible. So hereafter I shall strive to be contented with my lot" (*Zixi*, ch. 15). The bittersweet simplicity of this fairy tale's moral imbues it with an undercurrent of irresolution, for most such stories feature the attainment of impossible goals, not their rejection. Indeed, one of the chief pleasures of fantasy novels is precisely their ability to depict alligators climbing trees, owls swimming, and characters transforming themselves into who they truly are. Yet for a novel written approximately forty years before Christine Jorgensen's trailblazing gender confirmation surgery, Zixi's encounter with the little girl is a poignant reminder that many trans people of this era might draw such a resigned conclusion, that the dream of living as their true gender and sex would not be realized, even in the pages of fantasy novels. At the same time, with Ereol shifting between female and male incarnations and with regal advisors so attracted to female finery that they cannot resist trying on a rainbow-threaded cloak, *Queen Zixi of Ix* simultaneously demonstrates that not all trans dreams need be dismissed as impossibilities.

In contrast to the trans themes running throughout *The Enchanted Island of Yew* and *Queen Zixi of Ix*, *John Dough and the Cherub* appears unconcerned with trans issues from its first page to its very last, until its final sentence.[18] The opening chapters introduce John Dough, a life-sized gingerbread man animated by the Great Elixir; the plot focuses on his efforts to evade his chief antagonist, Ali Dubh, who hopes to eat this life-sized and animate cookie, thus to enhance his own longevity.[19] Throughout *John Dough and the Cherub* Baum adheres to the standard narrative arc of his fantasy novels, in which odd adventurers encounter odd antagonists until a final resolution is achieved, with little to indicate that gender stands as one of its primary interests. In this adventure's conclusion, John Dough is proclaimed king of Hiland and Loland with Chick the Cherub, his companion throughout his travels, appointed to serve in the honorary role of Head Booleywag.[20] The novel ends with these words: "The Records of the Kingdom say very little of Chick's later history, merely mentioning the fact that the King's most valuable assistant was the Head Booleywag, who grew up to be the especial favorite of all the inhabitants of the island. But, curiously enough, the Records fail to state whether the Head Booleywag was a man or a woman" (*Dough*, ch. 19). It is a rather stunning conclusion, for readers must confront their ignorance of this key aspect of Chick's identity and more so, that Baum purposefully withheld this information until virtually taunting them in his final sentence.

Many readers likely did not notice that Chick's gender was left unspecified; many others likely assumed that a cherub might simply be genderless, or perhaps they defaulted to the expectation that Chick was a boy, given the predominance of males as protagonists in much fiction of this era. Regardless of these interpretive possibilities, Baum never specifies the character's gender or sex, instead referring to Chick as a "child," "it," and "little one," as in this passage introducing the character:

> The child had fair hair, falling in fleecy waves to its shoulders, but more or less tangled and neglected. It had delicate features, rosy cheeks, and round blue eyes. When these eyes were grave—which was seldom there were questions in them; when they smiled—which was often—sunbeams rippled over their blue surfaces. For clothing the child wore garments of pure white, which reached from the neck to the ankles, and had wide flowing sleeves and legs, like those of a youngster's pajamas. The little one's head and feet were bare, but the pink soles were protected by sandals fastened with straps across the toes and ankles.
>
> "Good morning," said John, again smiling and hoping he had not stared too rudely. "It gives me great pleasure to meet you."

"My name's Chick," replied the child, laughing in sweet trills, while the blue eyes regarded the gingerbread man with evident wonder. (*Dough*, ch. 5)

Baum employs such ambiguous language throughout the novel and thus undercuts the male/female binary by highlighting its inefficacy to delineate any aspect of Chick's gender and sex. John Dough's potentially rude staring suggests his initial surprise at his new acquaintance's indeterminate gender and sex, yet if readers assume that Chick must then be genderless, the novel's concluding call for child readers to identify Chick definitively as female or male undercuts the coherency of this theory. As J. L. Bell observes, "Chick presents a bigger challenge to our notion of gender because the character does not magically slip from a male body to a female one. Chick occupies a place between the two sexes. Baum, a chicken expert, knew the name 'Chick' was doubly appropriate for this child: chicks had been hatched in incubators for years, and chicks are notoriously difficult to sex."[21] Indeed, the chicken Billina of the *Oz* novels refers to the difficulty of sexing hatchlings in her backstory, mentioning that "when I was first hatched out no one could tell whether I was going to be a hen or a rooster" (*Ozma*, ch. 2). Bell's observations require further calibration, however, because Chick no longer "occupies a place between the two sexes" if readers are solicited to definitively label the character as male or female. Readers of Baum's fiction encounter so many varieties of unusual and unexpected beings—many of whom are human or humanoid, many of whom are not—that an ungendered child cherub need not initially appear as a particularly unusual figure. Baum then insists that readers confront the enigma of this character's gender and remedy the ambiguity by assigning a conclusive answer that the text never addresses in its previous chapters.

The issue of Chick's gendered identity returns in *The Road to Oz*, in which Baum includes cameo appearances of royal figures from across his fantasy fiction—including Queen Zixi of Ix, Santa Claus, the Queen of Merryland, John Dough, and Chick the Cherub—who travel to Oz to celebrate Ozma's birthday. In contrast to *John Dough and the Cherub*, in which Chick's sex is overlooked until the novel's final sentence, Dorothy immediately comments on this issue. The narrator asserts that "John Dough's Head Booleywag at once became a prime favorite," with Chick's sex then becoming a topic of discussion:

"Is it a boy or a girl?" whispered Dorothy.
"Don't know," said Button-Bright.

"Goodness me! what a queer lot of people you are," exclaimed the rubber bear, looking at the assembled company. (*Road*, ch. 21)

Dorothy is accustomed to speaking her opinions rather forcefully and occasionally rudely, such as when she states, "You're just *awful* stupid, Button-Bright" (*Road*, ch. 2), but now her whisper indicates that she realizes her question is potentially offensive. Button-Bright's terse response of "Don't know" could be taken as his lack of interest in this topic, but because this is his preferred answer to virtually any question, it is difficult to discern much significance in it. The rubber bear, Para Bruin by name, then asks Dorothy and Button-Bright to acknowledge the queerness of the assembled company, for the roster of celebrants of Ozma's birthday ranges from the Tin Woodman to the Hungry Tiger, from Billina the chicken to Jack Pumpkinhead, with an assortment of otherwise unexpected and eccentric figures. Para Bruin's words are directed to, or at the very least include, two cisgendered human children, and thus he points out the inherent queerness of any construction of gender, even the genders of those who inhabit a widespread cultural norm but query the gender and sex of another.

As Baum's son and biographer Frank Joslyn Baum documents, his father's publishers resisted his genderless portrayal of Chick the Cherub and "told him that he could not leave the story that way because children demanded detailed information about the characters they liked." Baum reportedly replied, "I wrote the story as I felt it. . . . I cannot remember that Chick the Cherub impressed me as other than a joyous, sweet, venturesome and loveable child. Who cares whether it is a boy or girl?" Baum refused to answer the question definitively, and the issue was resolved when the publishers opted to turn this character into a marketing ploy by printing with the novel a "green ballot . . . bound into the front of the book, so that the reader might express his opinion and the reason for it in twenty-five words or less. Prizes were offered for the best answers with the top prize of one hundred dollars in gold" (see figure 2.3).[22] In sum, Baum insisted that Chick the Cherub remain ungendered, the publishers insisted on the character being gendered, and the book's child readers were asked to resolve this dispute between adults. *John Dough and the Cherub* stands as a striking example both of the gendered freedoms in Baum's fictions and of widespread gender policing in the culture in which it was published, with this character both liberated from and then metatextually reinstated into the prevailing gendered order.

In Baum's fantasy fictions, magic productively complicates questions of trans identity, for it reminds readers that what they might presume they know about characters, if they base these presumptions on supposedly immutable

Figure 2.3. "Is the Cherub Boy or Girl?" advertisement, from the December 1906 issue of the *Ladies' Home Journal*.

characteristics like sex, remains forever in flux. In a final example of these dynamics in Baum's fantasy novels, the title of *The Lost Princess of Oz* captures its plotline—Ozma has mysteriously disappeared and a team of adventurers must find her—but in a puzzling moment they are told that Ozma can be found in a nearby hole. There, they find not Ozma but Button-Bright, and so the Lavender Bear posits, "Perhaps Button-Bright is Ozma," an idea that Dorothy peremptorily rejects based on her perceptions of the immutability of sex: "And perhaps he isn't! Ozma is a girl, and Button-Bright is a boy" (*Lost*, ch. 20). Yet only a few pages later, Dorothy remembers the likelihood of magical enchantments in Oz and muses aloud, "I wonder if she's been transformed into Button-Bright?" She then demands of the boy: "Are you Ozma? Tell me truly!" (*Lost*, ch. 20). Button-Bright remains Button-Bright, and the adventurers later learn that Ozma was transformed into a golden peach pit and that Button-Bright ate the surrounding fruit and then pocketed the golden pit. On the whole, then, this scenario flirts with a trans storyline as it then segues into one with surprising erotic undertones, with Button-Bright consuming fruit—an enduring symbol of sexuality—that hides his queen within it. In Baum's fantasy worlds ever open to trans possibilities, gender and sex are rendered eternally suspect, always open to renegotiation and reimagination.

TRANS ADVENTURE TALES

Baum's leading trans and gender-atypical characters in his fantasy works, including Ozma, Prince Marvel, and Chick the Cherub, play the role of protagonists, with their elastic adaptability to gender key to their attractiveness and charisma. In contrast Baum's trans characters in his nonfantasy fiction—Valcour in Schuyler Staunton's *The Fate of a Crown* and Tato in Edith Van Dyne's *Aunt Jane's Nieces Abroad*—inhabit adversarial roles yet ultimately emerge as plucky and likable antagonists who upset stifling cultural norms and thus model for the protagonists the liberating possibilities of transgression. Both novels feature American protagonists—Robert Harcliffe in *The Fate of a Crown*, the eponymous nieces and their Uncle John in *Aunt Jane's Nieces Abroad*—who travel to foreign lands depicted as exotic sites of intrigue: Brazil in the former, Sicily in the latter. As these cisgendered American protagonists confront unfamiliar landscapes and find themselves surrounded by conspirators, kidnappers, and other nefarious malefactors, Baum's trans characters contribute to the sense of danger threatening the heroes while ultimately revealing themselves as sympathetic figures. Unlike Ozma, however, Valcour and Tato are depicted as retransitioning into female characters, despite the freedoms they enjoyed as men.

Moreover, it is significant that readers first meet Valcour and Tato as male characters, unlike such cross-dressing characters as Shakespeare's Viola in *Twelfth Night* and Rosalind in *As You Like It*. Viola and Rosalind exploit gender's porousness and assume masculine identities to pursue their objectives, including objectives of heteroerotic attraction, and so Shakespeare's audiences realize from these plays' beginnings that these characters remain—or will return to their lives as—cisgendered women underneath men's attire. Contrasting this vision of cross-dressing as an open secret, Baum cloaks Valcour's and Tato's gender play throughout much of these novels, thereby more powerfully disrupting the coercive force of ideological normativity. In effect, these trans characters have their own unique stories to tell about their gendered desires, and thus their storylines highlight the freedoms available to young women who reject the social limitations placed upon their sex and instead live as men.

The Fate of a Crown tells the (astonishingly convoluted) tale of American Robert Harcliffe's exciting adventures in Brazil, which begin when his Uncle Nelson proposes that he travel there to serve as the personal secretary of one of their clients, revolutionist Dom Miguel. Initiating the novel's gendered themes, Harcliffe sees this journey as an opportunity to prove his masculinity: "Uncle Nelson's sudden proposal gave me a thrill of eager interest best explained by that fascinating word 'danger.'... Would I, a young man on the threshold of life, with pulses readily responding to the suggestion of excitement and adventure, leave my humdrum existence in a mercantile establishment to mingle in the intrigues of a nation striving to cast off the shackles of a monarchy...? My answer was assured" (*Fate*, ch. 1). In Brazil, Harcliffe joins league with the revolutionaries fighting for democracy against the repressive forces of Emperor Pedro II, and the novel's (mostly male) cast of characters include statesmen from this period of Brazilian history, including Floriano Piexoto and Deodoro da Fonseca. Indeed, Harcliffe comments on their respective merits: "To see the two leaders together one would never suspect that history would prove the statesman [i.e., Piexoto] greater than the general" (*Fate*, ch. 10). By the novel's end, Harcliffe's actions have contributed to the revolution's success, as his comrade Bastro affirms: "There is no doubt but General Fonseca, at Rio, has before now gained control of the capital, and that the Revolution is successfully established" (*Fate*, ch. 20). Baum writes historical fiction with little concern for accuracy, with his interest more evident in the genres of adventure and romance and in the many dangers that Harcliffe must overcome.

Male protagonists of adventure novels readily prove their masculinity through conquests both martial and amatory, and alongside Harcliffe's contributions to the revolutionaries' wartime efforts he woos and wins the lovely Lesba. Counterbalancing this love plot, Harcliffe is relentlessly pursued by the spy Valcour, who is revealed to be a woman as part of the novel's shocking finale. The initial encounter between Harcliffe and Valcour, who introduces himself as Senhor Manuel Cortes de Guarde, bears hints of homoerotic attraction: "On deck I met a young gentleman of rather prepossessing personality who seemed quite willing to enter into conversation. He was a dark-eyed, handsome Brazilian, well dressed and of pleasing manners.... He loved to talk, and I love to listen" (*Fate*, ch. 2). By stressing both Valcour's eagerness to speak with Harcliffe and Harcliffe's attention to Valcour's attractiveness, as well as the mutuality of their burgeoning friendship, Baum appears to present the two men as sympathetic allies, but Harcliffe soon overhears his acquaintance conspiring to assassinate him in order to obstruct the revolutionaries' efforts. Realizing the threat that Valcour poses, Harcliffe muses: "Evidently it was far from safe to involve one's self in Brazilian politics. My friend Valcour... was a spy of the Emperor, masquerading under the title of Senhor Manuel Cortes de Guarde. A clever fellow, indeed, despite his soft, feminine ways and innocent chatter, and one who regarded even murder as permissible in the execution of his duty to Dom Pedro. It was the first time in my life I had been, to my knowledge, in any personal danger, and the sensation was rather agreeable than otherwise" (*Fate*, ch. 2). Readers see a clue to the future revelation of Valcour's sex in Harcliffe's reference to his "soft, feminine ways," and Harcliffe delights in the dangers afforded by this murderous adversary who straddles the border between male and female. Indeed, he acknowledges his rather bizarre hope to maintain a friendship with his would-be assassin: "Attracted toward [Valcour] in spite of my discoveries, I made several attempts to resume our former friendly intercourse; but he recoiled from my overtures and shunned my society" (*Fate*, ch. 3). Similarly, when Harcliffe is arrested while posing under the alias Andrea Subig, Valcour reveals his (Harcliffe's) true name, with Harcliffe again noting the man's femininity: "The spy spoke in his womanish, dainty manner" (*Fate*, ch. 13).

Notwithstanding these clues to Valcour's sex, Harcliffe perceives his adversary as a man and thus assumes his heterosexuality as well. In the labyrinthine storyline of his romantic pursuit of the beautiful Lesba, the sister of the revolutionary Francisco Paola, Harcliffe becomes convinced that Valcour loves Lesba: "Now, in a flash, the truth came to me. Valcour was still at the mansion—Valcour, [Lesba's] accomplice; perhaps her lover" (*Fate*, ch. 19). Harcliffe senses a heteroerotic attraction that, were he correct, would then be revealed as a lesbian affair upon Valcour's eventual regendering. Discussing with Valcour the relationship between Lesba and the villainous Captain de Souza, Harcliffe obliquely accuses him (Valcour) of attempting to seduce her: "Ah; and [Lesba] laughed at the dear captain, as we all heard. But you, senhor, made an effort to induce her to change her mind—did you not?" Valcour replies that it would be better that Lesba "should die than marry this brutal Captain de Souza"; Harcliffe finds confirmation for his viewpoint in his words: "This speech seemed to confirm my suspicion that Valcour himself loved Lesba" (*Fate*, ch. 22). Discerning a heteroerotic passion that does not exist between Lesba and Valcour, and thus viewing Valcour as his competitor for Lesba's affections, Harcliffe perceives an erotic triangle among the three. In effect, he relies on the age-old script of homosocial competition so that he can prove his devotion to Lesba, not realizing that his trans foe has rewritten this script for him.

As Baum subtly limns a homoerotic undertone in Valcour's early relationship with Harcliffe, so too does the spy apparently indulge in homoerotic relationships with other men, notably the revolutionaries Mazanovitch and Francisco Paola. While ostensibly sworn enemies with these men, Valcour unexpectedly expresses deep affection for them. For example, when observing an encounter between Valcour and Mazanovitch, Harcliffe notes that "the eyelids of Mazanovitch for an instant unclosed, and in that instant so tender a glance escaped them that Valcour trembled slightly, and touched with a gentle, loving gesture the elder man's arm" (*Fate*, ch. 9). In another such scene, Harcliffe reports to Mazanovitch of the enmity between Valcour and Francisco Paola—"Valcour is a most persistent foe to the cause.... It would have pleased you to watch him struggle with Paola for the mastery, while the Emperor was by. Ah, how Paola and Valcour hate each other!"—a revelation to which Mazanovitch responds cryptically, as recorded in Harcliffe's reaction: "Mazanovitch turned his passionless face toward me, and it seemed as though a faint smile flickered for an instant around his mouth" (*Fate*, ch. 21). Mazanovitch's smile is left unexplained at the moment but hints that he understands that the passion between Valcour and Francisco Paola is likely not based on mutual enmity.

Immediately prior to the revelation of his female sex, Valcour undertakes an act of great bravery by rescuing Francisco Paola from the villainous Captain de Souza. De Souza shoots at Paola, with Harcliffe observing, "Paola was ... helpless to evade the bullet; but Valcour, who had nearly reached him, turned suddenly at my cry and threw himself in front of Paola just as the shot rang out" (*Fate*, ch. 23). The earlier hints of latent desire between Valcour and both Mazanovitch and Francisco Paola now appear blatantly homoerotic, as these men openly affirm their affection for him. Harcliffe states that "Mazanovitch dashed aside his captors and sprang to the spot where Valcour lay" and records the man's words: "'Oh, my darling, my darling!' he moaned, raising the delicate form that he might pillow the head upon his knee. 'How dared they harm you, my precious one! How dared they!'" (*Fate*, ch. 24). One might well presume these words indicate Mazanovitch's grief for his fallen lover. Baum accelerates the scene's queer tension by depicting Francisco Paola as equally enamored by Valcour: "Taking one of the spy's slender hands in both his own he pressed it to his heart and said in trembling tones: 'Look up, sweetheart! Look up, I beg of you. It is Francisco—do you not know me? Are you dead, Valcour? Are you dead?'" (*Fate*, ch. 24). The homoerotic frisson of the scene, as two men tenderly care for their wounded "darling" and "sweetheart," then dissipates as Valcour's sex is revealed: "A gentle hand pushed him aside, and Lesba knelt in his place. With deft fingers she bared Valcour's breast.... I found myself regarding the actors in this remarkable drama with an interest almost equaling their own. The bared breast revealed nothing to me, however; for already I knew that Valcour was a woman" (*Fate*, ch. 24). With these words Harcliffe claims that he perceived the gendered illusion created by Valcour's clothes and recognized her morphological sex cloaked underneath. This passage is confused and confusing, however, for he then quotes Lesba's words to Valcour's father—"Fear nothing, Captain Mazanovitch . . . the wound is not very dangerous, and—please God!—we will yet save your daughter's life"—and reports his reaction, "His daughter! How much of the mystery that had puzzled me this simple word revealed" (*Fate*, ch. 24). What did Harcliffe know, and when did he know it? These contradictory statements, put forth on the same page, treat Valcour's sex as both an open and an impenetrable secret, one that Harcliffe never previously discloses to readers, asserts he long knew, and now proclaims as the resolution to an enigma. Throughout these various possibilities, Valcour's sexed body remains cloaked until it is bared for the world to see, in a sex-reveal scene that coincides with her acceptance of her female body and her future as a wife and mother. With her gender, sex, and even sexuality reframed for readers, Baum depicts a kiss that only a few pages before would have read as daringly homoerotic: "The girl [Valcour] was awake and apparently much better, for she smiled brightly into the face Paola bent over her, and showed no resentment when he stooped to kiss her lips" (*Fate*, ch. 24).

Following the revelation of Valcour's gender, Lesba explains Valcour's reason for adopting masculine attire and her familial relationship to Mazanovitch:

> "She is the daughter of captain Mazanovitch, who, when her mother died, took delight in instructing his child in all the arts known to the detective police. . . . When Mazanovitch was won over to the Republican conspiracy his daughter, whose real name is Carlotta, refused to desert the Emperor, and from that time on treated her father as a traitor, and opposed her wit to his own on every occasion. The male attire she wore both for convenience and as a disguise; but I have learned to know Valcour well, and have found her exceedingly sweet and womanly, despite her professional calling." (*Fate*, ch. 24)

In the early twentieth century, given the traditional view that detective work falls within an inherently masculine sphere, a storyline of a father teaching his daughter the art of detection thematizes gender transgression. Baum also deploys this trope in his Mary Louise series, as John O'Gorman assists his daughter Josie in her efforts to solve the mysteries that Mary Louise encounters. Notably, though, Josie does not don masculine attire in her adventures, and so *The Fate of a Crown* adopts a deeper transgressive theme in its gender play. Moreover, in this passage readers learn that Valcour's birth name is Carlotta, and while one might expect her to reclaim this name now that her feminine identity has been revealed, the characters continue to refer to her as Valcour, as her body adapts to her new gendered circumstances: "Meantime Valcour mended daily, and the roses that had so long been strangers to her pale cheeks began to blossom prettily under the influence of Francisco's loving care" (*Fate*, ch. 25).

In addition to Valcour, Baum portrays in *The Fate of a Crown* another character whose gender performance confuses Harcliffe: Francisco Paola. Similar to the male characters painted with distinctively feminine characteristics and other potential trans touches discussed earlier in this chapter, Francisco Paola is repeatedly viewed by Harcliffe in feminine terms, as in this assessment: "Somewhat older than his bewitching sister, his features were not without a sort of effeminate beauty, of which he seemed fully aware" (*Fate*, ch. 4). He also describes him as "exhibit[ing] a queer mingling of folly and astuteness" (*Fate*, ch. 5). Effete and narcissistic, Francisco Paola irks Harcliffe, who castigates the man for his apparent lack of masculinity: "God forbid that I should ever meet with such another man as Francisco Paola again! Deep or shallow, coxcomb or clever conspirator, true man or traitor—it was as impossible to read him or to judge his real character as to solve the mighty, unfathomable secrets of Nature" (*Fate*, ch. 17). Following Valcour's transformation into womanhood, Francisco Paola similarly transforms into a culturally approved version of masculinity: "And there was no simper upon Paola's face then, you may be sure. Since the tragedy at Bastro's that disagreeable expression had vanished forever, to be replaced by a manliness that was the fellow's most natural attribute, and fitted his fine features much better than the repulsive leer he had formerly adopted as a mask" (*Fate*, ch. 25). Curiously, Francisco's unrequited affections for Valcour effeminized him, or was the cause of his effeminacy the revolution itself? Baum traces an effect—Francisco's restored masculinity upon uniting with Valcour—without explaining its cause. War confuses gender categories for these Brazilian revolutionaries, while they employ the inherent confusion of gender, its internal inconsistencies and contradictions, to advance their interests.

The Fate of a Crown ends with gendered and erotic normativity ostensibly restored, as Valcour/Carlotta and Francisco Paola marry, as do Lesba and Harcliffe. But following such a bizarre chain of events, normativity bears queer undercurrents that cannot be fully quelled. When a woman who formerly lived as a man marries a man formerly perceived as excessively feminine, such a union stretches the boundaries of heteronormativity beyond its circumscribing force. Even their names carry hints of queerness: Valcour's deadname of Carlotta is mentioned once but then remains unspoken; *Paola* ends with the feminine *-a* of Romance languages; and *Lesba* is reminiscent of *lesbian*. Harcliffe laughs at the incongruities and surprises of his South American adventures, remarking, "In no other country than half-civilized Brazil, I reflected, could such a drama have been enacted" (*Fate*, ch. 24). At the novel's end, however, Harcliffe and Lesba remain in Brazil rather than returning to New Orleans (except for winter vacations), and so they reside in the topsy-turvy gendered world of South America rather than returning to the United States and its gendered norms (although it is worth wondering how well New Orleans represents any such norms). "It was here that our little Valcour was born," Harcliffe adds (*Fate*, ch. 25), yet it is curious that he does not specify whether their newborn child is a boy or a girl. Named after the child's aunt who lived as an uncle, the infant Valcour stands at the novel's end as a promise of a trans and transgressive future. Like Chick the Cherub in Baum's *John Dough and the Cherub*, the image of a child of unspecified sex powerfully disrupts the reproductive fantasy key to so much cisgendered fiction.

Baum's other trans antagonist in his nonfantasy fiction, Tato in *Aunt Jane's Nieces Abroad*, proves strikingly adept in shifting his gender performance while pursuing his goals, primarily financial ones as part of his father's criminal endeavors. Uncle John, the wealthy benefactor of Aunt Jane's nieces (Patsy, Beth, and Louise), encounters Tato while hiking in the Sicilian mountains, unaware that this young boy assists his father in his nefarious kidnapping syndicate. The narrator recounts Uncle John's initial reaction to Tato: "To his surprise he found a boy standing there and looking at him with soft brown eyes that were both beautiful and intelligent. . . . He was slender and agile . . . yet the most attractive thing about this child was his face, which was delicate of contour, richly tinted to harmonize with his magnificent brown eyes, and so sensitive and expressive that it seemed able to convey the most subtle shades of emotion. He seemed ten or twelve years of age, but might have been much older" (*Abroad*, ch. 16). This portrait, which concentrates on Tato's physical characteristics, offers few clues to his morphological sex, although the phrase "elfish character" captures the complexity of his gender presentation because in many instances elves straddle the borders between masculinity and femininity (*Abroad*, ch. 16). Upon meeting his captor Victor Valdi, also known as Il Duca, Uncle John witnesses a scene of familial affection: "[The cigars] were brought by Tato, who then sat in the duke's lap and curled up affectionately in his embrace, while the brigand's expression softened and he stroked the boy's head with a tender motion. Uncle John watched the little scene approvingly." Valdi's slip of the tongue identifies Tato's concealed sex—"My child is a linguist. . . . Sh—he has been taught English, German and French, even from the days of infancy"—and Uncle John thus resolves the mystery of this enigmatic figure: "Ah, I have solved one mystery, at any rate. Tato is a girl!" (*Abroad*, ch. 18). It appears that, had the duke not accidentally outed his daughter, Uncle John would have remained convinced of his masculine identity, and as with the confusion over when Harcliffe perceived Valcour's female sex, Tato's cross-dressing proves both wholly convincing and utterly transparent. Later, when Beth wonders of Tato's whereabouts and asks, "Where's that girl?" Kenneth replies, "Tato, my dear coz, is a boy," to which Beth scoffs: "You must be blind . . . not to recognize a girl when you see one. A boy, indeed!" (*Abroad*, ch. 22). Kenneth sees a boy, Beth sees a girl, with Baum's description of the character leaning decidedly toward an elfishness that defies binary categorization. At the very least, after divulging that this male-presenting character is female by sex, Baum mentions that Tato's fifteenth birthday is approaching, yet nothing in Tato's physical description alludes to the physical maturation of primary and secondary sexual characteristics.

Baum struggles to develop a coherent reason for Tato's cross-dressing, floating a variety of unsatisfying answers to this question. The strength of the answer could ultimately be found in the author's failure to give a reason, in that his character's male identity provides sufficient reason in itself. This answer, however, requires assuming Baum's motivations rather than interpreting the novel's words, which focus on Valdi's preference for a male son. In a discussion with his mother, the leader of their band of criminals, Valdi states: "Had I a son to inherit your business, a different thought might prevail; but I have only Tato, and a girl cannot be a successful brigand." Here the duke implies the necessity of Tato's masculine performance, in that he requires a son for the physically taxing word of brigandage. His mother rejects his words and cites herself as an example of a woman succeeding in a traditionally male domain: "'Why not?' cried the old Duchessa, contemptuously. 'It is the girl—always the girl—you make excuses for. But have I not ruled our domain—I, who am a woman?'" (*Abroad*, ch. 20). The duchess exposes the illogical basis of Tato's masculinity, and Tato similarly ascribes her masculine clothing to her father's desires: "I live in the mountains, where dresses catch in the crags, and bother a girl. And my father has always been heart-broken because he had no son, and likes to see me in this attire" (*Abroad*, ch. 23). These passages collectively suggest that a patriarchal preference for male children, rather than a young girl's innate desire to have her male gender confirmed, motivates Tato's cross-dressing.

Following Uncle John's escape from the kidnappers, both Tato and his father proclaim their ambition to redeem him (Tato) from both criminality and masculinity. Valdi promises his peaceful plans for the future, which include a cisgender future for his trans son: "Quietly we will disband our men and go away. In another land we live the respectable life, in peace with all, and Tato shall be the fine lady, and forget she once was a brigand's daughter" (*Abroad*, ch. 20). Significantly, the omniscient narrator—whom readers should ostensibly believe—confirms Tato's desire to emulate her new American friends: "The sweet young American girls had made a strong impression upon the lonely Sicilian maid, and she dreamed of their pretty gowns and ribbons, their fresh and comely faces, and the gentleness of their demeanor" (*Abroad*, ch. 23). Valdi cites admiration for Patsy, Beth, and Louise as a determinative factor in Tato's desire to reconcile with them: "As for Tato, she has been charmed by the young American signorini [sic], and longs to be like them. So we come to ask that you forgive the wrong we did you, and that you will now allow us to be your friends" (*Abroad*, ch. 27). As the book nears its conclusion, Tato appears to be adopted into the nieces' extended family unit—"Tato was now one of the family"—and Patsy affirms Tato's gendered position in it: "we already love you as if you were our little sister" (*Abroad*, ch. 28). In her reformation from lawbreaking boy to beautiful young girl, Tato's fairylike qualities are stressed, thus gracing the novel with the fairy-tale elements so common throughout Baum's corpus. Even when she dresses shabbily, in "a gray cloth gown, ill-fitting and of coarse material," the narrator assures readers that "no costume could destroy the fairy-like perfection of her form or the daintiness of her exquisite features" (*Abroad*, ch. 27). "Tato now looked more like a fairy than ever," the narrator states approvingly (*Abroad*, ch. 28), with this romanticized femininity apparently resolving the gender crisis that his cross-dressing instigated.

But in a final reversal that leaves many questions unanswered, Tato robs Uncle John and the nieces of their money, leaving behind a letter confessing his crime: "You tricked me once; but I have tricked you at the last, and the final triumph is mine." Tato ends this letter with proclamations of love and identifies himself as a "Sicilian tomboy" (*Abroad*, ch. 29). Tomboys confuse categories of gender, sex, and sexual orientation, a topic ably explored by Michelle Ann Abate, who unpacks the ways in which they subvert the "boundaries between male and female, adult and child, heterosexual and homosexual, masculine and feminine," as well as "between blackness and whiteness."[23] The nieces and Tato return to their respective homes, with Tato's performance of exaggerated, fairylike femininity revealed to be a facade for hoodwinking gullible American tourists, rather than any sincere desire to assert her long-cloaked femininity. This tomboy, it appears, will not be tamed.

Valcour and Tato prove likable, sympathetic characters as they challenge the uniformity of cisgenderism, yet it should be noted as well that their portrayals as nonwhite, or non-fully-white, characters correspond with their gender transgressions. Certainly, Baum's white female protagonists in his Aunt Jane's Nieces and Mary Louise series do not undermine visions of cisgendered femininity to the extent of Valcour and Tato. As he travels from New Orleans to South America in *The Fate of a Crown*, Robert Harcliffe stereotypes the people he will find at the end of his journey—"already I knew that Brazil was a dangerous country and sheltered a hot-headed and violent people" (*Fate*, ch. 3)—and thus should the trans touches of Valcour's character be viewed as part of Baum's othering of Brazilian characters? Likewise, Tato's unruly gender performance coincides with her depiction as a Sicilian bandit. Reflecting the anti-immigrant stance against Italians in the early twentieth-century United States, Italians and Italian Americans also suffer contumely, with Baum's characters referring to them with a pejorative term. After his kidnapping ordeal ends, Patsy asks Uncle John, "Did you think your nieces would let you be robbed by a bunch of dagoes?" (*Abroad* 291). Although never specified as Italian immigrants, the antagonistic workmen of *Aunt Jane's Nieces on Vacation* are depicted as "rough foreigners" (*Vacation*, ch. 9) who do not speak English (*Vacation*, ch. 19), with one character assessing them thusly: "Most of the workmen are foreigners, and all of them rude and reckless" (*Vacation*, ch. 15). Because Baum never specifies how these hundreds of foreigners entered the United States, it raises the likelihood that they are not foreigners but immigrants denied their identity as new citizens of the United States. In *Tamawaca Folks* Wilder comments on a neighbor, "Professor Graylor . . . used to be a rich man, but spent everything he had to convert the heathen dagos of the Windy City" (*Tamawaca*, ch. 3). As Jennifer Guglielmo, Salvatore Salerno, and others discuss in their volume *Are Italians White? How Race Is Made in America*, Italian Americans were often denied the privileges of whiteness after immigrating to the United States, and Baum's novels reflect the ways in which race is variably constructed alongside a person's nationality, ethnicity, and gender performance.[24] With Valcour and Tato, Baum's stereotyped visions of Brazilian and Italian characters as less civilized and less mannered than his white heroines coincide with their surprising gendered freedoms.

As a whole, Baum's trans tales subvert early twentieth-century expectations of gender and sexual morphology, and thus demand that readers look beyond initial depictions to see the bodies and desires of the characters who camouflage themselves—or were camouflaged by others. Ozma wins a kingdom, Prince Marvel enjoys an adventure, Chick the Cherub flummoxes publishers and child readers, Valcour fights revolutionaries, and Tato dupes American tourists through their ready acceptance, and even exploitation, of the porousness of both gender and sex. Although readers can see trans desires regulated or rechanneled in some of these texts, such as when the little girl of *Queen Zixi of Ix* learns not to pine for that which she cannot attain and when Valcour of *The Fate of a Crown* resumes life as a woman, in so doing they overlook the ways in which the transgressions cannot be recoded simply as a detour toward the character's ultimate acceptance of normativity, especially with Valcourt's deadname of Carlotta left behind. The transgressions linger; they persist beyond any sense of closure achieved by these novels' resolutions in the unknowability of the trans characters' desires and the intrusive act of questioning their bodies. The narrator asks readers to determine Chick the Cherub's sex, but they cannot resolve this conundrum in any meaningful way beyond the recognition of their own desires concerning Chick. In refusing to depict trans characters returning to the constraints of the sex assigned them at birth, Baum envisions gender and sex as plastic and malleable, determinative but not determined, and thus ever open to further negotiation and exploration as these characters chart their paths forward, and not only in the fantasy world of Oz.

Chapter 3

QUEER EROTICISMS IN OZ AND ELSEWHERE

> "These folks are all trying to do something queer,
> and most of them are doing it."
> —CHICK THE CHERUB (*DOUGH*, CH. 7)

In an extraordinary statement expressing his ambition to reframe standard erotic plotlines, Baum proclaimed of his fairy tales that there would be "no love and marriage in them."[1] As discussed in the first chapter, he also stated that he sought to create with his Oz series "a modernized fairy tale, in which the wonderment and joy are retained and the heartaches and nightmares are left out" (*Wonderful*, "Introduction"), and so it is noteworthy that his narratives do not conclude with the "and they lived happily ever" formula of fairy tales, which is surely intended to stimulate "wonderment and joy" from readers as they witness the heterosexual bliss of traditional matrimony. Furthermore, in removing romance and marriage from his tales, Baum aligns these themes with the "heartaches and nightmares" that he also avoids, which suggests his ambivalence toward depicting heteroeroticism as a whole. With heteroerotic desires frequently marginalized in the Oz series and Baum's other fictions, queer desires and queer eroticisms emerge to fill this absence. As dandies, mollycoddles, and fashion plates, many of Baum's male characters buck long-standing gendered norms of masculine identity and behavior, with other such characters expressing their strong distaste for female companionship. Some of Baum's men engage in heteroerotic relationships only owing to their firm adherence to the protocols of etiquette, while others form long-term homosocial bonds with their male friends, even to the point of resembling a fantasy version of queer marriage, as is notably the case with the Scarecrow and the Tin Woodman. Further developing his themes of male homosocial attachment, Baum depicts several instances of two men united in one body; many of these characters express their deep affection for each other and thus resemble gay married couples, or at the very least, committed partnerships. Finally, this chapter's concluding section addresses a miscellany of Baum's puzzlingly queer eroticisms, including fetishists of cloth and fat, a masochist, and the enigma of the Shaggy Man's Love Magnet, which makes him irresistible to everyone, except perhaps the most dedicated of gardeners.

As with so many instances of queerness in children's literature, readers are often left with puzzling hints of homoerotic desire rather than clearly communicated meanings, as the following short scene from *Queen Zixi of Ix* illustrates. While battling Queen Zixi's army, King Bud's general Tollydob pauses to request a favor from his colleague Tellydeb, who wields magically stretchable arms: "Yet I can never resist admiring a fine soldier, whether he fights for or against me. For instance, just look at that handsome officer riding beside Queen Zixi—her chief general, I think. Isn't he sweet? He looks just like an apple, he is so round and wears such a tight-fitting red jacket. Can't you pick him for me, friend Tellydeb?" The end result of this exchange falls into the logic of the story's battle, as Tellydeb "stretched out his long arm . . . and dragged his victim swiftly over the ground until he was seized . . . and firmly bound with cords" (*Zixi*, ch. 13). Engaged in battle, armies fight and men are captured, and so the hints of erotic desire in Tollydob's request are mostly squelched with this man's arrest. At the same time, Tollydob's attention to the "handsome officer," his appreciative eye for this man's close-fitting uniform, and his comparison of the man to an apple he desires to pluck and consume all contribute a frisson of queer desire to an otherwise comic battle scene. To argue that Tollydob should be read as a gay man risks drawing an anachronistic conclusion to a comic encounter among the topsy-turvy revels of children's literature, but to overlook the queerness of his desires and his appreciation of male beauty risks bleaching the text of its complexity. Baum engages with eroticisms well beyond the limits of the heteronormative but most frequently through sideways approaches, demanding readers to ponder the variability of desire in fictional worlds while also allowing plausible deniability to refute the proposition that two men might actually consummate their desire for each other.

OF GIRL-HATERS, DANDIES, MOLLYCODDLES, AND BAUM'S OTHER QUEER MALE IDENTITIES

Throughout Baum's fictions, readers encounter a range of girl-haters, dandies, mollycoddles, and other atypically gendered male characters suggestive of, but not correlative with, queerness. One cannot simply presume that Baum intended for these figures to be interpreted as gay men, particularly because dandyism blurred the borders between the normative and the queer in late nineteenth-century and early twentieth-century Britain and the United States of America. Not all dandies of this era were queers, and not all queers were dandies, but sufficient overlap between the categories raises the issue of how these many dandies contribute to the gendered themes of Baum's novels.[2] Oscar Wilde stands as the definitive exemplar of the era's queer dandies, and as Joe Lucchesi observes, "After Oscar Wilde's 1895 sodomy conviction, the image of the elegantly attired gentleman became indelibly associated with decadent male homosexuality."[3] Similar to the interpretive challenges surrounding *dandy*, the noun *mollycoddle* denotes "an effeminate male," although not necessarily a homosexual man. Nonetheless, the prefix *molly*, as in *mollyhouse* (a male brothel) and *mollymop* (a synonym for *mollycoddle*), refers to male homosexuality, and so the word can be used to connote without denoting homosexuality.[4]

A common trope of children's literature portrays the boys versus the girls, a children's version of the battle of the sexes in which a character or characters register their antipathy toward the other sex for little reason beyond this assumed otherness. For example, in *Sky Island* Trot meets Button-Bright and asks him, "Do you like girls?" He replies, "Not very well.... Some of 'em are pretty good fellows, but not many" (*Sky*, ch. 1). Button-Bright's dislike for girls is acknowledged but then recedes to the background of his character, and he travels with his fellow female adventurers without further expressing misogynistic viewpoints. Baum's older girl-haters, however, exhibit subtly queer traits. In *Mary Louise* the country lad Bub trumpets his misogyny: "They's gals there. I hate gals.... Any sort o' men critters I kin stand, but gals gits my goat" (*Mary*, ch. 13). One might presume that at fifteen years old Bub might begin reassessing his views of girls and women, yet he persists with his contumely: "To me ... ev'rything in skirts is gals. The older they gits, the more ornery, to my mind. Never seen a gal yit what's wuth havin' 'round" (*Mary*, ch. 15). In the Boy Fortune Hunter series, Uncle Naboth expresses his disdain for women; protagonist Sam Steele likewise rejects female companionship. In the Aunt Jane's Nieces books, Kenneth Forbes, who is sixteen years old in the series' first novel, initially despises females. "I hate all girls!" he cries (*Nieces*, ch. 13). As Kenneth becomes acquainted with Patsy, Beth, and Louise, his fear of women lessens—"All [Kenneth's] reserve and fear of women seemed to have melted away as if by magic" (*Nieces*, ch. 16)—yet queer hints to his characterization remain. In a subsequent novel of the series in which Kenneth campaigns for election to the state legislature, voters recoil at his candidacy with terms that attack his masculinity: "Some called Kenneth a 'prig' and declared that he was 'stuck up' and conceited.

Others said he was a 'namby-pamby' without brains or wit. But there were a few who had occasionally talked with the boy, who understood him better, and hinted that he might develop into 'quite a man' in time" (*Work*, ch. 2). Indeed, the raison d'être for Kenneth's campaign emerges in his distaste for advertising billboards that mar the countryside's beauty: "It's a crime to allow these signs to flaunt themselves in our prettiest scenes. My instinct revolts at the desecration" (*Work*, ch. 3). Has Kenneth Forbes matured from a girl-hating namby-pamby into heterosexuality, or does he remain a queer aesthete in the tradition of Oscar Wilde? Baum leaves the question unanswered.[5]

While in most instances they are distinct from girl-haters, dandies dress to attract attention, with their interest in fashion and their personal appearance indicative of an underlying vanity that nears narcissism. Baum's fantasy and juvenile fictions teem with dandies, particularly in his Land of Oz, which features three leading characters adopting this mannered lifestyle. Most significantly, the Tin Woodman is fastidiously concerned with his appearance, despite the fact that, as a tin man, he does not require clothing. The Scarecrow confirms, "My friend was ever inclined to be a dandy, and I suppose he is now more proud than ever of his personal appearance" (*Marvelous*, ch. 11); the narrator agrees that the Tin Woodman is "something of a dandy [who] kept his tin body brilliantly polished and his tin joints well oiled" (*Patchwork*, ch. 27). The Woggle-Bug, another recurring protagonist, "dressed like a dandy and was so full of knowledge and information (which are distinct acquirements), that he had been made a Professor and the head of the Royal College" (*Emerald*, ch. 5). Scouring the countryside for Ozma after her kidnapping, the Frogman travels in natty attire, as noted when he "arranged his necktie and smoothed his beautiful vest and swung his gold-headed cane like a regular dandy" (*Lost*, ch. 17). In Baum's fantasy land Mo, Prince Zingle's kite flies him to a land of civilized monkeys, who are shocked by his strange form. They determine that they must have evolved from such a primitive creature, but a foppish simian expresses his horror at such a thought: "'Heaven forbid!' cried a dandy-monkey, whose collar was so high that it kept tipping his hat over his eyes. 'If I thought such a creature as that was one of my forefathers, I should commit suicide at once'" (*Mo*, ch. 12). While not precisely a specimen of Wildean wit, this fop-monkey's words could be archly articulated to elevate their queer undercurrents: "If *I* thought such a creature as *that* was one of *my* forefathers, *I* should commit *suicide* at once."

As is well attested in LGBTQ+ history, the rise of urban centers throughout the twentieth century, particularly in the aftermaths of the world wars, contributed to the evolution of queer culture, as queer people left their small-town roots for the greater freedoms of large cities.[6] The vast majority of

Baum's fictions, however, were published before World War I, and aside from such exceptions as *Aunt Jane's Nieces in Society*, he more frequently sets his novels in fantasy and rural locales than in metropolises. Notwithstanding the unlikelihood of locating dandies in bucolic outposts, Aunt Jane's nieces, while vacationing in the hamlet of Millville, meet Nib Corkins, "the dandy of the town" (*Millville*, ch. 3), and while vacationing in a remote area of Sicily, they encounter the villainous duke's doctor, "a dandified appearing man who was very slight and thin of form but affected the dress and manners of extreme youth" (*Abroad*, ch. 18). The narrator of *The Flying Girl* introduces the baroquely named Mr. H. Chesterton Radley-Todd, nicknamed "Chesty," as both a dandy and a mollycoddle: "He was six feet and three inches tall and dressed like a dandy. People estimated him as a mollycoddle at first acquaintance" (*Flying*, ch. 21). Despite this effeminizing characterization, Chesty is enraptured by Orissa Kane, the eponymous flying girl of this two-novel series: "[Chesty] was thinking how good it was to find a girl not wrapped up in herself, but unselfish enough to admire others at her own expense. A pretty girl, too, Chesty concluded with a sigh, as he watched her prepare to start. What a pity he had lived all of twenty-one years and had not known Orissa Kane before!" (*Flying*, ch. 26). In this instance any presumption that Chesty's dandyism masks his queerness is apparently dashed, and it should be noted that *dandy* can also be used ironically, such as in the depiction of Hayes in *The Boy Fortune Hunters in Alaska* as "a big ruffian who was called 'Dandy Pete,' in derision, because he was so rough and unkempt" (*Alaska*, ch. 10).

Although the erotic lives of most of these dandies are left unexplored, Baum's *Phoebe Daring* includes in its cast of characters Mr. Holbrook, the handsome new lawyer in the novel's setting of a small southern town; this novel's conclusion obliquely points to the possibility of a queer partnership. According to the narrator, Mr. Holbrook is "something of a dandy" (*Phoebe*, ch. 2), and Phoebe and her friends find him attractive: "Neither had expected to find so young a man or one so handsome and well dressed" (*Phoebe*, ch. 5). This novel's plot focuses on Phoebe's efforts to exonerate an innocent young man, Toby Clark; she succeeds in this ambition, and so one might expect the novel to conclude heteronormatively, as a romance blossoms between them because their future happiness is assured owing to Phoebe's role in Toby's inheritance of a sizable fortune. Toby Clark, however, envisions a different partnership in his future: "I'm going to college. Some day, though, I'll be a lawyer, too, Mr. Holbrook, and then—who knows?—we may go into partnership together" (*Phoebe*, ch. 26). Toby evades a romantic partnership with his female savior and aspires to a business partnership with the town dandy. At the very least, Baum's evasion of the love plot—and in this instance for the much less popular form of the "business plot"—highlights the extent of his preference for depicting homosocial male friendships over heteroerotic couples. In a related scene from *Phoebe Daring*'s companion novel, *The Daring Twins*, readers witness a moment of intimacy between two men: "Mr. Ferguson slowly rose and laid an arm across the banker's shoulder. The gesture was strangely caressing, as between one man and another" (*Twins*, ch. 25). With Toby Clark linked in future partnership to a handsome dandy, with Phoebe's romantic interests left undeveloped, and with Mr. Ferguson "strangely caressing" his friend, Baum skirts the heteronormative conclusions so frequently celebrated in juvenile fiction, with other such evasions evident throughout his corpus.

HOMOSOCIAL COUPLES AND THE ETIQUETTE OF COMPULSORY HETEROSEXUALITY IN OZ

As with the ending of *Phoebe Daring*, in many instances Baum resists the heteronormative impulse of narrative conclusions that feature marriage, coupledom, and the formation of a new family unit. In his Oz novels, Baum foregrounds a view of sexuality incongruent with any presumption of heterosexuality, heteroeroticism, and heteronormativity, for, quite simply, heteroerotic romantic passion is virtually absent in Oz and his other fantasy works. When questing about on their adventures, the protagonists may dine or lodge with some configuration of a nuclear family, but none of the numerous featured characters in the series—including Dorothy, the Scarecrow, the Tin Woodman, the Cowardly Lion, Ozma, Glinda, Billina, the Hungry Tiger, Button-Bright, Scraps the Patchwork Girl, Tik-Tok, Cap'n Bill, Trot, Betsy Bobbin, the Shaggy Man, the Wizard, Toto, Eureka, the Woggle-Bug, and the Sawhorse—are linked in a heterosexual pairing. In contrast, several of these characters, while enjoying a wide range of friends, are paired with a character of the same sex, establishing the predominance of homosocial pairings throughout Oz, including Dorothy and Ozma, the Cowardly Lion and the Hungry Tiger, and, as discussed in more detail subsequently in this chapter, the Scarecrow and the Tin Woodman. Cap'n Bill and Trot are paired but not romantically attached, and the primary exception to the anti-heteroeroticism of Oz appears in Uncle Henry and Aunt Em, the old and childless couple who adopted Dorothy when her parents died, along with a few other married minor characters (e.g., Dr. Pipt and Dame Margolotte).[7] Indeed, even when, in a storyline reminiscent of the Persephone myth, the Nome king Ruggedo threatens to abduct the fairy Polychrome into his underground lair, he reassures her that she need not fear his sexual appetite: "Remain here and live with me and I'll set all these people free. You shall be my daughter or my wife or my aunt or grandmother—whichever you like—only stay here to brighten my gloomy kingdom and make me happy!" (*Tik-Tok*, ch. 17).[8] Ruggedo includes "wife" as one of Polychrome's four options, yet he appears surprisingly open to other forms of kinship, ones in which she would not be expected to sexually consummate their undesired relationship. Even in Baum's pseudonymously published works, heterosexual unions are often evaded, despite the primacy of the marriage plot for so much juvenile fiction.

The queerness of Oz is part of its utopian characterization: it is a fairyland where magic brings happiness and contentment to all of its citizens, despite the peculiarities of their gendered identities in regard to constructions of heteronormativity. Yet owing to Baum's resistance to depicting heteroerotic love and marriage, procreation is mostly absent, and when procreation nonetheless occurs, it is decidedly asexual. Numerous creatures are magically brought to life in the Oz series, including the Scarecrow (*Wonderful*, ch. 4), the Sawhorse (*Marvelous*, ch. 4), the Gump (*Marvelous*, ch. 17), Tik-Tok (*Ozma*, ch. 4), the Glass Cat (*Patchwork*, ch. 2), and Scraps (*Patchwork*, ch. 5). In these instances, magic facilitates the asexual creation of new life forms, in contrast to the mostly barren populace that no longer evinces any interest in reproduction, and it is worthwhile pondering, even within a fantasyland, how creatures such as scarecrows, sawhorses, and glass cats could reproduce, should they desire to do so. Even when new life arrives to bring companionship to the lonely and assistance to the distressed, reproduction in Oz is firmly divorced from eroticism and sexual attraction. Furthermore, it is unclear whether children could be born in Oz because the fairy magic that makes the land a queer utopia also renders it into a state of eternal equilibrium, if not of endless stasis, as explained in its backstory: "From that moment [when Queen Lurline enchanted the land] no one in Oz ever died. Those who were old remained old; those who were young and strong did not change as years passed them by; and children remained children always, and played and romped to their hearts' content, while all the babies lived in their cradles and were tenderly cared for and never grew up.... [S]o seldom was there anything to worry over that the Oz people were as happy and contented as can be" (*Woodman*, ch. 12). In such a land, the asexuality ascribed to children can never metamorphose into the heterosexuality of adults. The magic of Oz affects—or infects—Dorothy such that she can never mature into a sexually experienced woman but must always remain a sexually innocent girl: "She could not grow big, either, and would always remain the same little girl who had come to Oz, unless in some way she left that fairyland or was spirited away from it" (*Glinda*, ch. 1). If no child ages in Oz, the utopia is predicated upon a rejection of heterosexual procreation: it is unnecessary, and thus irrelevant to the formation of the social order.

Thus, the paradox of Oz is that it represents a queer utopia predicated upon the antisocial and anti-erotic rejection of heteronormative reproduction: its foundational utopian identity necessitates the eternal presence of children but not their continual procreation into the future. In contrast to the fantasy of Oz that celebrates queerness while simultaneously rejecting heterosexual eroticism, the rejection of fertility within much of modern Western society is ideologically linked to the denigration of nonreproductive sexualities, as Lee Edelman posits: "If, however, there is *no baby* and, in consequence, *no future*, then the blame must fall on the fatal lure of sterile, narcissistic enjoyments understood as inherently destructive of meaning and therefore as responsible for the undoing of social organization, collective reality, and, inevitably, life itself."[9] In Oz, however, one can celebrate nonreproductive sexuality while simultaneously celebrating the child; here queers are not blamed for or denigrated as a result of the failure of heterosexual reproduction, because reproduction is not a cultural goal of any relevance. Baum's fictions fracture the ideological celebration of fecund heterosexuality by reimagining the meaning and necessity of romantic networks.

If the ending of "they lived happily ever after" defines the heteronormative valence of the fairy tale as a genre, the Oz books cannot be easily construed as replicating the sexually and ideologically normative dynamics of such texts. By employing queer-friendly themes, by upsetting traditional gender roles in its construction of a fairyland utopia, and by reimagining the necessity of heterosexuality and reproduction within its antisocial critique of normativity, Baum infuses his Oz books with such queer oddness that the ideological and sexual foundations of fairy tale and myth are fractured. As Adrienne Rich theorized the force of compulsory heterosexuality as an ideological construction, so too do expectations of compulsory heterosexuality function in much of narrative history, yet Baum frequently depicts the acquiescence to compulsory heterosexuality as a matter of politeness and etiquette rather than of erotic desire.[10] Along these lines, even when it appears that a heterosexual couple may be developing in Oz, such narrative expectations are more likely to be dashed than fulfilled. *Rinkitink in Oz* concludes with the handsome Prince Inga visiting the poor maiden Zella. The narrator, to erase any aspersions against this hero's heterosexuality, admonishes readers "not [to] think that Inga was a molly-coddle" (*Rinkitink*, ch. 3), and a fairy-tale ending might depict their wedding so that the prince can continue his family dynasty and the maiden can escape her poverty. No such match takes place.

Instead, a homosocial couple is formed, as the cursed goat Bilbil metamorphoses back into his human form of Prince Bobo and promises to remain forever with King Rinkitink: "As for Prince Bobo, he had become so greatly attached to King Rinkitink that he was loth to leave him" (*Rinkitink*, ch. 23). In complementary contrast, *The Scarecrow of Oz* stands as one of Baum's rare fantasy works ending with the union of a heterosexual couple, in this instance between Princess Gloria and her suitor Pon. As the novel approaches its end, the couple, having overcome daunting magical obstacles, embrace: "Without an instant's hesitation she threw herself into Pon's arms and this reunion of two loving hearts was so affecting that the people turned away and lowered their eyes so as not to mar the sacred love of the faithful lovers" (*Scarecrow*, ch. 19). This celebration of their love cannot wholly overshadow the fact that their relationship sprang not from mutual affection but from etiquette, as Pon explains his love for Gloria in rather tepid terms: "Up to that time I had not thought of loving Princess Gloria, but realizing it would be impolite not to return her love, I did so" (*Scarecrow*, ch. 10). A civil obligation rather than a stirring passion, Pon's love discounts heteroerotic attraction as a motivating force in romance. Also, when Princess Gloria states, "I am unhappy because they will not let me love Pon, the gardener's boy," Trot responds brusquely: "Well, never mind; Pon isn't any great shakes, anyhow, seems to me.... There are lots of other people you can love" (*Scarecrow*, ch. 12). Hardly a sentimentalist, Trot views romance as inherently transactional.

As the above examples demonstrate, heteroerotic attraction is often evaded, denigrated, or politely acquiesced to in Baum's storylines, and the intersecting storylines of the Scarecrow, the Tin Woodman, and Scraps the Patchwork Girl demonstrate additional ways in which Baum acknowledges heteroerotic attraction only to dismiss it, and thus the ways in which he privileges homosocial partnerships. A flagrant example of unresolved heterosexual attraction occurs between the Scarecrow and Scraps:

> "Forgive me for staring so rudely," said the Scarecrow, "but you are the most beautiful sight my eyes have ever beheld."
> "That is a high compliment from one who is himself so beautiful," murmured Scraps, casting down her suspender-button eyes by lowering her head. (*Patchwork*, ch. 13)

This flirtatious scene lays the groundwork for male/female romance (albeit between a straw man and a quilted woman), and the Scarecrow aspires to pursue this newfound friendship: "We must be better acquainted, for never before have I met a girl with such exquisite coloring or such natural, artless manners" (*Patchwork*, ch. 13). Indeed, the Tin Woodman appears equally smitten by the lovely Patchwork Girl; the narrator records that he "gazed upon her in mingled wonder and admiration" (*Patchwork*, ch. 26). Based on these passages, readers might expect an erotic triangle to evolve, in which the Tin Woodman and the Scarecrow vie for Scraps's affections. In his foundational work on triangulated desires, René Girard suggests that, when two lovers pursue a shared beloved, the tensions generated culminate in conflict, and in her work on the latent queerness of erotic triangles, Eve Sedgwick explains that "in any erotic rivalry, the bond that links the two rivals is as intense and potent as the bond that links either of the rivals to the beloved." She further notes "that the bonds of 'rivalry' and 'love,' differently as they are experienced, are equally powerful and in many senses equivalent."[11] It is stunning to consider how many masterworks of literature would be lost without the intersecting plots of love and competition.

 Baum, however, pairs neither the Scarecrow nor the Tin Woodman with Scraps in any type of romantic relationship and instead concentrates on their deep friendship. Indeed, if any couple in Oz models the heartfelt affection of a long-term relationship, it is these two fast friends. As mentioned earlier, the Tin Woodman is described as a dandy, and while the Scarecrow is never painted with such terms, his interest in his appearance is adumbrated when Ozma gives him "a silver jar of complexion powder" (*Ozma*, ch. 20). The furnishings of the Tin Woodman's palace stress the significance of these men's friendship—"On the walls hung several portraits, that of the Scarecrow seeming to be the most prominent and carefully executed" (*Marvelous*, ch. 11)—and their union is presented, in the words of the Scarecrow, as a lifelong commitment: "'I shall return with my friend the Tin Woodman,' said the stuffed one, seriously. 'We have decided never to be parted in the future'" (*Marvelous*, ch. 24). Later in the series, the narrator describes the depth of their friendship: "There lived in the Land of Oz two queerly made men who were the best of friends. They were so much happier when together that they were seldom apart" (*Little*, "The Scarecrow and the Tin Woodman"). In this passage the queerness of the two men is located in their bodies constructed respectively of tin and straw, but their relationship likewise establishes them as a unique pairing in Oz, as few other friendships are described in such singular terms. In another such scene, the narrator stresses their shared emotional bond: "At times they spoke to one another of curious things they had seen and strange adventures they had known since first the two had met and become comrades. But at times [the Tin Woodman and the Scarecrow] were silent, for these things had been talked over many times between them, and they found themselves contented in merely being together, speaking now and then a brief sentence to prove they were wide awake and attentive" (*Woodman*, ch. 1). The simple pleasure of each other's company unites them in homosocial intimacy. W. W. Denslow's front-matter illustration in the first edition of *The Wonderful Wizard of Oz* captures the queer friendship of these two men by depicting them holding hands with their legs crossed.[12]

Of the many titles of the Oz series, *The Tin Woodman of Oz* most abundantly exposes the antiheteroerotic and homosocial themes at the heart of this queer utopia. A brief recounting of the Tin Woodman's backstory, in which a human named Nick Chopper transforms from a body of meat to one of tin, is necessary for the ensuing analysis. Prior to meeting Dorothy, as depicted in *The Wonderful Wizard of Oz*, Nick Chopper was engaged to a Munchkin Girl named Nimmie Amee, whose name suggestively indicates an excessive love.[13] Nimmie Amee worked for the witch with the silver shoes,[14] who opposed their marriage because she feared losing her servant. To halt their union, the witch cursed Nick Chopper's axe so that it would sever his various body parts. After each limb was cut off, the tinsmith Ku-Klip replaced it with tin. The Tin Woodman explains his transformation from carbon to tin-based life form: "In the Land of Oz . . . no one can ever be killed. A man with a wooden leg or a tin leg is still the same man; and, as I lost parts of my meat body by degrees, I always remained the same person as in the beginning, even though in the end I was all tin and no meat" (*Woodman*, ch. 2). One day the Tin Woodman rusted in the woods, was later rescued by Dorothy and the Scarecrow, and promptly forgot all about Nimmie Amee until the beginning of *The Tin Woodman of Oz*, when Woot the Wanderer queries him about his lost love and encourages him to find her.

The Tin Woodman of Oz thus begins with a fairly typical romantic plot: the Tin Woodman must undertake a quest to find his lost love, marry her, and live happily ever after with her. But in this utopian wonderland that rejects heteronormative procreation, the unfolding narrative proves just how antisocial and antierotic a force love can be. First, the Tin Woodman does not desire to pursue his lost beloved. He is known as the most loving man in Oz, as the narrator emphasizes: "The wonderful Wizard of Oz had given him an excellent heart to replace his old one, and he didn't at all mind being tin. Every one loved him, he loved every one; and he was therefore as happy as the day was long" (*Road*, ch. 15). When Woot reminds him of Nimmie Amee, his ability to love seems not quite as all encompassing as before. He explains to Woot that he loves everyone with his kind heart, but he does not possess a loving heart that would impel him to pursue a romantic relationship with a woman: "the Wizard's stock of hearts was low, and he gave me a Kind Heart instead of a Loving Heart, so that I could not love Nimmie

Amee any more than I did when I was heartless" (*Woodman*, ch. 2). The Tin Woodman excuses himself from the heterosexual imperative, claiming that his heart is designed to love all living creatures but not to love one woman exclusively in marriage. He only agrees to seek out his former girlfriend due to his sense of honor and responsibility: "I believe it is my duty to set out and find her. Surely it is not the girl's fault that I no longer love her, and so, if I can make her happy, it is proper that I should do so, and in this way reward her for her faithfulness" (*Woodman*, ch. 2). Similar to Pon falling in love with Princess Gloria owing to the strictures of etiquette, the Tin Woodman sees heterosexual union as an obligation to be bravely met rather than as a delight to be joyously sought. In the following dialogue, Woot exhorts the Tin Woodman to find pleasure in the courtship of a beautiful woman, but the reluctant lover sees only the disciplinary force of obligation:

> "It ought to be a pleasure, as well as a duty, if the girl is so beautiful," said Woot, well pleased with the idea of the adventure.
> "Beautiful things may be admired, if not loved," asserted the Tin Man. "Flowers are beautiful, for instance, but we are not inclined to marry them. Duty, on the contrary, is a bugle call to action, whether you are inclined to act, or not. In this case, I obey the bugle call of duty." (*Woodman*, ch. 2)

Like flowers, women are appreciated for their aesthetic value, yet such an homage to female attractiveness is accompanied with utter reluctance to pursue them. Only his sense of masculine honor, rather than a heteronormatively masculine sex drive, impels the Tin Woodmen on his quest to marry his long-lost fiancée.

During his journey to locate Nimmie Amee, the Tin Woodman discovers that he has a tin rival for her affections, and it thus appears that the narrative structure of the erotic triangle will govern this installment of the Oz series and that these two tin men will compete for the hand of their mutual beloved. The Tin Woodman's rival is a soldier named Captain Fyter, who wooed and won Nimmie Amee during the Tin Woodman's long absence, but this erotic triangle soon fizzles out, much like the one between the Scarecrow, the Tin Woodman, and Scraps. The wicked witch cast the same cruel spell on Captain Fyter, and so he too cut off his limbs one by one with his sword until nothing was left but a tin soldier. Having lost his heart, the Tin Soldier no longer loves Nimmie Amee ("As for that . . . I must admit I lost my ability to love when I lost my meat heart"), but similar to the Tin Woodman, he also decides to find and marry her out of a sense of duty ("Well, you see I had promised to marry her, and I am an honest man and always try to keep my promises" [*Woodman*, ch. 16]). The queerness of many erotic triangles arises in the competition between two men over one woman, which uncloaks the men's unresolved desire for each other, but in this instance, neither man wants to win Nimmie Amee, preferring the antieroticism of bachelorhood to the shared bliss of marriage:

> "If you have found such a heart, sir," said the Soldier, "I will gladly allow you to marry Nimmie Amee in my place."
> "If she loves you best, sir," answered the Woodman, "I shall not interfere with your wedding her. For, to be quite frank with you, I cannot yet love Nimmie Amee as I did before I became tin." (*Woodman*, ch. 16)

The function of the typical erotic triangle is to establish a narrative structure in which a heterosexual couple is created at the narrative's conclusion, such that the groundwork for procreation is prepared (even if such procreation is not depicted in the narrative itself). In their mutual desire to avoid marrying Nimmie Amee, and in their concomitant desire to avoid procreating with her, the Tin Woodman and the Tin Soldier enthusiastically reject the heteronormative imperative to reproduce. These tin men are indeed linked in a powerful bond, as Girard and Sedgwick posit, but their bond depends on the mutual rejection of heterosexuality rather than in its agonistic pursuit. The erotic triangle typically maps out the erotic energies of a social relationship in which, as the idiom proclaims, two's company, three's a crowd. In this incarnation, however, one is not the loneliest number; it's the preferred solution for avoiding heterosexual intercourse, and two is perfectly fine, but only if one's partner is also a man.

Readers might also wonder what exactly drives Nimmie Amee's erotic energies: while the Tin Woodman and Tin Soldier reluctantly compete for her hand in marriage, whom does she desire? The answer appears to be that she fetishizes tin to the extent that no meat-based man could ever win her affections; rather than a swooning young woman caught up in the delights of heterosexual attraction, she simply appreciates the aesthetic appeal of shiny metal. Captain Fyter describes how his tin body aided immeasurably in courting her:

> "She told me the [Tin Woodman] was nicer than a soldier, because he was all made of tin and shone beautifully in the sun. She said a tin man appealed to her artistic instincts more than an ordinary meat man, as I was then.... [F]inally Nimmie Amee permitted me to call upon her

and we became friends. It was then that the Wicked Witch discovered me and became furiously angry when I said I wanted to marry the girl. She enchanted my sword, as I said, and then my troubles began. When I got my tin legs, Nimmie Amee began to take an interest in me; when I got my tin arms, she began to like me better than ever, and when I was all made of tin, she said I looked like her dear Nick Chopper and she would be willing to marry me." (*Woodman*, ch. 16)

The question of why Nimmie Amee finds tin such a compelling component in her beloveds is never answered beyond her declarations regarding the metal's aesthetic appeal, yet certainly procreation becomes impossible when attempted between creatures respectively composed of meat and tin. (Does a tin man ejaculate oil?) Sexual attraction is very rarely depicted in these children's books, but it seeps into this scene, not to advance the cause of heterosexual romance, but to make such attractions outlandish, ridiculous, and ultimately terrifying. Who would pay the price of winning a woman's love if it necessitated the amputation of all of one's body parts? Although the biology of meat-based life forms is frequently derided in Oz, the gruesome and horrific violence inflicted upon these men—in which they suffer every possible metaphoric castration in the loss of their limbs, as well as the actual castration of their penises—renders heterosexual eroticism morbidly unattractive and undesirable.

This intriguing narrative reaches its climax when the Tin Woodman and the Tin Soldier find Nimmie Amee, but they discover that, during their long absence, she has married another man: Chopfyt. In yet another instance of asexual reproduction in Oz, the tinker Ku-Klip created Chopfyt out of the discarded body parts of Nick Chopper and Captain Fyter, assembling their hacked-off and leftover limbs together with Magic Glue. Ku-Klip recounts the project of making a man: "First, I pieced together a body, gluing it with the Witch's Magic Glue, which worked perfectly. . . . [B]y using a piece of Captain Fyter here and a piece of Nick Chopper there, I finally got together a very decent body, with heart and all the trimmings complete" (*Woodman*, ch. 18). Chopfyt is thus the triunal offspring of male reproduction, necessitating the bodies of two men and the creative energies of a third. Except for the Witch's Magic Glue that binds the two male bodies together, Chopfyt is a creature corporeally and psychically constructed by and from men. In a nod to Nimmie Amee's sexual attraction to metal, Chopfyt bears one limb made of tin, which marks Ku-Klips's role in his genesis; he is a hybrid figure of meat and metal symbolizing the past and present identities of the Tin Woodman and the Tin Soldier.

Instead of representing the "child" of the Tin Woodman and the Tin Soldier, the son who should serve as the apple of their eyes, Chopfyt symbolizes the external incarnation of their own rejected qualities. Any paternal or kindred instincts that the Tin Woodman and the Tin Soldier might feel for Chopfyt are negated by the creature's surly disposition. The first vision of Chopfyt emphasizes his rude and unappealing characteristics: "A man . . . was lazily reclining in a easy chair, and he . . . turned his eyes on the visitors with a cold and indifferent stare that was almost insolent. He did not even rise from his seat to greet the strangers, but after glaring at them he looked away with a scowl, as if they were of too little importance to interest him" (*Woodman*, ch. 22). After calling him such disparaging names as a "Nobody" and a "mix-up" (*Woodman*, ch. 22), the Scarecrow, Woot, and the Tin Woodman discuss their dislike for him:

> "Your old parts are not very polite, I must say," remarked the Scarecrow, when they were in the garden.
> "No," said Woot, "Chopfyt is a regular grouch. He might have wished us a pleasant journey, at the very least."
> "I beg you not to hold us responsible for that creature's actions," pleaded the Tin Woodman. "We are through with Chopfyt and shall have nothing further to do with him." (*Woodman*, ch. 23)

This scene bizarrely reconfigures Jacques Lacan's description of the mirror stage in which identity formulates in response to the perceived differences between the self and the external world: the Tin Woodman and the Tin Soldier desire to see a reflection of themselves in their offspring, yet they see only unattractive qualities instead. Lacan outlines the function of the mirror in that it "may on occasion imply the mechanisms of narcissism, and especially the diminution of destruction or aggression. . . . But it also fulfills another role, a role as limit. It is that which cannot be crossed."[15] Narcissism is negated in this encounter, as the image of Chopfyt allows no opportunity for the Tin Woodman and Tin Soldier to revel in the perfection of their own reflection; rather, Chopfyt points to the monstrous limits of heterosexuality in regard to the tin men's construction of their selves. He is the hideous reconfiguration of their bodies who must likely undertake, as part his household responsibilities, the onerous task of sexual intercourse with Nimmie Amee. Although antisocial in his interactions with his "fathers," as a husband he must participate in the sociality of marriage, which is built on a heterosexual foundation rejected by the Tin Woodman and the Tin Soldier.

The extent to which the Tin Woodman and the Tin Soldier reject Chopfyt is frighteningly apparent in their offer to Nimmie Amee to kill him and then to reclaim their lost body parts:

> "If you don't like him," suggested the Tin Woodman, "Captain Fyter and I can chop him up with our axe and sword, and each take such parts of the fellow as belong to him. Then we are willing for you to select one of us as your husband."
> "That is a good idea," approved Captain Fyter, drawing his sword.
> "No," said Nimmie Amee; "I think I'll keep the husband I now have. He is now trained to draw the water and carry in the wood and hoe the cabbages and weed the flower-beds and dust the furniture and perform many tasks of a like character. A new husband would have to be scolded—and gently chided—until he learns my ways." (*Woodman*, ch. 22)

Nimmie Amee's unromantic view of married life dismisses heterosexual attraction and affection in favor of a husband's domestic utility. Perhaps unsurprisingly for a woman who was formerly bound to serve a witch, she finds more benefit in a man trained to tend to her household needs than in either of the two men with whom she was romantically involved. Likewise, the Tin Woodman rejoices in his escape from domesticity and encourages the Tin Soldier to join him in his happiness free from heterosexual domestic obligations: "Be thankful. It is not our fate to hoe cabbages and draw water—and be chided—in the place of this creature Chopfyt" (*Woodman*, ch. 22). A happy ending is achieved at the conclusion of this fairy tale, with the three "lovers" in the erotic triangle each achieving their respective goals, yet no one in this triangulated affair sought the erotic attachment ostensibly at its base. In this most antisocial of erotic triangles, freedom is found in the dismissal of heterosexual attraction, and the Tin Woodman can escape from any lingering heteroerotic obligations back to the pleasures of homosocial companionship with the Scarecrow.

As unsettling as the vision of Chopfyt may be, the image of two male characters united for life in a single body recurs in Baum's fictions, and while it stretches credulity to interpret these figures as gay married couples, their unions are presented as lifelong attachments and, in some instances, preferable to female companionship. Images of two humans united in one body date back millennia, as evident in Plato's *Symposium*, which explains the origins of human sexuality, both heterosexuality and homosexuality, through such mythic figures. In this historic dialogue, Aristophanes first explains that there are three genders—"male and female" as well as "a third one, [a] combination of these two." Originally, "the shape of each human being was a rounded whole, with back and sides forming a circle," but Zeus punished humanity by cutting each person into two pieces. "Since their original nature had been cut in two, each one longed for its own other half," Aristophanes continues, with queer people created from this process: "Those women who are cut from the female gender are not at all interested in men, but are drawn much more towards women.... Those [men] who are cut from the male gender go for males."[16] As discussed in this volume's Introduction, the Ki-ki of *The Enchanted Island of Yew* exemplify Baum's penchant for such mutually constituted men, and *Dot and Tot in Merryland* features another such curiously formed man when the eponymous protagonists meet Mr. Split, who hooks his separate parts together: "the right half of Mr. Split placed his flat side close to the left half's flat side and then with both hands he hooked the two halves together with little brass hooks. Then Mr. Split looked more like a complete man, although the left side was dressed in a bright red suit while the right side wore white, so it was easy to see where he was joined together" (*Merryland*, ch. 16). Little in this passage indicates that Mr. Split should be seen as two men newly merged into one, yet it is strikingly reminiscent of Plato's vision of a queer man divided from and then reunited with his lost half.

The queer undertones of such men are intensified in *Sky Island*, in which the tyrannous Boolooroo punishes wrongdoers by patching, a process explained by Jimfred Jonesjinks: "They cut two of us in halves and mismatch the halves—half of one to half of the other, you know—and then the other two halves are patched together. It destroys our individuality and makes us complex creatures, so it's the worst punishment that can be inflicted in Sky Island" (*Sky*, ch. 7). Jimfred Jonesjinks now constitutes one complete man, as does his counterpart Fredjim Jinksjones. The slicing and patching of criminals appears a gruesomely physical but also psychological punishment, and Jimfred Jonesjinks first stresses the likely mismatch between any two people so conjoined: "Then they match half of you to another person who has likewise been sliced, and there you are, patched to someone you don't care about and haven't much interest in" (*Sky*, ch. 7). Yet by the novel's end, Fredjim Jinksjones says to Jimfred Jonesjinks: "You and we are about alike, now, Jimfred, although we were so different before" (*Sky*, ch. 22). Not "you and me" but "you and we," the two (or four?) men—once separate, then spliced and patched together—now accept that they were forced into lifetime companionship with each other and find a mutuality previously unexpected. Moreover, Baum's patched men are prohibited from marrying women, as another character explains: "It's against the law for a patched man to marry anyone. It's regarded as half-bigamy" (*Sky*, ch. 20). For these men, once patched means always patched, with no erotic outlet except with this newly formed self. At the very least, these men, literally if fantastically, share their bodies with each other, in an apt metaphor of queer sexual intercourse.

In another of *Sky Island*'s storylines of the unexpected pleasures of homosocial patching and queer bonding, the Six Snubnosed Princesses offer to free the hero Ghip-Ghisizzle if he chooses a wife from among them; he replies, "Really, ladies, you must excuse me. I'd rather be patched than mismatched, as I would be with a lovely, snub-nosed wife. You are too beautiful for me; go seek your husbands elsewhere" (*Sky*, ch. 20). "Rather patched than mismatched": with this potent formulation, Ghip-Ghisizzle asserts his preference to be united corporally with Tiggle, a minor character who earned his punishment by performing one of Cap'n Bill's tasks, than to marry one of these admittedly unlikeable princesses. Indeed, when the Snubnosed Princess Indigo claims to know the location of Button-Bright's lost magic umbrella, which she will reveal if Trot compels Ghip-Ghisizzle to marry her, he refuses: "I'd like to help you . . . but nothing will ever induce me to marry one of those snubnoses." Trot counters that the Snubnosed Princess are physically attractive, but Ghip-Ghisizzle rebuts: "But when you marry a girl, you marry the inside as well as the outside . . . and inside these Princesses there are wicked hearts and evil thoughts. I'd rather be patched than marry the best of them" (*Sky*, ch. 27). Ghip-Ghisizzle escapes both patching and the Six Snubnosed Princesses, but in his preference for a spliced life with a man over marriage to an attractive, if disagreeable, woman, he appears to hope that, as with Jimfred Jonesjinks and Fredjim Jinksjones, a mutuality of homosocial spirit would grow to counterbalance the loss of heteroerotic possibility. Adhering to his stated prohibition against love and marriage in his fairy and fantasy tales, Baum envisioned instead a strikingly odd vision of homosocial companionship, one horrific yet somewhat resignedly endearing as two patched men embark on their new lives together.[17]

A QUEER MISCELLANY: FETISHISTS, A MASOCHIST, A NURSERY-RHYME TORCH SONG, AND AN AMOROUS BUT DUTIFUL GARDENER

Along with Baum's matched men and patched men who collectively undermine conceptions of masculinity and heteroeroticism, several characters further evince erotic queerness, although not gay identities, in their fetishes and masochistic desires. Thus, the "queer miscellany" adumbrated in this section's title captures the ways in which binary conceptions of sexuality attempt to circumscribe identities and desires but cannot staunch those that circulate beyond, or in excess of, such rigid borders. The very concept of a miscellany highlights the porousness of classifications, the failure of genres, and the surfeit of possibilities that can never be contained within taxonomies, thus suggesting the potential of queerness, however defined, whenever the need of a miscellany arises.

Similar to Nimmie Amee's fascination with tin, the Woggle-Bug fetishizes clothing, preferring a person's fashions over the person wearing the clothing and thus proving his indifference to sex as a determinate factor in desire. Baum's interest in window dressing is evident in the publication of his *The Art of Decorating Dry Goods Windows and Interiors*, and *The Woggle-Bug Book* captures the latent erotic power of visual design. Sauntering down the Main Street of an unnamed city, the Woggle-Bug pauses before a life-changing window display: "Presently he came to a very fine store with big plate-glass windows, and standing in the center of the biggest window was a creature so beautiful and radiant and altogether charming that the first glance at her nearly took his breath away. Her complexion was lovely, for it was wax; but the thing that really caught the Woggle-Bug's fancy was the marvelous dress she wore" (*Woggle-Bug* 4). Baum first misdirects his readers' attention, focusing on the "creature so beautiful and radiant" and her pleasing complexion. Seeing the word "creature," readers would likely presume that a living being has attracted the Woggle-Bug's attention, but Baum then reveals that this creature is a mannequin and that the Woggle-Bug prefers its "marvelous dress" to any beauty it would likely possess.

As much as the Woggle-Bug desires this dress, he cannot buy it because he has no money, and by the time he secures the necessary funds, it has been purchased. Normative gender is already demolished in this story as a highly magnified male insect pursues a woman's dress, and the Woggle-Bug then begins his quest to track down this lost fetishized object, moving from owner to owner, regardless of sex, gender, and ethnicity. As the narrator states, "It is very queer, when we think of it, that the Woggle-Bug could not separate the wearer of his lovely gown from the gown itself. Indeed, he had always made love directly to the costume that had so enchanted him, without any regard whatsoever to the person inside it; and the only way we can explain this remarkable fact is to recollect that the Woggle-Bug was only a woggle-bug, and nothing more could be expected of him" (*Woggle-Bug* 20). Because he is guided by his fetishized desire for the dress, the Woggle-Bug will engage in either heteroerotic or homoerotic relationships if they advance his ultimate purpose. He once again locates the dress, now owned by a Chinese American man. "Oh, my prismatic personification of gigantic gorgeousness—again I have found you!" the Woggle-Bug cries, and continues excitedly, "Be mine! Only be mine!" (*Woggle-Bug* 26). The humor of this passage arises in the Woggle-Bug's words to the dress being spoken in the immediate vicinity of the Chinese American man, even though the Woggle-Bug soon clarifies his intentions, "Never mind that! 'Tis your beautiful garment I love. Every check in that entrancing dress is a joy and a delight to my heart!" Bewildered by this unexpected declaration of devotion, this man's wife looks askance at the Woggle-Bug near her husband: "While the Woggle-Bug thus raved, the Chinaman's wife (who was Mattie De Forest before she married him) overheard the conversation, and decided this love affair had gone far enough" (*Woggle-Bug* 28). In contrast to the many ethnic slurs found in his fiction, Baum here introduces an interracial marriage without additional commentary, presenting it simply as a marriage rather than as one requiring comment, or worse, denunciation.

Despite this nod to racial egalitarianism in a romantic relationship, *The Woggle-Bug Book* exhibits Baum's casual racism in many other moments, thus again undercutting his otherwise progressive views. He refers to this Chinese American man as "the Chink" (*Woggle-Bug*, 26), and when Miss Chim, a chimpanzee, escorts the Woggle-Bug through her jungle, readers witness the following: "As they walked up the street they came to a big grey monkey turning a hand-organ, and attached to a cord was a little n----r-boy whom the monkey sent into the crowd of animals standing by to gather up the pennies, pulling him back every now and then by means of the cord." The narrator speaks the N-word, as Miss Chim then denigrates both Black and white people: "Those horrid things they call men, whether black or white, seem to me the lowest of all created beasts" (*Woggle-Bug*, 42). Along the Woggle-Bug's festishistic journey, Baum celebrates the character's queer desires while denigrating a range of characters of color. *The Woggle-Bug Book* ends, as many fairy tales do, with the protagonist and his love anticipating their "happy ever after," with the Woggle-Bug's words cementing this ending: "After all, this necktie is my love—and my love is now mine forevermore! Why should I not be happy and content?" (*Woggle-Bug*, 48). The gown that he initially admired has been cut and refashioned throughout its journey, and now only a necktie remains, yet the Woggle-Bug rejoices in their union. Whereas Baum so frequently dodges heteroerotic conclusions in his fantasy fictions, the Woggle-Bug wins his love, yet this affaire de coeur is only imaginable between a human-sized bug and a comely piece of cloth.

In another reference to fetishism, Baum incorporates a small story line of feederism, also referred to as fat fetishism and eater/feeder relationships, in which desire is expressed not primarily through fat itself but through the process of fostering another person's weight gain. Dina Giovanelli and Natalie Peluso theorize that "feederism sexualizes body fat, food consumption, and weight gain"; it is a "sexual practice which associates body fat with physical attractiveness, consumption with erotic behavior, and weight gain with sexual fulfillment."[18] In *John Dough and the Cherub*, the kinglet is enraged that Bebe Celeste, "a woman so exceedingly fat that she appeared to be much wider than she was long," has lost two ounces. He orders: "Take her away, guards, and stuff her with mashed potatoes and pate de foie gras. If she doesn't regain those two ounces in three days, she'll disgrace my kingdom, and I'll turn her over to the Royal Executioner" (*Dough*, ch. 5). Fatness falls within the carnivalesque tropes of children's literature, in that exaggerated bodies are often preferred to purportedly normative bodies, and while this scene falls to several regrettable stereotypes about fat people, it also suggests their desirability through the kinglet's passionate insistence that Bebe Celeste retain her stature. Similar but distinct from the Woggle-Bug's fetishization of a garment that prioritizes it over the sex of the person wearing it, the kinglet's fetishization of fatness evades the question of whether heteroeroticism plays any role in his desire: does the reputation of the kingdom depend on Bebe Celeste and her fat simultaneously or just on her fat? And who judges the land's reputation according to its fattest citizen? This short scene suggests a range of unexpected desires but also of disappointments, if those two missing ounces are not soon restored to Bebe Celeste's body.

Masochism would appear to be an unlikely theme in children's literature, and I do not propose that the toy alligator of *Dot and Tot in Merryland*, who encourages passersby to step on him so he can hear his squeak, should necessarily be interpreted as masochistic. On the other hand, with Nerle of *The Enchanted Island of Yew* readers encounter a character who appears more appropriate for Leopold von Sacher-Masoch's foundational opus of masochistic desire, *Venus in Furs* (1870), than for a children's fantasy novel. The protagonist Prince Marvel rescues Nerle from a thief only to find that he (Nerle) prefers his imprisonment. "I want to be miserable. It's the first chance I've ever had, and I'm enjoying my misery very much" (*Yew*, ch. 5), Nerle declares, and he also shares the roots of his masochistic desires in his childhood: "I once saw the son of one of our servants receive a flogging; and my heart grew light. I immediately begged my father to flog me, by way of variety; and he, who could refuse me nothing, at once consented" (*Yew*, ch. 6). As flogging is one of the key tropes of sadomasochism, so too is the masochist's enjoyment of humiliation, and Nerle recalls that he once inquired of a stranger undergoing many misfortunes, "Pray tell me how I can manage to acquire the misfortunes you have undergone. Here I have everything that I desire, and it makes me very unhappy." He then details the stranger's response and his unexpected enjoyment of it: "The stranger laughed at me, at first; and I found some pleasure in the humiliation I then felt" (*Yew*, ch. 6). When Nerle cries in anticipation, "Soon shall I be content, for these darts will doubtless pierce every part of my body" (*Yew*, ch. 10), the queer imagery of St. Sebastian's martyrdom is recalled, in which, in most images, a handsome, near-naked man is penetrated by a hail of arrows.[19]

Sadomasochistic relationships require both a sadist and a masochist, and while Prince Marvel never acts sadistically toward Nerle, Nerle thanks him for compelling him to exist in a subordinate position: "By forcing me to become your servant you have made me, for the first time in my life, almost contented. For I hope in your company to experience a great many griefs and disappointments" (*Yew*, ch. 6). Prince Marvel, initially perplexed by Nerle, later comes to understand his friend's unexpected pleasures. When they seek to enter the Hidden Kingdom of Twi, they must cut through a thick brier bush, and Nerle foresees great delights in his imminent pain. "The briers would probably prick me severely, and that would be delightful," he states, and he spiritedly volleys into the bush's thorns: "Nerle sprang from his horse to obey, but at the first contact with the briers he uttered a howl of pain and held up his hands, which were bleeding in a dozen places from the wounds of the thorns." Prince Marvel replies coolly, "Ah, that will content you for a time, I trust" (*Yew*, ch. 13). Indeed, some scholars theorize that the ultimate masochistic desire is for death, as expressed by Gilles Deleuze: "Beyond Eros we encounter Thanatos; beyond the ground, the abyss of the groundless; beyond the repetition that links, the repetition that erases and destroys."[20] Baum depicts this dark desire for his audience of children. Upon meeting the doughty Prince Marvel, Nerle ponders his own demise, hoping that any incipient death pains will be prolonged: "if you should prove my superior in skill I beg you not kill me at once, but let me die a lingering death." Prince Marvel wonders why Nerle would express such a wish, to which the masochist replies: "Because I shall suffer more, and that will be delightful" (*Yew*, ch. 5). By the end of *The Enchanted Island of Yew*, Nerle is apparently cured of his masochistic longings: "He did not seem as unhappy as usual, and when the prince inquired the reason, his esquire answered that he believed the excitement of their adventures was fast curing him of this longing for something he could not have. As for the pleasure of suffering, he had had some experience of that, too, and it was not nearly so delightful as he had expected" (*Yew*, ch. 22). A reformed masochist, Nerle experiences sufficient pain to quench his pleasure in it, with his unruly yearnings a testimony to the varieties of desires expressed in Baum's fantasylands.

Finally, whereas Baum's Shaggy Man neither shares his body with another man nor expresses fetishistic or masochistic desires, his Love Magnet compels men to love him, with the ensuing dialogue carrying romantic overtones. Requiring the assistance of Johnny Dooit to cross the desert surrounding Oz, the Shaggy Man summons him with two lines of verse that resemble a mashup of a nursery rhyme and a torch song: "*Dear Johnny Dooit, come to me. / I need you bad as bad can be*" (*Road*, ch. 11). When the Shaggy Man and Betsy Bobbin are condemned to death for entering the Rose Kingdom, he employs his Love Magnet on the Royal Gardener, who then rhapsodizes: "Oh, you lovely, lovely man! How fond I am of you! Every shag and bobtail that decorates you is dear to me—all I have is yours!" (*Tik-Tok*, ch. 6). Seeking to press his advantage, the Shaggy Man flirts with his words and his gestures: "'Don't you love me, Gardy?' asked Shaggy, carelessly displaying the Magnet." Torn between desire and duty, the Royal Gardener replies, with his obligations ultimately triumphing: "'I do. I dote on thee!' answered the Gardener earnestly; 'but no true man will neglect his duty for the sake of love. My duty is to drive you out, so—out you go!'" (*Tik-Tok*, ch. 6). In Baum's fantasy fictions, not every queer desire can be sated, yet on the whole, queer desires are featured more prominently than heteroerotic ones, thus proving by their commonness the discontent provoked by normative regimes.

As much as this chapter has focused on Baum's overarching rejection of heteronormative plotlines in so much of his fiction, it would be remiss not to acknowledge that some of his pseudonymous novels, grounded more in realist than in fantasy settings and intended for adult readers, allow for the well-worn narrative conclusion of heteroerotic marriage. His anonymously published *The Last Egyptian* ends with Aneth Consinor and Gerald Winston planning their wedding in Luxor; and, in John Estes Cook's *Tamawaca Folks: A Summer Comedy*, the revelation that Susie Smith is "the only, only child of the great Agamemnon Smith, the richest Standard Oil magnate after Rockefeller himself!" paves the way for her engagement to protagonist Jim Everton (*Tamawaca*, ch. 13). Indeed, Everton is described in terms that stress his normative sexuality: "[Jim] had purposely concealed his occupation while on vacation, in order to enjoy a bit of feminine society, of which he was as wholesomely fond as every boy ought to be" (*Tamawaca*, ch. 6). In Schuyler Staunton's *Daughters of Destiny*, Janet Moore reunites with her husband, Herbert Osborne, also known as Ahmed Khan, with this cross-cultural union meriting the approval of Janet's dour and prejudiced aunt:

"There was no doubt of Aunt Lucy's democracy, yet it was amusing to note her pride in the fact that Janet was the wife of an Eastern potentate of the importance of Ahmed Khan" (*Daughters*, ch. 24). Here again Baum endorses an interethnic marriage, despite the many calumnies expressed against Asian men elsewhere in his fiction and, in particular, in this novel.[21] In Suzanne Metcalf's *Annabel: A Novel for Young Folks*, Dr. Meigs inquires of Will Carden if he is "in this young lady's company pretty often these days." Will "glance[s] shyly" as Annabel stands "with downcast eyes, her face suffused with blushes"; Will then states fondly, "Of course I am. Annabel's an old chum" (*Annabel*, ch. 18). Edith Van Dyne evades romance for the first four Mary Louise novels, but the final installment, *Mary Louise Adopts a Soldier*, features Baum's most sentimental account of heteroerotic attraction: "The blaze of light turned to the soft dusk of twilight as Danny stood and gazed at her. Then simply, naturally, and with an infinite tenderness Danny Dexter stepped through the door and took Mary Louise in his arms" (*Soldier*, ch. 27). But even here evidence of Baum's antiheteroerotic tendencies arises, for it is more likely than not that this scene was penned by Emma Speed Sampson, the author who continued Baum's Mary Louise novels after his death.[22] Moreover, as discussed in chapters 6 and 7, Baum avoids heteroerotic plotlines in his Boy Fortune Hunters and Aunt Jane's Nieces series, sometimes to an eye-raising extent.

With such a prodigious output of fiction, it is unlikely that Baum could have entirely evaded depicting heteroerotic desire, particularly in his more realist fictions for older readers, but in complementary contrast, virtually any author of his era could have easily evaded depicting homoerotic and other queer desires. Baum daringly portrays a range of nonnormatively gendered men and prioritizes homosociality in other instances, and includes a range of erotic behaviors fetishistic in their expression. With heteroeroticism sidelined in much of his fantasy work, although represented more proportionately in his pseudonymous fictions, queer identities emerge not merely as expressions of carnivalesque inversion but as fundamental reimaginings of gender and desire. With these queer eroticisms always celebrated, never denigrated, readers see new visions of kinship, community, and lifelong companionship. The startling image of Jimfred Jonesjinks and Fredjim Jinksjones, it turns out, envisions a union preferable to the ones offered to Baum's contemporary queer readers by the Western society in which they lived, proving the necessity of fantasy fiction for imagining whimsical new ways of being that might just have a glimmer of truth in them.

Chapter 4

THE QUEER CREATURES OF OZ AND ELSEWHERE EAT ONE ANOTHER

"Queer things happen in the Land of Oz."
—POLYCHROME, THE RAINBOW'S DAUGHTER, ENCHANTED INTO
THE FORM OF A CANARY (*WOODMAN*, CH. 8)

Even if Baum intended for the word *queer* to refer exclusively to the odd and the eccentric with no relation to matters of sexuality, it is striking that Oz's eccentricity undoes its facade as a utopian realm and demarcates the impossibility of normativity for its eclectic range of queer creatures. In these ostensibly halcyon lands populated by benevolent fairies, talking animals, and other marvelous creatures, Oz and Baum's other fantasy settings embrace a wide-ranging and ecumenical community in which various queer species interact peacefully, yet a recurrent theme of cannibalism undermines this egalitarianism. The need to eat and the ensuing search for food—daily activities that undergird biological existence—are never overlooked in Oz, and this bodily realism deflates the utopian fantasy of these modern-day fairy tales. The frequent focus on food, cooking, and eating, along with the ways in which these activities create and undermine civilization, provides a strong countercurrent to elements of Oz that constitute it primarily as a utopian wonderland.[1] Osmond Beckwith suggests that the "internal evidence" of the Oz series "must contradict the sentimental idea that Oz was intended as a planned Utopia,"[2] and by observing who eats what—or whom—in Oz and Baum's other fantasy lands, readers see the ways in which the author subverts his utopia through food's paradoxical role in society. Cooking and eating together should build the queer community of Oz, yet such fundamental and quotidian processes simultaneously highlight cultural tensions in that the social order must be readdressed at almost every meal. Through the perpetual threat of cannibalism in Oz, one never knows if one will be the diner or the dined upon. Consequently, even normative identities in Oz and Baum's other fantasy landscapes are queer (in the sense of odd or eccentric), because under these conditions no sense of normativity can function as an effective yardstick against which creatures might assess one another.

THE CANNIBALISTIC QUEERNESS OF FOOD, COOKING, AND CONSUMPTION IN OZ

Food and cooking are central to the creation and maintenance of a social structure, and in Baum's fantasy fiction they define the parameters of civilization and civilized behavior. Kara Keeling and Scott Pollard, in their study of consumption in children's literature, posit that "the sociocultural contexts of food reveal . . . fundamental understandings of the child and children's agency and [enrich] the interpretation of [children's literature]."[3] Speaking more generally, Claude Lévi-Strauss outlines the pivotal role of food and food preparation in cultivating a society: "The art of cooking is not entirely situated on the side of culture. Since it corresponds to the demands of the body, and is determined in each of its modes by the particular way in which, in various contexts, man fits into the world, cooking, being situated between nature and culture, has as its function to ensure their articulation one with the other. It belongs to both domains, and reflects this duality in each of its manifestations."[4] In theory, the raw ingredients of food belong to the realm of nature, whereas the cooking process adheres to the realm of civilization; in practice, these borders frequently dissolve owing to the close intermingling of the steps necessary to consume food, including hunting, gathering, storing, and preparing the various ingredients of a meal. Cooking cannot be discretely taxonomized under rubrics of either nature or culture because it is central to their complex interrelationship, as it is also key to the propagation of a culture and its norms. And whereas foodstuffs and their consumption may appear to be widely divergent from the concerns of queer theory, both food and sexuality can be ideologically conscripted to define the (ab)normality of a culture's citizens, and thus surprising convergences emerge.

In many ways, food serves a civilizing function for the various queer denizens of Baum's fantasylands. The texts suggest that, if creatures have access to a sufficient food supply, they will evolve to a higher level of sophistication, intelligence, and social involvement. Aunt Em brings her American prejudice against mosquitoes to Oz, but the Tin Woodman ensures her that such fears are now misguided:

> "We have some very large mosquitoes here, which sing as beautifully as song birds," replied the Tin Woodman. "But they never bite or annoy our people, because they are well fed and taken care of. The reason they bite people in your country is because they are hungry—poor things!"
>
> "Yes," agreed Aunt Em; "they're hungry, all right. An' they ain't very particular who they feed on. I'm glad you've got the 'skeeters educated in Oz." (*Emerald*, ch. 24)

In this beneficial paradigm of the role that food plays in civilization, mosquitoes participate in a higher level of culture simply because they are well fed. Aunt Em's preconception of the antagonistic relationship between mosquitoes and humans—predicated on her dislike of serving as a food source for parasitical insects—fades in light of their educated nature in Oz. This exchange also indicates that food supplies are essential to education, as the basic necessity of nourishment must be met before cultural development can be attained.

This ideal example of educated mosquitoes, who are successfully integrated into society once their food supply is guaranteed, is counterbalanced by numerous examples of creatures who disrupt Oz's queer social order through their cannibalistic appetites. Similar to cooking, cannibalism also defines a civilization and its social structure, according to Peggy R. Sanday: "Cannibalism is never just about eating but is primarily a medium for nongustatory messages—messages having to do with the maintenance, regeneration, and, in some cases, the foundation of the cultural order."[5] In this light, cannibalism demarcates a society's mores by defining the parameters of civilized and uncivilized behavior. As William Arens ponders, "What could be more distinctive than creating a boundary between those who do and those who do not eat human flesh?"[6] When attending a dinner party in a civilized society, one rightly expects to be served dinner, not to be served *as* dinner.

In a fairyland, however, boundaries demarcating cultural clusters are remarkably fluid, as humans, talking animals, and magical creatures all live together in a functioning society. Thus, as is evident throughout this chapter, simply defining cannibalism poses a difficult task when applied to the queer land of Oz: if humans eat sentient, intelligent, and anthropomorphized animals in a magical kingdom, are they cannibals? Certainly, equality among the various creatures in many ways establishes the necessary conditions for their (mostly peaceful) coexistence. As Andrew Karp suggests, "[Baum] sees no fundamental distinction between the animate and inanimate world, between the pastoral and mechanical world, or between the inanimate and natural worlds. In Oz, anything and everything can be 'alive' and, consequently, worthy of respect and rights, from rainbows to silverware to robots to rag dolls."[7] Alison Lurie likewise notes, "In the world of Oz, acceptance of minority rights is taken for granted."[8] By definition, cannibalism requires mutuality between the diner and the dined upon: if a meat-based life form is eaten by a different species, it has certainly encountered a carnivore but not necessarily a cannibal. The playful paradox of defining cannibalism in a queer fairy kingdom appears when Jack Pumpkinhead offers his guests pumpkin pies:

> The pumpkin-headed man welcomed his visitors joyfully and offered them several delicious pumpkin pies to eat.
> "I don't indulge in pumpkin pies myself, for two reasons," he said. "One reason is that were I to eat pumpkins I would become a cannibal, and the other reason is that I never eat, not being hollow inside." (*Emerald*, ch. 25)

The paradox of a pumpkin eating a pumpkin suffuses this scene with humor, yet it also upends the culinary rules of real life, in which one should never see a dining companion devour a foodstuff cooked from the same material as the host. From a realistic perspective, it is ridiculous to argue that pumpkin-eating represents cannibalism, yet the sheer pleasure of much children's literature arises in the contradictory and precarious balance between the rules of the real world and the queer rules of the fictional and fantastic "reality" of the text. Such is the appeal of children's literature, in that the adult nightmare of cannibalism is transformed into a humorous (yet nonetheless threatening) dynamic in interpersonal relationships. Carolyn Daniel points out that cannibalism "dissolves the difference between the eater and the eaten,"[9] and in a queer land of magic and magical creatures, this distinction has been muddied before diners sit down together at a table.

In many volumes of children's literature, interspecies cannibalism (although an oxymoronic term) disrupts the supposedly egalitarian social structures that embrace a multitude of queer creatures. By describing their fellow denizens of Oz as the raw ingredients of food rather than as fellow cooks who prepare food for civilized consumption, characters of the series highlight the fault lines within the social order. As one might expect of the series, cannibalism frequently characterizes some of its antagonists. For example, the mischievous Kiki learns the magic of transformations and then describes how he would attack a potential enemy: "I will transform myself into a lion and tear him to pieces, or into a bear and eat him up" (*Magic*, ch. 3). Likewise, the rebellious Jinjur plans to serve Jack Pumpkinhead as a tart, to feed the Tin Woodman to goats, and to cook the Woggle-Bug into "a Hungarian goulash, stewed and highly spiced" (*Marvelous*, ch. 15). Even Dorothy, the heroine of the series, faces consumption when she encounters Yoop the Giant:

> "But this is a lonely place, and no good meat has passed by my cave for many years; so I'm hungry."
> "Haven't you eaten anything in many years?" asked Dorothy.
> "Nothing except six ants and a monkey. I thought the monkey would taste like meat people, but the flavor was different. I hope you will taste better, for you seem plump and tender." (*Patchwork*, ch. 20)

The untamed aggression and unrestrained hunger depicted in these scenes—not just defeating but devouring an adversary—delineates the antisocial nature of the impetuous, power-hungry, and ravenous Kiki, Jinjur, and Yoop. Not surprisingly, their brutish appetites construct them as the antagonists that the more civilized denizens of Oz must conquer if they are to maintain the queer order of their utopian realm.

Cannibals are usually viewed as the debased Other to a civilization that deems itself superior to this monstrous reflection of itself. In a conversation between Dorothy and the talking hen Billina, it is apparent that cannibals are recognized throughout the civilized world as savage beings and that aligning intelligent animals with cannibalism debases them as monstrous:

> "I'm a trifle hungry, myself," declared the yellow hen.
> "Why don't you eat the egg?" asked the child. "You don't need to have your food cooked, as I do."
> "Do you take me for a cannibal?" cried the hen, indignantly. "I do not know what I have said or done that leads you to insult me!" (*Ozma*, ch. 2)

Billana's offense at being accused of cannibalistic tendencies highlights the depth of Dorothy's unintentional insult. Matthew Beaumont acknowledges that "the emblematic figure of the cannibal historically has functioned in imperial discourse as the ultimate emblem of enlightened civilization's dark other,"[10] and readers see such a moment of culture clash when Billina believes Dorothy has credited her with cannibalistic tendencies simply because the chicken's dietary tastes differ from hers. Cannibalism structures the social order in scenes such as these, highlighting the ways that various characters position themselves in relation to the ultimate act of savagery. Rather than a means of upholding Baum characters' respectively queer qua eccentric identities, dietary practices stress their differences and the challenges of maintaining Oz's utopian veneer.

Surprisingly, though, such uses of cannibalism to underscore the unappealing traits of malevolent characters or to accentuate cultural clashes are eclipsed by its use to illustrate the fractured social order of Oz in respect to its more likable inhabitants. That is to say, the good characters of the series are just as likely, if not more likely, to engage in these quasi-cannibalistic acts, thus proving the universality of queerness and the impossibility of fairyland normativity. In this regard cannibalism functions not merely to construct the Other but to criticize the denizens of the ostensibly superior civilization. This view of cannibalism, expressed by Michel de Montaigne in his famed essay "Of Cannibals," permits the citizens of the "enlightened" culture to see themselves anew by viewing cannibals as their reflections: "So we may well call these people barbarians, in respect to the rules of reason, but not in respect to ourselves, who surpass them in every kind of barbarity."[11] Protagonists of the Oz series use the threat of consumption against their adversaries, such as when the Wizard threatens to metamorphose three imps—cleverly named Imp Olite, Imp Udent, and Imp Ertinent—into pigs to dissuade them from their destructive habits. The Wizard threatens that "unless the horrid creatures behave themselves hereafter, they are liable to be killed and eaten. They would make good chops, sausages or roasts" (*Little*, "Ozma and the Little Wizard"). His words reflect the belief that creatures, if they cannot be effectively civilized, should be quickly consumed to serve a constructive role in the maintenance of the social order. Furthermore, when the Tin Woodman, the Tin Soldier, the Scarecrow, Polychrome, and Woot the Wanderer come upon the home of Professor Grunter and Mrs. Squealina Swyne, the pigs react suspiciously to these strangers: "If you are butchers," warns Mrs. Swyne, "you'd better run away and avoid trouble." Woot explains to the pigs that they need not fear the travelers because their appetites bear no threat: "Do not be afraid of us, Mrs. Swyne, for we are harmless travelers. The tin men and the Scarecrow never eat anything and Polychrome feasts only on dewdrops. As for me, I'm rather hungry, but there is plenty of food in your garden to satisfy me" (*Woodman*, ch. 20). Woot's words soothe Mrs. Swyne, yet they simultaneously hint at the problem of food in the queer social order of Oz: although Woot promises to partake of a vegetarian meal, he does not disavow his carnivorous appetite. In a land of intelligent and anthropomorphized animals, ostensible parity between the animal and human communities is subverted by the possibility of interspecies cannibalism, because the smiling guests allowed into a home might turn around at any moment and devour their hosts. The egalitarian facade of this queer land of Oz is continually undermined in scenes such as these, because talking animals cannot truly represent the equals of other characters if they must always protect themselves from being killed, cooked, and eaten. As Tess Cosslett points out, "Animal characters do not guarantee a cosy, protected space" for readers of children's literature,[12] and this threat of interspecies cannibalism puts bared teeth in the background of the Ozian utopia.

Despite the threat of cannibalism to annihilate and digest, it also works to establish equality between opposing cultural clusters. If humans are eaten by another creature and this consumption is identified as cannibalism, a basic parity is thus acknowledged between the devoured and the devourer. For instance, Scoodlers are two-faced humanoid creatures with one side black and the other white, and Dorothy recognizes her shared humanity with these monstrous antagonists, even as she quails at their gustatory habits:

> "But what do you want us for?" asked the shaggy man, uneasily.
> "Soup!" they all shouted, as if with one voice.
> "Goodness me!" said Dorothy, trembling a little; "the Scoodlers must be reg'lar cannibals." (*Road*, ch. 9)

In labeling the Scoodlers as cannibals, Dorothy acknowledges her basal kinship with these queer figures. The taxonomical similarity necessary for cannibalism constructs cannibals as both the Same and the Other: they are the monstrous reflection of an ostensibly civilized species, and thus they are coded to represent the barbarism of an uncivilized race, yet these beings must be sufficiently recognizable to be construed as cannibals rather than as predators.

As evident in the tensions between Dorothy and the Scoodlers, cannibalism defines the relationships among various people with possibly antagonistic relationships, but it also underscores the tensions among groups constituted as allies. In some fraught encounters, the threat of eating acquaintances and friends is linked to emotional cathexis. When the Hip-po-gy-raf requests permission to eat the Scarecrow's straw, he couches his desire to consume the Scarecrow with words of friendship: "Oh, how I love straw! I hope you don't resent my affectionate appetite?" (*Woodman*, ch. 19). Anthropologists distinguish between, in Susanne Skubal's words, "exophagy or aggressive cannibalism and endophagy or affectionate cannibalism," with the former directed outside the community and the latter directed inside of it.[13] The idea of an "affectionate appetite" humorously underscores the ways in which eating does not solely signify aggression and disharmony in Oz, even when the diner and the potentially dined upon do not agree on the dietary propriety of the meal in question. In a related moment from *Dot and Tot in Merryland*, one of Baum's books for young children, a candy man recalls an acquaintance who fell down a hill and broke into seventeen pieces: "Oh, as he was ruined beyond repair, we divided him up among the neighbors who loved him best, and ate him the next morning for breakfast." Dot is horrified by this admission. "But this is horrible.... You are all cannibals," she cries; the candy man does not recognize the term *cannibal* and so Dot defines it as "people who eat each other." The man amiably agrees: "Oh, then we are cannibals, sure enough" (*Merryland*, ch. 8). Embracing his queer identity as a cannibal or, perhaps more accurately, refusing to accept that cannibalism could render him nonnormative in any way, this candy man forces Dot to reconsider her perceptions of the social order. Queer theory is primarily concerned with nonnormative erotic desires and identities, yet here it can be extended to the queer dietary practices of the Hip-po-gy-raf and others who consume (or seek to consume) those whom they view with apparently sincere affection.

In this manner the ideal function of food to build community gives way to more predatory and animalistic appetites, in which friends turn against friends when faced with the threat of hunger. In the following exchange, the Woggle-Bug advocates a dietary pleasure that the Tin Woodman finds horrifying:

> "As for me," said the Woggle-Bug, "I think that I could live for some time on Jack Pumpkinhead. Not that I prefer pumpkins for food; but I believe they are somewhat nutritious, and Jack's head is large and plump."
> "How heartless!" exclaimed the Tin Woodman, greatly shocked. "Are we cannibals, let me ask? Or are we faithful friends?" (*Marvelous*, ch. 16)

This exchange highlights the fragile balance between food and friends in Oz: surely one would never eat a friend, yet the different races and species that inhabit Oz frequently define one another in relation to food. Furthermore, this incident is hardly an isolated moment in the texts, and similar incidents disrupt the queer social fabric of Oz, such as when the Scarecrow suggests cooking Billina: "Heat is just in her line.... If she is nicely roasted, she will be better than ever" (*Ozma*, ch. 9). The Scarecrow's declaration here is all the more surprising because he does not eat and would not therefore benefit from consuming Billina. Given the Woggle-Bug's suggestion to eat Jack Pumpkinhead, it is only fitting that another character praise a diet of insects, and Billina demonstrates her prioritizing of food over friends in her appetite for bugs: "The bugs and ants that I find here are the finest flavored in the world ... and there are plenty of them. So here I shall end my days" (*Ozma*, ch. 21). Issues of personal identity are frequently mediated through food, and the lurking possibility of interspecies cannibalism exposes the fractures within the utopian fantasy of Oz. In this world of fantastic and queer creatures, a highly magnified Woggle-Bug might betray an animated pumpkin at any moment, leaving a man made of tin shocked by the dissolution of the social order and a chicken planning her next delicious meal of bugs.

Even if one defines cannibalism solely as humans eating humans, one can never be exactly sure what (or whom) one is eating in Oz, because many creatures have been magically transformed from one entity to another. In the following passage from *Rinkitink in Oz*, King Rinkitink advocates eating the talking goat Bilbil:

> Then [Rinkitink] seemed thoughtful for a moment and turning to Inga he asked: "Do you think, Prince, that if the worst comes, we could eat Bilbil?"
>
> The goat gave a groan and cast a reproachful look at his master as he said: "Monster! Would you, indeed, eat your old friend and servant?"
>
> "Not if I can help it, Bilbil," answered the King pleasantly. "You would make a remarkably tough morsel, and my teeth are not as good as they once were." (*Rinkitink*, ch. 5)

A sly humor pervades this scene in that Rinkitink and Bilbil play the parts of longtime friends who enjoy their bickering immensely, as Rinkitink states on one such occasion: "But this is a jolly quarrel ... and it is the way Bilbil and I often amuse ourselves" (*Rinkitink*, ch. 6). On this occasion the joke nonetheless appears to have gone a little too far to suit Bilbil's taste. In consideration of their friendship, it is unlikely that Rinkitink would follow through on his threats, but if he did, he would later learn that he dined on human flesh. Toward the end of this narrative, the Wizard reveals that the goat Bilbil is really "the unhappy Prince of Boboland," whom a "cruel magician transformed" (*Rinkitink*, ch. 21). The earlier scene, in which interspecies cannibalism is threatened, retroactively appears to be one of true cannibalism. Thus, in Oz, because one can never know if one's meal is what it appears to be or is merely an illusion, one's relationship to food threatens the core of personal identity and communal civilization predicated upon one's observance of community dietary laws. That is to say, if any creatures in Oz believe that they adhere to the norms of a civilized appetite, they are likely to find themselves nonnormative, and thus queer, after consuming what they believed to be a wholly innocuous meal.

As the issue of food and the potential for cannibalism define the queer social structure of Oz, so too does the distinction between the raw and the cooked contribute to a breakdown of the social order. Lévi-Strauss divides food into three categories—the raw, the cooked, and the rotten—and differentiates among these categories with his observation that "the raw state constitutes the unmarked pole, whereas [the cooked and the rotten] are strongly marked, although in opposite directions: the cooked being a cultural transformation of the raw, and the rotten its natural transformation."[14] The raw should represent primitivism (in that a culture lacks the necessary skills and tools to serve food other than in its uncooked state), and the cooked should represent civilization (in that a culture has sufficiently mastered fire and tools to heat food). In the following dialogue between Billina and Dorothy, the social implications of this distinction crumble:

> "What are you doing?" asked Dorothy.
> "Getting my breakfast, of course," murmured the hen, busily pecking away.
> "What do you find?" inquired the girl, curiously.
> "Oh, some fat red ants, and some sand-bugs, and once in a while a tiny crab. They are very sweet and nice, I assure you."
> "How dreadful!" exclaimed Dorothy, in a shocked voice.
> "What is dreadful?" asked the hen, lifting her head to gaze with one bright eye at her companion.
> "Why, eating live things, and horrid bugs, and crawly ants. You ought to be 'shamed of yourself!" (*Ozma*, ch. 2)

Dorothy defines a culture by its food, and here she attempts to shame Billina into accepting her argument that raw, live food corresponds with a degraded appetite and therefore a degraded and antisocial identity.[15] As Carolyn Daniel outlines in her analysis of food in children's literature, "certain foods impart certain qualities to the eater, that is, you are (or you become) what you eat."[16] Showing no awareness of the cultural construction of food, especially in regard to the odd social structures of Oz, where she might expect that different cultural rules are in effect, Dorothy applies her culinary ideology to the appetites of chickens to lead Billina to a higher understanding of food and culture.

Billina, however, refuses to be cowed by Dorothy's shaming of her appetite. As the dialogue continues, she defends her dietary predilections by pointing out the inherent contradictions hidden within societies that define themselves through cooked food:

"Goodness me!" returned the hen, in a puzzled tone; "how queer you are Dorothy! Live things are much fresher and more wholesome than dead ones, and you humans eat all sorts of dead creatures."

"We don't!" said Dorothy.

"You do, indeed," answered Billina. "You eat lambs and sheep and cows and pigs and even chickens."

"But we cook 'em," said Dorothy, triumphantly.

"What difference does that make?"

"A good deal," said the girl, in a graver tone. "I can't just 'splain the diff'rence but it's there. And, anyhow, we never eat such dreadful things as *bugs*."

"But you eat the chickens that eat the bugs," retorted the yellow hen, with an odd cackle. "So you are just as bad as we chickens are."

This made Dorothy thoughtful. What Billina said was true enough, and it almost took away her appetite for breakfast. As for the yellow hen, she continued to peck away at the sand busily, and seemed quite contented with her bill-of-fare. (*Ozma*, ch. 2)

Here, Billina forces Dorothy to confront the hypocrisy of defining civilization through "the cooked." If one of the purposes of cooking is to proclaim civilization, such self-pronouncements must eventually fail, in that cooking only whitewashes the ingestion of the raw by other animals before they themselves are cooked. Furthermore, Billina's sly reminder to Dorothy that she (Dorothy) eats chicken brings to mind the cannibalistic nature of such consumption in a fairy kingdom. Billina's implicit comparison—it is surely no worse to eat live bugs than cooked chickens—subverts the culinary basis of social distinction, thus upending the social order itself. The chicken gains the upper hand in her debate with Dorothy by dissolving differences between the raw and the cooked in light of Dorothy's appetite, which appears potentially cannibalistic in her queer new surroundings.

Chickens metonymically represent the breakdown of Oz's social order in relation to food, because their queer status—are they foodstuffs or are they friends?—refutes definitive answers. The issue of eating chickens is addressed in *The Emerald City of Oz*, and it is apparent that chickens are considered inappropriate for consumption. Billina triumphantly reports to Dorothy that, since her arrival in Oz, chickens "are never eaten or harmed in any way, as chickens are in your country" (*Emerald*, ch. 7). This line hints at the primitivism of the United States of America, a country insufficiently civilized to treat chickens other than as a food source. Aunt Em cements Billina's stereotype of the savage American when she naively gives some advice on feeding chickens prior to cooking them. Billina responds disgustedly to her suggestions:

> "Broilers!" exclaimed Billina, in horror. "Broil my chickens!"
> "Why, that's what they're for, ain't it?" asked Aunt Em, astonished.
> "No, Aunt, not in Oz," said Dorothy. "People do not eat chickens here. You see, Billina was the first hen that was ever seen in this country, and I brought her here myself. Everybody liked her an' respected her, so the Oz people wouldn't any more eat her chickens than they would eat Billina."
> "Well, I declare," gasped Aunt Em. "How about the eggs?"
> "Oh, if we have more eggs than we want to hatch, we allow people to eat them," said Billina, "Indeed, I am very glad the Oz folks like our eggs, for otherwise they would spoil."
> "This certainly is a queer country," sighed Aunt Em. (*Emerald*, ch. 14)

Aunt Em's exasperation is warranted, as the dietary laws of Oz once again serve to confuse rather than to clarify social structures. If chickens are not to be eaten in Oz because the animals are accorded a social status basically equivalent to humans and fairies, why then are eggs—the fetuses of the chicken world, if you will—treated with such gustatory nonchalance? Billina herself advocates their consumption (although she would never eat an egg herself), and eggs are frequently used as weapons against the great nemeses of Oz, the Nomes (e.g., *Tik-Tok*, ch. 18; *Rinkitink*, ch. 20; and *Magic*, ch. 4). Thus, chickens appear to straddle the border between the fully human and the fully animal: they are an acceptable culinary supply in one form, yet they metamorphose upon hatching into a taboo foodstuff and thus inhabit both the status of a norm and its antithesis.

The queer status of chickens is fraught with confusion, and so too is the status of humans within a fairy kingdom, who cannot maintain any claim to normativity owing to their odd surroundings. A variety of magical beings inhabit these lands, and humans are frequently derided as "meat people" who suffer the many vagaries of biological existence. The Scarecrow pities "meat people [who must] shut their eyes and lie still during the dark hours" (*Scarecrow*, ch. 20). Likewise, the Tin Woodman refers to humans as "clumsy meat people" and points out the advantages of straw and tin bodies in his colloquy with the Scarecrow: "You and I do not eat meat, and so we are spared the dreadful bother of getting three meals a day" (*Lost*, ch. 26). The Sawhorse likewise denounces the utility of a meat-based body: "I must point out to you the fact that you are all meat creatures, who tire unless they sleep and starve unless they eat and suffer from thirst unless they drink. Such animals must be very imperfect, and imperfect creatures cannot be beautiful" (*Lost*, ch. 10). Here again readers see that food defines the queer society of Oz, but humans are now accorded a lower level in the hierarchy because their meat bodies must continually be fed and tended. Indeed, as a meat-based life form, the human body is potentially constituted as an entrée in cannibalistic feasts. Like chickens, humans both are and are not privileged life forms in fairyland, and their borderline status affects their position in the shifting social landscape of Oz.

THE QUEER IMPOSSIBILITY OF A VEGETARIAN UTOPIA

In creating a fairy world in which eating meat is so fraught with fears of cannibalism, Baum might have turned to vegetarianism as a reasonable solution to these narrative tensions, and his refusal to do so highlights the essential nature of queerness for his fictions. In terms of the ingredients of food and food preparation, vegetables mediate between the raw and the cooked because they may be served in either fashion, in contrast to meat, which is typically cooked.[17] At times Baum appears to move in such a direction, as when he lushly describes a vegetarian meal: "The platter was fairly heaped with a fine stew, smoking hot, with many kinds of vegetables and dumplings and a rich, delicious gravy. . . . There were several other dishes on the table, all carefully covered, and when the time came to remove these covers they found bread and butter, cakes, cheese, pickles and fruits—including some of the luscious strawberries of Oz" (*Emerald*, ch. 14). This meal erases any potential dietary tensions, because none of the characters attending the feast must confront the cooked body of a member of their species served on the dinner table. Likewise, in *The Lost Princess of Oz*, Baum introduces a minor character who adheres to a vegetarian diet as penance for a cannibalistic act. This ferry boat driver atones for his crime of cooking a bird-egg omelet—a dietary transgression predicated upon the creation of food from a respected life form—by eating and serving only "fruit and bread, which was the only sort of food he had" (*Lost*, ch. 14).[18] Also, lunchbox trees bloom in these fairylands (*Ozma*, ch. 3), which again highlights the potential for organic solutions to meat-based dilemmas.[19] In passages such as these, vegetarianism would apparently solve the dietary dilemma of friends eating friends in Oz.

Baum underscores the ways in which queer carnivores might turn against one another at any moment, and in the final analysis, vegetarianism also fails to offer any lasting redemptive possibilities to the culinary problems in this utopia. For just as the many races and species of creatures in Oz make it impossible to define social structures in relation to food, so too do animated vegetables fracture any attempt to establish a hierarchy among living creatures. When the Wizard kills an aggressive vegetable, the dichotomy between meats and vegetables collapses:

> As the two halves of the Sorcerer fell apart on the floor [Dorothy] saw that he had no bones or blood inside of him at all, and that the place where he was cut looked much like a sliced turnip or potato.
> "Why, he's vegetable!" cried the Wizard, astonished.
> "Of course," said the Prince. "We are all vegetable, in this country. Are you not vegetable, also?"
> "No," answered the Wizard. "People on top of the earth are all meat. Will your Sorcerer die?"
> "Certainly, sir. He is really dead now, and will wither very quickly. So we must plant him at once, that other Sorcerers may grow upon his bush," continued the Prince. (*Dorothy*, ch. 3)

Because vegetables live, think, and act together in a civilized, if hostile, manner, it is difficult to differentiate between vegetables and animals regarding their shared condition as animated and sentient beings. Also in this passage, the Wizard identifies humans as meat, thus demarcating humanity by its ability to serve as nourishment, not by any faculties of reasoning or emotion. The differences between meats and vegetables evaporate in light of their shared status as cognizant beings, but then how could one eat a vegetable while recognizing it as a sentient life form?

In light of such factors, vegetarianism cannot resolve the problems inherent in a meat-based diet in Oz, but Baum offers another potential solution in the Shaggy Man's pill meals. A recurring motif in Baum's fictions, pill meals also appear in *The Boy Fortune Hunters in Yucatan*, when the heroes "made some very excellent soup from a small tablet" (*Yucatan*, ch. 15), and in *The Master Key*, when the Demon of Electricity gives tablets to the child protagonist Rob, in which "are stored certain elements of electricity . . . capable of nourishing a human body for a full day" (*Key*, ch. 3). Likewise, Ajo of *Aunt Jane's Nieces Out West* eats a diet of "food-tablets," although Patsy advises him to partake of regular food and to "Fletcherize—chew your food, you know" (*West*, ch. 9).[20] Each of the Shaggy Man's pills, the remarkable invention of Professor Woggle-Bug, "contains soup, fish, roast meat, salad, apple-dumplings, ice cream and chocolate drops, all boiled down to this small size, so it can be conveniently carried and swallowed when you are hungry and need a square meal" (*Patchwork*, ch. 11). It could be argued whether these magical pills would actually alleviate the dietary tensions of eating in an ostensibly civilized fairy kingdom: if the fish and roast meat are merely boiled down into pill form, the ingredients of the pill still necessitate that one animal die to feed another. Regardless of this issue, many of the inhabitants of Oz reject these pill meals simply because they strip away the pleasure of consuming food. A disagreement ensues between the Shaggy Man and the Woozy about the merits of these pills, with the Shaggy Man declaring, "One should only eat to sustain life," and the Woozy asserting, "I don't care for it. I want something I can chew and taste" (*Patchwork*, ch. 11). The Shaggy Man advocates the more ethical view in this exchange, as his utilitarian view of food mitigates against excessive consumption that relies on finding one creature who must die to feed another, but the Woozy asserts the more popular opinion that dining provides a pleasurable experience that should be savored and enjoyed.

BANQUETS, FEASTS, AND BAUM'S QUEERLY CANNIBALISTIC COMMUNITIES

The Woozy's opinion about the pleasure of dining holds sway in this queer fairy kingdom, and scenes of sharing food together in feasts occur frequently in the Oz novels, typically to celebrate the successful preservation of the social order. These Ozian banquets are grand and lavish events in which community is formed through the ritual serving and ingesting of food. Pondering the cultural function of feasts to arrange and cement social hierarchies, Roy C. Wood declares that "status symbolism is conveyed and reinforced by the actions of the donor in selecting what may be deemed an appropriate environment for the meal in terms of the excellence and expense of the meal."[21] At the same time, these Ozian feasts also depict the fault lines among the queer creatures of this social order, in that the different species are stationed at different tables: "But what amused the jolly King most were the animal guests, which Ozma always invited to her banquets and seated at a table by themselves, where they talked and chatted together as people do but were served the sort of food their natures required" (*Rinkitink*, ch. 22). Such scenes of segregated dining undermine the ostensibly egalitarian social structure of Oz, and the differences in a creature's form—animal or human—are linked to differences in dietary preferences. In a similar dining scene celebrating Ozma's birthday, the guests are separated presumably due to their differences in size: "On this especial birthday of the lovely girl

Ruler, a long table was set in the royal Banquet Hall of the palace, at which were place-cards for the invited guests, and at one end of the great room was a smaller table, not so high, for Ozma's animal friends, whom she never forgot" (*Magic*, ch. 22). Certainly, some of the animals at this table, such as Toto and Billina, would need a smaller table, but the Cowardly Lion, the Hungry Tiger, and Hank the Mule would likely be of appropriate size to eat at a human-sized dining table. The hierarchy associated with a dining table reveals the ways in which a civilization prioritizes its members, and in Oz, the animals are accorded a lower place in the social structure owing to their biological forms, as well as owing to their appetites.

As much as food disrupts community and fractures the harmony of Oz as a queer utopia, it is important not to lose sight of the fact that these books are designed to delight, entertain, and amuse. Certainly, many of these dining and cannibalistic scenes are quite funny, and the Hungry Tiger's primary narrative purpose appears in his humorous desire to eat his companions and any fat baby that might cross his path. The conflict between the Hungry Tiger's appetite and his conscience that forbids him from succumbing to his bestial desires weaves a running joke throughout the series: "A fat baby, I want a fat baby.... A nice, plump, juicy, tender, fat baby. But, of course, if I had one, my conscience would not allow me to eat it. So I'll have to ... forget my hunger" (*Ozma*, ch. 14). On another occasion, he politely asks a maid for permission to eat her: "You certainly look delicious.... Will you kindly give me permission to eat you?" (*Ozma*, ch. 9). After Dorothy declares her willingness to summon the dangerous Nome King, the Hungry Tiger sees an opportunity to feast upon her remains: "'Do,' said the Hungry Tiger; 'and if he makes hash of you I'll willingly eat you for breakfast tomorrow morning'" (*Ozma*, ch. 11). Such aggressive posturing bears no real threat, and readers also learn that the Hungry Tiger would never eat a baby. When the opportunity finally arrives, and he finds "a nice fat baby sitting in the middle of the street and crying as if in great distress," he nurses the anxious child and then returns it to its mother. The story concludes with his realization that his reputation is inextricably linked to his appetite: "For, had I eaten that fat baby, I would not now be the Hungry Tiger. It's better to go hungry, seems to me, than to be cruel to a little child" (*Little*, "The Cowardly Lion and the Hungry Tiger"). He also confesses to Dorothy that his dietary urges are mostly a facade designed to promote an illusion of ferocity: "'Hush, Dorothy,' whispered the Tiger; 'you'll ruin my reputation if you are not more discreet. It isn't what we are, but what folks think we are, that counts in this world. And come to think of it Miss Polly would make a fine variegated breakfast, I'm sure'" (*Road*, ch. 17). The Hungry Tiger showcases the ways in which aggressive appetites build humor in the Oz books, with his continual threats dismissed by his friends as the innocuous posturing of a gentle ally.

As raw food represents the natural world untouched by humanity, so too are appetites themselves natural, and in the final analysis, they can never be fully tamed. One cannot prevent hunger pangs; they are an integral part of existence as a biological life form. Thus, despite the ways in which hunger both threatens and upholds the queer social structures of Oz, Baum stresses that appetites are natural and cannot be denied. Dorothy's kitten Eureka may appear heartless in her desire to eat tiny talking piglets, but she merely reiterates that she is responding to the demands of her body:

> "May I eat one of them?" asked the kitten, in a pleading voice. "I'm awfully hungry."
> "Why, Eureka," said Dorothy, reproachfully, "what a cruel question! It would be dreadful to eat these dear little things."
> "I should say so!" grunted another of the piglets, looking uneasily at the kitten; "cats are cruel things."
> "I'm not cruel," replied the kitten, yawning. "I'm just hungry." (*Dorothy*, ch. 5)

Eureka here advocates a decidedly utilitarian view of pigs: when one is hungry, she nonchalantly argues, anything edible metamorphoses into an acceptable food supply. The kitten's appetite threads throughout *Dorothy and the Wizard in Oz* to undermine the group cohesion of the cheerful band of adventurers, and it reappears when she makes another request for a meal:

> "Please, Mr. Wizard, may I eat just one of the fat little piglets? You'd never miss *one* of them, I'm sure!"
> "What a horrid, savage beast!" exclaimed a piglet; "and after we've been such good friends, too, and played with one another."
> "When I'm not hungry, I love to play with you all," said the kitten, demurely; "but when my stomach is empty it seems that nothing would fill it so nicely as a fat piglet." (*Dorothy*, ch. 11)

Friendship is jettisoned in favor of food, but Eureka refuses to be shamed into denying her appetite. Civilization depends on groups of people interacting for their mutual benefit, but Eureka underscores the limits of any civilized order: if the food supply breaks down, chaos is imminent. While dining together is one of the great communal experiences of civilized existence, the actual act of consuming food is ultimately a singular act because each separate body must find and devour its own food, or that existence will cease.

Likewise, when Toto attacks Billina, presumably to eat her, his natural appetite undermines the social order. Billina links the dog's eating habits to his inability to talk and thus to his status as an uncivilized and lower life form. For Billina, only a savage would eat a chicken: "'What a brute!' croaked Billina, glaring down at the little dog." She then dismisses him as insufficiently cultured to prevent his acting on such basic instincts as hunger: "'The miserable thing can't talk,' said Billina, with a sneer" (*Road*, ch. 14). Talking and communication serve as integral factors in participating in a civilization, and so Billina labels Toto as brutishly uncivilized in his failure to communicate and in his animalistic appetite. Billina, however, is mistaken, and readers later learn that Toto can indeed talk: like every other American animal that finds itself in Oz, he discovers his latent ability to speak in the fairy kingdom (e.g., *Tik-Tok*, ch. 25; *Lost*, ch. 6). Toto merely performs the role of a mute in Oz, hiding his intelligence and civilized nature so that he can act in accordance with his natural urges to eat any nearby food source. In a civilized land but with an uncivilized appetite, Toto hides his vocal abilities so that he can respond to the natural appetites that motivate him.

In forming civilizations communities attempt to defy nature, but Baum demonstrates in Oz that even the most utopian of communities faces internal dissolution through the force of natural appetites that renders all of his characters queer. Everyone enjoys eating together as a community, but in the final analysis, the individual obligation to consume sufficient food for oneself trumps more altruistic and benevolent attitudes. Natural appetites cannot be denied, yet the tension between nature and civilization demonstrates just how challenging it is to maintain any civilization, queer or otherwise. And so readers should not be terribly surprised when the protagonists of the Oz books display traits reflective of their animalistic instincts, as when Dorothy realizes that the Cowardly Lion could never conquer his taste for meat: "The Lion had stolen away and found a breakfast to his liking; he never told what it was, but Dorothy hoped the little rabbits and the field mice had kept out of his way" (*Lost*, ch. 12). The Cowardly Lion knows enough about how society functions to keep quiet about his appetite, but it lurks in the background of Oz, and one never quite knows when cravings for food will upset long-standing relationships. Indeed, even Dorothy, despite her overarching kindness, behaves rather antagonistically and imperiously when questions of food arise. In her encounter with the sentient baked goods of Bunbury, she suggests these creatures should readily sacrifice themselves to her and her friends' appetites: "'See here,' said Dorothy, determined to defend her pets. 'I think we've treated you all pretty well, seeing you're eatables an' reg'lar food for us.... But Toto and Billina can't be 'spected to go hungry when the town's full of good things they like to eat, 'cause they can't understand your stingy ways as I do'" (*Emerald*, ch. 17). Perhaps most shockingly, she herself breaks the taboos against chicken consumption, showcasing her own natural inclinations in opposition to civilized dietary codes. Long after commencing her friendship with Billina, Dorothy dines with the king of the foxes, as the narrator reports: "Foxes, as you know, are fond of chicken and other fowl; so they served chicken soup and roasted turkey and stewed duck and fried grouse and broiled quail and goose pie, and as the cooking was excellent the king's guests enjoyed the meal and ate heartily of the various dishes" (*Road*, ch. 4). Although never depicted in the series, one can well imagine Dorothy's apology to Billina for enjoying such a cannibalistic meal, predicated upon an appeal to the natural order: "Oh, Billina! I was just so very hungry . . ."

Baum's queerly cannibalistic themes run beyond the Oz novels to his other fantasy works, further attesting to the challenges of imagining utopian lands without social fault lines. More than any other of Baum's works, *John Dough and the Cherub* elevates cannibalism into its guiding plotline, in the story of a gingerbread man evading those seeking to devour him. "To destroy life is murder," he exclaims to one hungry woman, who responds nonchalantly: "But to destroy gingerbread isn't.... And I can't see that it's cannibalism to eat a man if he happens to be cake, and fresh baked. And that frosting looks good" (*Dough*, ch. 4). The villainous Ali Dubh hopes to consume John Dough so that he will live eternally off the remnants of the Great Elixir that animated the gingerbread man: "Evidently it was the Arab's intention to find him and insist upon eating him; and John Dough did not want to be eaten at all" (*Dough*, ch. 4). The characterization of Ali Dubh carries several anti-Arab stereotypes, also apparent in the fact that Ali Dubh is himself pursued by Arab men with "dark, beady eyes [that] proclaimed them children of the desert" (*Dough*, ch. 1). Also in this novel, the monstrous and villainous Mifkets, with coconut-shaped heads, pear-shaped bodies, short legs, and long arms, claim themselves as the ancestors of Arabs, as their king affirms: "In some parts of Arabia the people speak exactly as we do; so the Arabs are probably descended from our race" (*Dough*, ch. 13; for further description of the Mifkets, see *Dough*, ch. 11).[22] In this allusion to Darwin's theories of evolution, Baum imagines nonwhite peoples as descended from monstrous Others. Yet as much as John Dough fears being consumed by others, his companion Chick the Cherub urges him to share the restorative features of his dough flesh: "Well, then, why don't you let the Princess eat the rest of your left hand, and get well? The hand isn't any use to you since Black Ooboo ate off the fingers." John refuses, but Chick replies: "if *I* was gingerbread you can just bet I wouldn't be so stingy with myself" (*Dough*, ch. 13). Facing such emotional pressure, John Dough eventually relents: "I'm going to save the Princess before I'm gone entirely.... Not that I have overcome my dislike to being eaten, you understand, but ... Ali Dubh is sure to get me in time, and before that happens I want to do one good deed, and help the little girl to regain her strength and health" (*Dough*, ch. 14). With John Dough offering his queer body as the gingerbread of life, he serves as a Christlike figure, yet one who expresses his willingness to sacrifice himself for others only hesitantly, horrified by the idea of himself as a comestible. The innate and animalistic instinct for self-preservation here cedes to the image of a man allowing others to feed upon him, privileging their desires over his for the preservation of a queer social order in which identities and desires are always as contingent as one's next meal. Moreover, as much as *John Dough and the Cherub* revels in the construction of a queer social order, the novel depicts characters of color as John Dough's primary cannibalistic antagonists, thus introducing troubling racial tropes into Baum's fantasylands.

Through his culinary and cannibalistic themes, Baum creates fantasy novels and fairylands populated by whimsically queer characters with dangerous appetites, with violent consumption frequently a possible outcome of encounters even among friends. Such savagery is mostly humorously expressed, yet as Martin Gardner explains of Baum's conflicted sense of his violent themes: "It is all done in such an offhand, preposterous way that it is hard to imagine how children could be disturbed by it, but evidently Baum himself later decided that this kind of comedy is best soft-pedaled" (*Mo*, x). Toothless cannibalism, in other words, yet if there is no savagery in the bite there nonetheless can be no utopia in such a world where friends and foes shift so frequently at the dinner table. As Baum does not effectively demarcate between the eater and the eaten, the cannibal and the consumed, in the odd, eccentric, topsy-turvy, and queer lands of Oz and his other fantasy realms, it is both of little surprise but of great wonder that, as the previous chapters demonstrated, any boundaries between male and female, between normative and nonnormative, are similarly destabilized throughout his queer corpus.

Chapter 5

JOHN R. NEILL

Illustrator (and Author) of L. Frank Baum's Queer Oz
and Elsewhere

>OH MEOW.
>
>—WRITTEN ON A PLACARD WORN BY DOROTHY'S CAT EUREKA,
>
>IN AN ILLUSTRATION BY JOHN R. NEILL

John R. Neill (November 12, 1877–September 19, 1943), the illustrator of all of the Oz novels except the first, aligned the queerness of L. Frank Baum's texts with his drawings. On the one hand, this is not surprising: a novel's illustrations should cohere to its narrative content, with the author and artist collaborating to some degree on how their respective contributions should best harmonize. On the other hand, it was equally plausible that Neill would attempt to tame the queerness unleashed by Baum's texts or simply ignore it altogether; that he chose not to do so demonstrates the wider utility of queerness for capturing the carnivalesque world of Oz. Following the success of *The Wonderful Wizard of Oz*, Neill needed to visually capture, in Baum's words, "this queer Land of Oz" (*Wonderful*, ch. 4) in a manner consistent with the author's vision, thereby to ensure the continued popularity of the fledgling series. With queerness, both in its primary denotations of odd and eccentric and in its nascent slang connotations relating to homosexuality, playing such a key role in Baum's themes, Neill was charged with creating an equally queer visual world. His many illustrations exploit the carnivalesque freedoms of children's literature in visions of exuberance and excess; moreover, many feature sexual images and erotic undercurrents.

Baum first collaborated with W. W. Denslow on *The Wonderful Wizard of Oz*, which sparked the series' initial success through the enchanting union of Baum's fantasy and Denslow's quirky illustrations, but they soon parted ways. Baum's wife, Maud, reported tersely, "Denslow got a swelled head, hence the change."[1] Indeed, Baum apparently alludes to his conflicts with illustrators in his short story "The Girl Who Owned a Bear," in which a bear who springs to life from the pages of a children's book claims, "That author is as disappointing as most authors are," to which a similarly animated donkey brays, "But he's not as bad as the artist" (*American*). Neill began his career as an illustrator for such newspapers as the *New York Evening Journal*, the *Philadelphia Inquirer*, and the *Philadelphia North American* before turning his attention to illustrating children's books.[2] Today he is primarily remembered for his collaboration with Baum during the first two decades of the twentieth century, yet he was a prolific artist throughout the era known as the Golden Age of American Illustration, which featured the talents of such luminaries as Norman Rockwell, Jessie Willcox Smith, N. C. Wyeth, Maxfield Parrish, and Winslow Homer—and, of course, W. W. Denslow, Neill's predecessor in Oz. Neill's pictures adorn all of Baum's remaining Oz books, as well as such works as *John Dough and the Cherub*, *The Sea Fairies*, and *Sky Island*. Given his vast publishing interests Baum collaborated with several other illustrators as well, including Maxfield Parrish (*Mother Goose in Prose*), Maginel Wright Enright (*Policeman Bluejay*), Ike Morgan (*The Woggle-Bug Book*), Pauline M. Batchelder (*The Daring Twins*), F. Y. Cory (*The Master Key*), Alice Carsey (*Mary Louise and the Liberty Girls*), Joseph W. Wyckoff (*Mary Louise Adopts a Soldier*), and more. Baum died in 1919, with *The Magic of Oz* and *Glinda of Oz* appearing posthumously, yet numerous additional Oz books were published following his demise, most notably Ruth Plumly Thompson's twenty-one titles—many of which Neill also illustrated.[3] Neill himself authored four Oz books following Baum's death: *The Wonder City of Oz*, *The Scalawagons of Oz*, *Lucky Bucky in Oz*, and *The Runaway in Oz*. From his first Oz drawings for *The Marvelous Land of Oz* (1904), the sequel to *The Wonderful Wizard of Oz*, Neill staked his career on Baum's wonderland and maintained his allegiance for the ensuing four decades until his demise, all the while infusing the books with an additional queer subtext through several suggestive drawings.

As much as Baum's use of *queer* carries connotations of queerness beyond the odd or merely unusual, an in-text advertisement for the Oz books, included among the front matter of the original edition of *The Lost Princess of Oz*, encourages adults to enjoy the pleasures of this children's utopia. "Develop your child's imagination with the wonders of a Fairyland that has a message to grown-ups as well," the advertisement proclaims, as it also extols the "Gay picture jackets" of the series as a key selling point. While an argument that *gay* in this instance intentionally denotes homosexuality would be ridiculous, the intriguing play of language cannot disbar such a subtext entirely. While the copywriter of this advertisement for the Oz books presumably intended no queer meaning to their words, language subverts intentional meanings on numerous occasions—and, by so doing, exposes other truths. This advertisement also declares that adult readers will discover Baum's message for them, pointing to the double coding of much children's literature that embeds two narrative levels—an apparently innocent one for children, with a correspondingly more suggestive one for adults—into a single text. Along these lines, while it is impossible to make any claims about artistic intentionality in Neill's illustrations, they align with a queer sensibility as they also highlight the intriguing process of narrative and pictorial interpretation, in which what one sees speaks to one's own desires for representation and transgression, yet these visions simultaneously emerge from within the boundaries of another's creations.

NEILL'S QUEER ILLUSTRATIONS OF BAUM'S OZ BOOKS

Neill's illustrations of Oz enjoy widespread acclaim, particularly for their wealth of detail and their vibrant energy, with characters appearing to be perpetually in motion as they act and react to the bizarre circumstances of life in a fairyland. Michael Riley extols Neill's "visual whimsy," which surfaces in his many "richly detailed drawings [that] provide a running commentary on the story,"[4] and James Thurber affirms, "Too much cannot be said for the drawings of Mr. John R. Neill. . . . [H]is pictures were far superior to those of Mr. W. W. Denslow. . . . After doing more than three thousand drawings . . . he keeps up beautifully."[5] Likewise, Jack Snow comments, "The Neill style . . . combines rare beauty with great charm and a captivating sense of humor,"[6] for his illustrations highlight key elements of the various characters' personalities. For instance, in his iconic portrait of Scraps the Patchwork Girl, strands of her hair fly to the left as her left leg kicks out to the right, while her right patchwork foot contorts in upon itself as she stands en pointe. The resulting image, a patchwork body drawn from a geometric mishmash of shape and tone, epitomizes the joy and vivacity of one of Baum's most beloved characters. Neill mostly refrains from captioning his illustrations for the Oz series, but for this image he quotes Baum's text—"I HATE DIGNITY"—to exuberantly pronounce what the picture displays: a body incapable of restraint (*Patchwork*, ch. 11; see figure 5.1). This portrait introduces a single character in all of her stunning individuality, bringing to life Baum's character as a unique and inimitable personality. Moreover, many of Neill's illustrations feature a dazzling array of activity and bustle.

Figure 5.1. With its exuberant mix of emotion, energy, and geometry, Neill's masterful rendition of Scraps the Patchwork Girl brings to life Baum's creation.

H. Nichols B. Clark, focusing on Neill's detailed illustration of "Drinking the Health of Princess Ozma of Oz" (*Road*, ch. 23), declares, "Neill, with his deft craftsmanship, creates a visual cornucopia which sparkles with crystal stemware and jewel-like architectural details. He truly transports us to a wonderland."[7] Surprisingly, and despite Neill's skills and the acclaim modern critics bestow upon him, Baum expressed dissatisfaction with his work. Rebecca Loncraine attests that Baum "wrote to Reilly [his publisher] asking for a new illustrator, 'who could infuse new life and a spirit of fun into the Oz characters, which in Mr. Neill's hands are now perfunctory and listless.' But he later retracted his words, admitting to Reilly that 'perhaps no author is ever satisfied with his illustrator, and I see my characters and incidents so differently from the artist that I fail to appreciate his talent.'"[8] In another letter to his publishers Baum again criticized Neill: "What we need is more *humorous* pictures."[9] Despite Baum's hesitations, Neill's drawings today stand as the definitive renditions of Oz through their eclectic arrangement and irrepressible energy.

As an example of the tense dynamics framed between an author's words and an artist's image, it is evident that Neill markedly changes the tenor of some of Baum's scenes, at times by escalating their violence. Conjuring a strangely gruesome image, he depicts Jack Pumpkinhead stabbing one of his pumpkinheads while sitting beside a pile of discarded pumpkinhead "corpses" (*Patchwork*, ch. 19); readers know that Jack Pumpkinhead must carve a new head before his current one decays, but stabbing is not carving. Similarly, in *The Sea Fairies* Princess Clia assures Trot that the mermaids' swordfish troops "are among our most valued and faithful servants, guarding the entrances to the gardens which surround our palace," calming any fear she might feel. Neill, however, draws Trot with her eyes raised and her hands pulled back in fright, with a swordfish's bill appearing to have impaled her (*Sea*, ch. 4; see figure 5.2). The two-dimensional drawing, with Trot's body in front and the swordfish's bill in back, creates the illusion of impalement because much of the bill cannot be seen behind her body. This issue could have been easily resolved by drawing the bill in front of her body so that viewers would see the sword in its entirety and thus know that it does not penetrate Trot. With every image that he drew for the Oz books, Neill needed to conform to some degree to Baum's words while finding the freedom to interpret them to his own sense of their potential, whether for increased violence, humor, or any other such affective response. And as Neill enhanced the violence of some of Baum's scenes, he similarly escalated the queerness of others.

Neill's drawings convey queer attractions in a manner both strikingly obvious yet subtle, but even his bolder depictions of desire require explication due to the prevailing assumption of innocence as a primary virtue of children's literature. In contrast, to point out the sexual symbolism of much artwork intended for adult patrons often requires little decoding: to take one example, only the most willfully naive of viewers would deny the erotic frisson of Georgia O'Keeffe's flowers, many of which resemble female genitalia in their curves, clefts, and hollows. Still, when artists tackle subjects presumed to be devoid of sexual content, or when it is presumed that sexual content would only contaminate such subject matter, some spectators refuse to see the sexual images embedded in artworks despite their insistent visibility. Leo Steinberg's masterful study *The Sexuality of Christ in Renaissance Art and in Modern Oblivion*, which examines depictions of Jesus's genitalia, standing erect or otherwise noticeably situated in various artworks, provides a compelling example of a preference for modesty among some spectators. Steinberg notes that the foregrounding of Jesus's penis in these artworks "has been tactfully overlooked for half a millennium."[10] So too with eroticized elements of much children's literature and its illustrations: few discuss the implications of sexuality in these texts, presuming that erotic content does not—that it should not—exist in this forum, and thus these readers overlook the evidence before their eyes.

Figure 5.2. Baum assures readers that swordfish troops are harmless, yet they appear quite menacing in Neill's illustration, which creates the illusion that one has stabbed Trot. Such moments demonstrate Neill's predilection for liberating himself from Baum's texts.

Furthermore, as much as artists encode sexuality into various artworks, viewers must recognize their erotic force—whether latent or blatant—for it to signify as such. As Clifford Bishop and Cristina Moles Kaupp argue, "No work of art, whatever its content, can become erotic without the activating force of the spectator's gaze."[11] Here again the possibility emerges for illustrations ostensibly directed for children's consumption to camouflage their erotic content, for many children will not recognize the sexual images they unwittingly peruse. Young readers may not yet possess the necessary knowledge to realize that a drawing subtly suggests that the characters are engaging in a sex act, or to perceive the illustrated double entendre of an everyday object assuming vaginal, phallic, or other erotic connotations. The double coding of children's literature, in effect, assumes the unlikelihood of children comprehending certain aspects of the storylines and illustrations, while they are nevertheless clearly on display. To take a preliminary examination of such dynamics, when Neill illustrates the scene in which the villainous Nomes

"FOR GOODNESS SAKE, WHAT SORT OF A BEING ARE YOU?"

Figure 5.3. Neill obscures Jim the Cab-Horse's penis, presumably because the image would be too provocative for a children's book.

mock Ozma, he depicts fourteen Nome faces, with their bodies dissolving into air and one another but with several of their hands rising up, with one of the hands, in the lower center, limp-wristed (*Ozma of Oz*, ch. 11). The stereotype of the limp-wristed queer man dates back centuries, and Thomas King traces it as far back as John Bulwer's seventeenth-century treatise titled "Alphabet of Manual Expressions." King concludes that "wagging the hand was not only effeminate as a gesture, it indicated an inherent effeminacy of the subject."[12] Young children are not likely to know this stereotype and so would remain ignorant of its likely meaning. In complementary contrast, many very young children have learned the difference between a penis and a vagina, yet the image of Jim the Cab-Horse, which is drawn to show the animal in a side view from tail to head, places a black blot of dense cross-hatching where his penis should be, thereby protecting child readers from the rather banal image of a horse's appendage, which they would see on any trip to a farm (*Dorothy*, ch. 16; see figure 5.3).

While most of Neill's illustrations appear simply to depict the actions of Baum's stories, elements suggestive of human genitalia disrupt the presumed

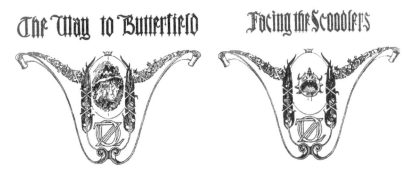

Figures 5.4 and 5.5. Chapter-opening vignettes from chapter 1 and chapter 9 of *The Road to Oz*, which match the general structures of female genitals, including a vagina, uterus, fallopian tubes, and ovaries.

correlation between text and image in other drawings. For example, the chapter-opening vignettes of *The Road to Oz* strikingly resemble the general contours of female genitalia. The bottom of these images mimics the vaginal vestibule, with two wheaty leaves approximating vaginal walls. The scrolls at their far left and right stand in the position of ovaries, with filigree serving as the fallopian tubes connecting to the illustration's central circle, which is placed within the overarching framework as the uterus. Most humorously, Neill puts a character in the "uterus" of each of these images, with the first inhabited by the fully-grown Shaggy Man and a later one with one of the adversaries the adventurers face, a Scoodler. With the Shaggy Man looking rather old with his unkempt hair, and with the Scoodler resembling a newborn infant with his two front teeth set in a bawling mouth, Neill parodies the birth of the various characters, no matter their age (*Road*, ch. 1 and ch. 9; see figures 5.4 and 5.5). Neill employs a similar vaginal design for the chapter-opening vignettes in *Rinkitink in Oz*, although its more open format lessens its resemblance to female genitalia.[13] On these chapter pages, the text itself is oddly formatted, in that the first five lines of text are short and centered, in contrast to the following seven lines of text that are flush left and right to the margin. The text formatting thus approximates a phallus, or at least a protrusion, that nears Neill's vaginal illustrations. Certainly, Baum's experiences with the *Aberdeen Saturday Pioneer* offered him ample opportunity to explore layout and design, resulting in, as Nancy Tystad Koupal states, "the usual pizzazz that Baum's touch gave to the publication" (*Landlady*, 107). In *The Lost Princess of Oz*, this formatting is repeated, with Neill's opening chapter illustrations wider and more open (and thus less obviously representing a vagina but still yonic in shape), with the oddly formatted text now penetrating the image.

Such play with genital imagery appears in several other of Neill's illustrations, and additional examples include when Cap'n Bill and Trot, after eating magical berries and shrinking down to miniature size, cut their way through a sunbonnet. Similar in spirit to the chapter-opening vignettes of *The Road to Oz*, the tear in the bonnet is suggestive of vaginal imagery, and it likewise parodies childbirth, as these two characters—neither of whom is an infant—peer forth from the hole to life anew (*Scarecrow*, ch. 5). In their later adventures in *The Magic of Oz*, Cap'n Bill and Trot encounter a magic tree that dispenses a variety of fruits, and Neill depicts Trot holding a pair of round fruits across her chest, thus cheekily symbolizing her breasts (*Magic*, ch. 15). Indeed, Neill must alter the story so that Trot may hold these matching, spherical fruits, for Baum writes that she plucks a peach, a banana, and an apple from the tree—none of which should resemble the melonlike circles she holds. Neill's creative license freed him from the texts on numerous occasions. In another instance with a slightly queer inflection, Neill adds a character to Baum's *Ozma of Oz*. Recounting his origin story, Tik-Tok tells of his creators, the firm of Smith & Tinker, and the fates of its founders: the artist Mr. Smith painted a river so lifelike that he fell in and drowned, whereas Mr. Tinker made a ladder and climbed to the moon, where he "found it such a love-ly place that he de-cid-ed to live there" (*Ozma*, ch. 5). Baum does not mention that Mr. Tinker met a man there, but Neill's illustration depicts one—presumably the Man in the Moon—who opens his shutters and raises his hand in welcome, as Mr. Tinker raises his in return.

Neill often places phallic swords or other rodlike appendages suggestively between male characters' legs to approximate their penises, such as the long scepter across the Scarecrow's lap on the dedication page of *Dorothy and the Wizard of Oz* and when the Wizard cuts a vegetable sorcerer in half, with his sword plunged down to the creature's crotch (*Dorothy*, ch. 4). Illustrating the scene when the Saw-Horse steps into a rabbit hole and pitches his riders off, the horse's right rear leg is placed directly in front of Tip's crotch, thus suggesting an erect penis (*Marvelous*, ch. 12). In some particularly striking images, swords sport mushroom tips—certainly an anomalous and ineffective shape for a blade yet one that better matches the contours of the male member (*Ozma*, ch. 11; *Emerald*, ch. 4; *Tik-Tok*, ch. 9). Female characters wield phallic symbols in Oz as well, with Ozma's scepter as the most prominent of these images, such as in the suggestive illustration in which it lies across her lap, as Dorothy gently grasps it (*Dorothy*, ch. 19). In a particularly daring image with phallic shapes, Neill depicts the munchkin boy Woot the Wanderer coyly smiling as he grasps the long noses of the Tin Woodman and the Tin Soldier for the cover illustrations of *The Tin Woodman of Oz*, with the

Figure 5.6. Neill's cover illustration for *The Tin Woodman of Oz* features the very phallic noses of the Tin Woodman and the Tin Soldier, which the Munchkin boy Woot the Wanderer caresses.

Tin Soldier's sword further contributing to the scene's phallic symbolism. Noses have long been used to visually represent the penis, and Neill's Woot, balancing himself on the Tin Woodman's and the Tin Soldier's bent arms while grasping their phallic noses, brazenly suggests queer erotic possibilities among the three.[14] (See figure 5.6.) As suggested in the chapter "Queer Eroticisms in Oz and Elsewhere," *The Tin Woodman of Oz* represents one of Baum's most blatant forays into a queer storyline, and Neill's image indicates that he perceived the novel's erotic subtexts.

Further dismantling gender norms in his illustrations, Neill feminizes various male characters while correspondingly enhancing the masculinity of some female ones. Baum describes Prince Inga, the protagonist of *Rinkitink in Oz*, as a "manly little fellow, although somewhat too grave and thoughtful" (*Rinkitink*, ch. 1), but Neill's illustration stresses the character's feminine features, with his bobbed hair, almond eyes, and full lips imparting a gentle beauty to this ostensibly masculine figure. Part of the play of gender can also involve transposing genitalia between male and female characters, such as in Neill's illustration of Woot the Wanderer and Ozma in *The Tin Woodman of Oz*. In this image, Woot, who has been transformed into a Green Monkey, hopes that Ozma can return him to his human form. Neill clothes Woot in an apron to hide his simian genitalia, yet his paws are clasped in a manner to approximate the contours of a vagina. Ozma looms over the boy/monkey, pushing her scepter—long and phallic—down into the floor. (See figure 5.7.) The scepter exaggerates Baum's image, for he writes that Ozma "drew from her bosom a small silver Wand" to change the various enchanted characters back to their original forms (*Woodman*, ch. 13). The image requires a more imposing phallic symbol to accentuate the ironic transposition of genitalia between these two characters, embedding Neill's illustration with a humorous undercurrent that questions the purported prerogatives of masculinity.

As discussed previously, Baum's novels stress the close homosocial friendships between numerous characters, and some of Neill's illustrations imbue these relationships with hints of eroticism. As Baum records of the affection between Dorothy and Ozma: "Everything about Ozma attracted one, and she inspired love and the sweetest affection rather than awe or ordinary admiration. Dorothy threw her arm around her little friend and hugged and kissed her rapturously, and Toto barked joyfully and Button-Bright smiled a happy smile and consented to sit on the soft cushions close beside the Princess" (*Road*, ch. 20). Baum's words, which move from "sweetest affection" to kissing "rapturously," need not be depicted erotically, but Neill's illustrations show the two girls with lowered eyelids as their lips near, with the image frozen at the tantalizing moment before their kiss. Moreover, whereas Baum depicts the scene with onlookers, including Toto and Button-Bright, to dissipate its erotic charge, Neill's sketch focuses exclusively on this feminine embrace in a close-up. It should also be noted that, whereas Denslow painted Dorothy as a young child of about five or six years in *The Wonderful Wizard of Oz*, Neill updated her image, as Katharine M. Rogers observes: "Neill drew Dorothy as an older child, presumably with Baum's approval; he also dressed her fashionably, unlike Denslow's country child."[15] In this image Dorothy and Ozma appear to be more young women than girls, which heightens its potential eroticism. In a similar vein, Baum portrays the Cowardly Lion and the Hungry Tiger as intimate friends, and Neill's illustrations link the pair while also bedecking them with effeminizing ribbons—in the lion's mane, on the tiger's tail (*Ozma*, ch. 8). In this detail, Neill follows Denslow's lead, as his Cowardly Lion wears a ribbon in his mane (e.g., *Wonderful Wizard*, ch. 11). In another of Neill's portraits, the Cowardly Lion cradles the Hungry

Figure 5.7. Woot's clasped hands approximate a vagina, as Ozma towers above him.

Tiger's snout with his paw, looking down upon his friend adoringly—again with a ribbon decorating his mane (*Patchwork*, ch. 28; cf. a similar illustration in the front matter of *Magic*).

The friendship between the Scarecrow and the Tin Woodman brims with queer potential in Baum's texts. Numerous passages throughout the series comment on their close relationship, and Neill's illustrations of the Scarecrow and the Tin Woodman capture the latent suggestions of eroticism in their relationship, as did Denslow's drawings before him. Denslow's iconic illustration for *The Wonderful Wizard of Oz* depicts the Scarecrow and the Tin Woodman sitting together in a dandified pose, with their legs crossed as they clasp each other's raised hands, while perching on a rectangle detailing publication information. The joint of the Tin Woodman's eye conveys a gleam of gentle warmth, if not attraction, and he sports a natty bowtie, apparently made of tin as well. Denslow's illustration focuses neither on Dorothy, the book's protagonist, nor on the Wizard, its eponymous character, and instead foregrounds the strong friendship between two of its supporting characters. (See figure 5.8.) For the cover of *The Marvelous Land of Oz*, Neill depicts

Figures 5.8 and 5.9. Both Denslow's title-page illustration of *The Wonderful Wizard of Oz* and Neill's cover illustration of *The Marvelous Land of Oz* feature the homosocial friendship of the Scarecrow and Tin Woodman as the novels' defining images.

this pairing as well: the Scarecrow and the Tin Woodman sit on emeralds, and though they are separated, they reach out to each other and clasp hands, as the Scarecrow clutches his scepter and the Tin Woodman his axe. (See figure 5.9.) Other illustrations depicting the primacy of this relationship, with the two looking affectionately at each other, appear throughout the series (e.g., *Dorothy*, ch. 15; the cover illustration of *Emerald*; front matter illustration of *Magic*; table of contents illustration of *Glinda*). As he took over the job of illustrating Baum's Oz books, Neill first aimed for continuity between his drawings and Denslow's, but as Michael Patrick Hearn argues, Neill "felt even more confident with the next Oz book *Ozma of Oz* (1907) and broke completely free from Denslow's influence in *Dorothy and the Wizard of Oz* (1908)."[16] Part of Neill's liberation, it appears, involved elevating the erotic subtext of these images, pushing beyond Denslow's depictions of close friendship to more suggestive ones.

Given Baum's storylines, Neill must portray the Scarecrow and the Tin Woodman in numerous scenes, many of which stress their shared intimacy. When the two reunite in *The Marvelous Land of Oz*, the Tin Woodman cries, "My dear old friend! My noble comrade . . . how delighted I am to meet you once again!" Neill's illustration, captioned as "Caught the Scarecrow in a Close and Loving Embrace," shows the Tin Woodman smiling down at the Scarecrow as they hug, with Tip holding Jack Pumpkinhead's hand as they observe the pair (*Marvelous*, ch. 11). In *Dorothy and the Wizard of Oz*, a small sketch of the pair portrays the Scarecrow gazing up at his taller friend, who looks down, smiling, into his eyes (*Dorothy*, ch. 15), and a similar image can be found in the front matter of *The Magic of Oz*. The chapter-opening vignette of "The Loons of Loonville" in *The Tin Woodman of Oz* depicts the Scarecrow, the Tin Woodman, and the Munchkin boy Woot the Wanderer from the rear, with the Tin Woodman's hand placed gently on the Scarecrow's back, as he turns his head in his friend's direction (*Woodman*, ch. 4). To these examples numerous more could be added, for illustrations pairing the Scarecrow and the Tin Woodman can be found throughout the series, many of which teeter between the assumed asexuality of their homosocial bond and hints that deeper intimacies flourish.

Given these circumstances, at what point does a homosocial friendship between two fantastic creatures from a fairyland become recognizably queer? Most of Neill's drawings of the Scarecrow and Tin Woodman emphasize the close and innocently physical nature of their friendship, yet other images enhance their underlying erotic ambiguity and subtly indicate that their close friendship includes anal eroticism. In some drawings the Tin Woodman is oddly positioned behind the Scarecrow rather than standing by his side

(*Ozma*, ch. 7). The illustration captioned "All Were Immediately Dumped Out" features the Tin Woodman's head, which is topped with the phallic cylinder of an oil funnel, landing in close proximity to the Scarecrow's buttocks, after the Gump accidentally drops the riders from its unwieldy body. Despite the calamity that has befallen the adventurers, the Scarecrow, unhurt from the fall, finds reason to smile (*Marvelous*, ch. 18). In a scene from *The Tin Woodman of Oz* featuring an even more suggestive illustration, the Tin Woodman orders food to be brought for Woot the Wanderer, and, as Baum writes, "in a few minutes the servant brought in a tin tray heaped with a choice array of good things to eat, all neatly displayed on tin dishes that were polished till they shone like mirrors" (*Woodman*, ch. 1). Neill instead depicts an empty plate, with Woot holding an indeterminate foodstuff in his left hand and a phallic knife in his right. The Scarecrow bends slightly over the table, with the Tin Woodman positioned suggestively behind him. To read a hint of sodomy in this depiction may risk overinterpretation, yet Neill positions them similarly in an illustration from *Ozma of Oz*, with the Scarecrow in front bending his buttocks backward to the Tin Woodman's lifted crotch (*Ozma*, ch. 7). Returning to the prior scene of the Scarecrow, the Tin Woodman, and Woot the Wanderer, Neill sketches the furniture of the Tin Woodman's palace, as evident in the chair where Woot sits, with the images of the ruler and his dearest friend. (See figure 5.10.) This comic detail delights in its absurdity—few of even the most devoted couples, whether gay or straight, would ornament their furniture with their likenesses—as it also simply underscores what the Oz books repeatedly declare: that the relationship between the Scarecrow and the Tin Woodman exceeds the bonds of a simple friendship.

Counterbalancing the homosocial bond between the Scarecrow and the Tin Woodman, a heteroerotic attraction appears to ignite between the Scarecrow and Scraps the Patchwork Girl when they meet and comment on each other's beauty (*Patchwork*, ch. 13). Neill's illustration of this scene depicts the Scarecrow bending on one knee before Scraps, as if he were proposing marriage to her, and subsequent images in the novel link the pair, such as when they hold hands (*Patchwork*, ch. 26). On the other hand, Baum does not develop this relationship in the following novels of the series, and, in the opening illustration for the chapter "Ozma's Counsellors" in *Glinda of Oz*, Neill depicts the Scarecrow and Scraps linking arms, but with Scraps's left arm around the Tin Woodman's shoulder, which thus suggests a genial feeling of camaraderie among all of the Ozian adventurers (*Glinda*, ch. 14). Notwithstanding these hints of heteroerotic interest between the Scarecrow and Scraps, Neill illustrates the Scarecrow enjoying a much closer encounter

Figure 5.10. Whether or not one agrees that the positioning of the Scarecrow and Tin Woodman in this image is indicative of anal penetration, Woot waves his phallic knife suggestively, while the ornamentation of the Tin Woodman's chair points to the exaggerated nature of his homosocial friendship with the Scarecrow.

in another image suggestive of anal penetration in *Ozma of Oz*, when the private of Ozma's army, who is riding high in the air on an iron giant's arm, must jump off to safety. Baum sets the scene thusly: "The Scarecrow lay flat upon the ground and called to the man to jump down upon his body.... This the private managed to do, waiting until a time when he was nearest the ground and then letting himself drop upon the Scarecrow." Neill's accompanying drawing shows the private's buttocks landing directly on the Scarecrow's crotch; the Scarecrow smiles as the private's face registers his shock. The private's legs are spread in a sharp V-shape, which accentuates the focal point of the illustration as the intersection between the private's buttocks and the Scarecrow's crotch (*Ozma*, ch. 10).

Baum's colorful imagination envisioned many marvelous, magical beasts, and drawing them allowed Neill a congruent pleasure of creation, which he could enhance through the introduction of erotic elements. Baum describes the Hip-po-gy-raf as "a huge beast with a thick, leathery skin and a surprisingly long neck. The head on the top of this neck was broad and flat and the eyes and mouth were very big and the nose and ears very small" (*Woodman*, ch. 19). From this description Neill drew a beast resembling a penis, with its hunched shoulders approximating testicles, its neck a long shaft, and its head the tip of a penis. Furthermore, the plot requires the Hip-po-gy-raf to assist the Scarecrow and his companions in crossing a large ditch by riding

Figure 5.11. Polychrome strokes the phallic Hip-po-gy-raf, with her flowing dress symbolizing the orgasmic pleasure the creature enjoys.

on its elastic neck. As Baum explains, "When the head was drawn down toward the beast's shoulders, the neck was all wrinkles, but the head could shoot up very high indeed, if the creature wished it to" (*Woodman*, ch. 19). The dynamics described, signaled with the pun on *head*, match those of a flaccid penis becoming erect. Baum's account of these events include the Rainbow's Daughter, Polychrome, riding on the Hip-po-gy-raf's head, and in Neill's illustrations she strokes his neck/shaft, with her flowing gown, closely aligned to the creature's mouth, mimicking a spray of ejaculate. (See figure 5.11.) Again, Neill must ignore certain aspects of Baum's story so that his eroticized image will cohere, and in this instance, he overlooks Baum's detail that Polychrome carries "the bundle of the Scarecrow's raiment in her hand" (*Woodman*, ch. 19) so that he may position it in a more caressing gesture.

For his illustrations of *John Dough and the Cherub*, Neill faced the challenge of drawing Chick the Cherub, whom, as discussed in the chapter "Trans Tales of Oz and Elsewhere," Baum refrains from identifying by gender for the

BOY OR GIRL?

Figure 5.12. Neill's illustration of Chick the Cherub alerts readers to the gender play forthcoming in the text, with this caption deleted in other editions.

novel's entirety, until the final sentence poses the character's sex as a riddle to be resolved (*Dough*, ch. 19). The front matter of this novel includes Neill's illustration of Chick the Cherub accompanied by the rabbit Pittypat, along with the provocative caption, "Boy or Girl?" (*Dough* front matter; see figure 5.12). For those who have not yet read the book, the image is likely somewhat puzzling, for it is unclear whether the caption is directed at the rabbit or the human-looking character, nor do Pittypat and Chick stand as one of the book's definitive pairings. Rabbits, according to Lucia Impelluso, have long been "considered a symbol of lust and . . . sometimes appeared as a symbol of sensual pleasure in representations of love,"[17] and while there is little reason for proposing that Neill intends an amatory connection between cherub and beast in this image, the leporine illustration encourages viewers to contemplate its gendered subtexts. For later editions of *John Dough and the Cherub*, the caption of "Boy or Girl?" was deleted, leaving only the image of Pittypat and Chick, because the caption prepares readers for the gender play inherent in Chick's characterization, rather than allowing the full force of Baum's final sentence to register. Indeed, by pairing this gender-neutral image of Chick with Pittypat the rabbit, Neill encourages readers to misgender Princess Jacquelin, the character with whom Pittypat is more strongly linked. Baum describes Princess Jacquelin as "the loveliest and sweetest maiden that any one has ever looked upon; and so round and innocent were her clear and gentle eyes and so gentle and winning her smile, that to see her but once was to love her dearly. John . . . instantly accepted this shipwrecked waif as a real Princess, and from that moment worshiped loyally at her shrine" (*Dough*, ch. 11). Yet many readers would hardly expect gender to remain a stable construct in Baum's novels, given its variability in such previously published works as *The Marvelous Land of Oz*, *The Enchanted Island of Yew*, and *Queen Zixi of Ix*, and so it seems equally likely that some readers would be prepared for this princess to be revealed to be a boy. Neill's illustration of Chick kissing the Princess captures the ambiguity of Chick's gender and of the Princess's response, with Chick's left profile featuring a closed eye yet with the frontal image of the Princess capturing both eyes open (*Dough*, ch. 15).

For the two decades of their collaboration, Neill and Baum benefited from each other's talents. As a whole, children's literature is greatly enhanced through illustrations, which contribute a visual dimension to the narrative experience. Baum's queer Oz would have been bleached of its untamed excess if Neill had not brought along his own queer sensibility to their joint endeavors.

NEILL'S QUEER ILLUSTRATIONS OF HIS OWN OZ BOOKS

Following Baum's death in 1919, Ruth Plumly Thompson assumed authorship of the Oz series; Neill illustrated many of her works as well. After her *Ozoplaning with the Wizard of Oz* (1939), Neill wrote and illustrated four Oz books: *The Wonder City of Oz* (1940), *The Scalawagons of Oz* (1941), *Lucky Bucky in Oz* (1942), and *The Runaway in Oz* (1995, published posthumously, with illustrations by Eric Shanower).[18] Neill's stories are often disjointed, with no strong narrative thread linking the various adventures, as Hearn avers: "Although he was a fine illustrator, Neill had difficulty pulling all of his discordant ideas together into a coherent narrative."[19] Neill echoes much of Baum's narrative structure, as adventurers quest or otherwise rove across the marvelous land of Oz, encountering strange and exotic creatures along the way. He also adheres to many of Baum's plot points, including such repeated incidents as Jack Pumpkinhead needing to find a new pumpkin to replace his damaged head.[20] Moreover, he continues the Ozian tradition of gender switching. Baum's chicken Billina prefers to be called Bill, and in complementary contrast, Neill's horse, despite its name of Jennifer, is male: "The plow horse, though male, was named Jennifer. Before he had been born, his mother, a mare of strong opinions, had decided to name her first colt Jennifer because she liked the sound of the name" (*Runaway*, ch. 2). Neill also links many of his characters in homosocial pairings similar to Baum's Scarecrow and Tin Woodman, such as Lucky Bucky and the whale Davey, and Scraps the Patchwork Girl and Popla the plant. Readers might well imagine that Scraps, wearied that her attraction to the Scarecrow was never returned, now turns to lesbianism: "With deeper feeling than she had ever before shown, [Scraps] said, 'You're the most beautiful girl in Oz and the most wonderful traveling companion. We make a great team'" (*Runaway*, ch. 17). At the very least, they make a more satisfying team than Scraps and the Scarecrow.

Without question, Neill contributed most to Ozian lore through his illustrations, with his stories failing to match Baum's mix of fantasy, frivolity, and exuberance. *The Scalawagons of Oz* tells the tale of the Wizard giving every citizen of Oz a car, but it is hard to reconcile the magic of a fairy kingdom with the banality of traffic jams, as Scraps reports: "Public traffic jammed up hard / All along the boo-lee-vard!" (*Scalawagons*, ch. 23). Furthermore, as the third author of the Oz series, Neill needed to maintain consistency with its many previous novels and with the arcane rules of life in fairyland, and so continuity problems and other such contradictions inevitably arise. One such example is the question of whether children age in Oz. On this issue Baum declared that they did not (*Woodman*, ch. 12); in contrast, Neill's narrator asserts that, in Number Nine's family, "the stop-growing age . . . was ten for the girls and twelve for the boys" (*Wonder City*, ch. 5). Also, Neill's Dorothy explains that "in Oz everyone stops growing at the age he'd always like to be" (*Scalawagons*, ch. 17). Such small details do not significantly undermine the pleasures of the text, yet it suggests the difficulty of maintaining Baum's vision and the sense of wonder and surprise he cultivated throughout his fourteen Oz novels.

Neill's own Oz books, similar to Baum's, frequently foreground the homosocial and homoerotic attraction between the Tin Woodman and the Scarecrow. After the Tin Woodman has once again rusted and once again recovered, the Scarecrow responds with an outpouring of emotion: "'It's good to hear your voice again,' said the Scarecrow, with tears of happiness running down his cheeks. The two old friends embraced" (*Scalawagons*, ch. 14). Neill's images of the pair further accentuate their homosocial bond, such as when they dance, possibly a tango, and the Tin Woodman smiles sheepishly down on the Scarecrow, who raises his eyes to his friend. As the two concentrate on each other, an observing Flummox (a birdlike creature) appears to direct an arrow just below the Scarecrow's rear (*Bucky*, ch. 16; see figure 5.13). In another illustration, the Tin Woodman sits in the Scarecrow's lap during an all-male cruise on the whale Davey (*Bucky*, ch. 18; see figure 5.14). As they walk together in a drawing from *The Wonder City of Oz*, they both strike

Figures 5.13 and 5.14. In yet another suggestive image of the Scarecrow and the Tin Woodman, they gaze into each other's eyes while tangoing. Two chapters later, the Tin Woodman sits in the Scarecrow's lap while enjoying the homosocial pleasures of an all-male cruise. Not included in this portion of the two-page illustration is a male rabbit running off to join the fun, with a female rabbit angrily holding him back.

dandified poses—holding hands with arms linked, with the Scarecrow's body contorted outward, as the Tin Woodman smiles cheekily and the Scarecrow grins broadly (*Wonder City*, ch. 8). The sense of queerness that permeates Baum's Oz continues in Neill's scenes, for at this point in the series' evolution, gender play and homosocial bonds were too integral a part of the storylines simply to be forsaken. Still, as much as Neill continues Baum's play with Oz's queerness, he weaves heteroerotic attractions into his narratives, such as when the Munchkin boy Number Nine flirts with Jenny Jump. His eyes are "full of a warm blue light" when they meet (*Wonder*, ch. 4), and he later wheedles her to join him: "'Then why not come into my car,' pleaded Number Nine, with an unusually warm light in his blue eyes" (*Scalawagons*, ch. 14). Also, in a stunning image of heterosocial coupling unparalleled in Baum's Oz books, Neill depicts many of the characters dancing together in male/female pairs: the Wizard and Ozma, the Tin Woodman and Glinda, the Scarecrow and Dorothy, Number Nine and Jenny, Scraps and Jack Pumpkinhead, and Uncle Henry and Aunt Em, among others (*Scalawagons*, ch. 25).

Based on the preponderance of evidence presented in this chapter, it is clear that John R. Neill encoded sexual imagery in Baum's and his own Oz books, yet at the same time, some images simply leave one wondering. On the dedication page of *Dorothy and the Wizard of Oz*, Neill sketches Dorothy's cat Eureka, who sports a natty bowtie and holds a placard cheekily stating, "OH MEOW." I cannot conclusively argue that this image is a queer one, but the tonality—not just "meow" but "OH MEOW"—sounds so performatively gay, so reminiscent of many gay men I have known who indulge in a campy sense of play, that I can read the words only with a queer inflection. It is worth noting as well that Eureka speaks frequently in this novel yet never says "meow," and so this image, as with so many others, exemplifies the freedoms Neill took in illustrating Baum's characters. This image of Eureka, then, confronts me with the limitations of interpretation, for it raises the issue that what I see as queer may or may not accord with Neill's sensibilities. Does this natty, mincing cat suggest a queer sensibility transcending the temporal boundaries between gay cultures of the early twentieth and the early twenty-first centuries? (See figure 5.15.) Neill's play with vaginal, phallic, and other sexual images builds a transgressively erotic sensibility into the Oz texts, one that aligns with Baum's narratives, but at the same time, some of his illustrations, in their quirky humor, may align with a modern queer sensibility—whether my own or that of others—without necessarily depicting a latent eroticism in Baum's stories or in his illustrations. To the question, then, of whether Eureka is queer, I must confess myself perplexed yet simultaneously delighted by the possibility.

Figure 5.15. A queer cat? Eureka and the intriguing play of gay speech.

Like the most memorable songs that unite melodies and lyrics into a seamless whole, the finest children's literature features texts and images that cohere organically so that their mutual intricacies unfold in unison. Neill's illustrations of Oz accomplish this objective, matching the manic uncertainty and humor of life in a fairyland with images bursting with bustle, motion, and pleasure. Yet part of this pleasure, as it is part of the pleasure of Baum's novels, arises in the surprising depiction of Oz's eroticisms, which undermine the supposed innocence of children's literature while increasing Oz's depth, sophistication, and comedy.[21]

Chapter 6

CULTURAL PROJECTION, HOMOSOCIAL ADVENTURING, AND THE QUEER CONCLUSIONS OF FLOYD AKERS'S BOY FORTUNE HUNTERS SERIES

"We Meet Some Queer People"
—SAM STEELE, TITLE OF CHAPTER 3, *THE BOY FORTUNE HUNTERS IN THE SOUTH SEAS*

Published under the pseudonym Floyd Akers, L. Frank Baum's Boy Fortune Hunters series depicts Sam Steele's daring adventures across the globe, as this plucky youth pursues fabulous wealth and treasure while outwitting dangerous adversaries. Each of the series' six books follows a standard narrative arc, with Sam winning gold in *The Boy Fortune Hunters in Alaska* (1908), diamonds in *The Boy Fortune Hunters in Panama* (1909), buried treasure in *The Boy Fortune Hunters in Egypt* (1909), ancestral riches in *The Boy Fortune Hunters in China* (1909), rubies in *The Boy Fortune Hunters in Yucatan* (1910), and pearls in *The Boy Fortune Hunters in the South Seas* (1911). Oddly, Sam stands as the sole boy fortune hunter of the series' first two volumes, with his friends Joe Herring and Archibald "Archie" Sumner Ackley joining him in the third installment, *The Boy Fortune Hunters in Egypt*.[1] The three boys enjoy further exploits in China and the Yucatan peninsula; Archie, however, is dropped without mention for the final installment in the South Seas. Additional recurring characters include Sam's father, Dick Steele; Sam's uncle, Naboth Perkins; and fellow sailors Ned Britton, Bryonia, and Nux. As this brief cast of characters suggests, the boy fortune hunters inhabit an overwhelmingly male world, and numerous queer possibilities ensue from these narrative conditions.

Baum's adventure novels were inspired by novelists including Walter Scott and Robert Louis Stevenson—as acknowledged by Sam's ownership of their complete works (*Alaska*, ch. 5). H. Rider Haggard's corpus, notably such popular books as *King Solomon's Mines* (1885) and *She* (1887), also influenced their story lines. H. Alan Pickrell documents Baum's debts to Haggard: "the resulting novels quickly became weaker Haggard type plots: A series of jingoistic lost race novels in which the same things happen over and over again. . . . The natives to the area are hostile and want to kill the strangers, who have come to take away their treasures, but the female ruler saves them somehow and there is a last-minute escape in which some kind of fortuitous natural disaster figures. Baum seems to be retelling *King Solomon's Mines* and *She* over and over again."[2] Baum's series also engages with the burgeoning genre of science fiction, the popularity of which skyrocketed following the publication of such works as Jules Vernes's *From the Earth to the Moon* (1865) and *Twenty Thousand Leagues under the Sea* (1870) and H. G. Wells's *The Time Machine* (1895). Along these lines, *The Boy Fortune Hunters in Panama* features a car that travels on land and water, *The Boy Fortune Hunters in Yucatan* features a flying gas-jacket, and *The Boy Fortune Hunters in the South Seas* features a solo biplane. In line with prevailing trends of the adventure and science-fiction genres at the turn of the twentieth century, both of which foreground mostly male characters, Baum's protagonists represent a lionized form of boyish, daring masculinity that reflects the idealized but problematic values of their white, Western homeland. Baum's Boy Fortune Hunter books were published during the United States' pursuit of imperialist policies in different corners of the globe, and thus their geographical settings mirror the reach of US foreign policies, particularly for the volumes set in Central America and the South Pacific. As Ernest May summarizes, "In 1898–99 the United States suddenly became a colonial power. It annexed the Hawaiian Islands. Humbling Spain in a short war, it took Puerto Rico and the Philippines. In quick sequence it also acquired Guam and part of Samoa. . . . In an eighteen-month period it became master of empires in the Caribbean and the Pacific."[3] Not surprisingly, these imperialist episodes inspired a raft of jingoistic novels celebrating the United States' military strength.

And certainly, as is common with the imperialist adventure novels of this era, whether written for children or adults, the Indigenous characters whom Sam, Joe, and Archie encounter are frequently depicted with offensive stereotypes, for Baum consistently contrasts the villainy of the former to the bravery, derring-do, and intelligence of his white American heroes.[4] Bill Thompson summarizes this troubling dynamic in Baum's books: "The six Boy Fortune Hunters books are exciting adventure stories that remain more readable than many similar books by other authors of the day. They suffer, however, from their heroes' chauvinistic attitude toward other cultures, an attitude typical of the period during which these books were written."[5] In the series' many instances of cultural othering, Sam and his fellow protagonists ascribe positive values and motivations to themselves while projecting negative values and motivations onto their opponents, even when these protagonists and antagonists share strikingly similar objectives and actions. As Harold Anderson explains in his classic definition of projection: "A person is *projecting* when he ascribes to another person a trait or desire of his own that would be painful for his ego to admit. Since the act of projecting is an unconscious mechanism, it is not communicated to others nor is it even recognized as a projection by the person himself.... The fault or the unsavory desire or trait is still in the person's unconscious; it is not in the person or object on whom the projection is made."[6] Literary characters, as textual and imaginative creations, possess neither conscious nor unconscious nor subconscious minds, yet their authors imbue them with ideas and beliefs that are revealed both through their actions and through the contradictions exposed in the gap between their beliefs and actions. This pattern holds throughout many scenes in the Boy Fortune Hunter novels, in which Sam Steele denigrates an adversary with disparaging terms yet then reveals the similarity of their mind-sets. In an additional twist, Baum also depicts such moments of cultural projection coinciding with Sam's recognition of this dynamic, with the character in effect diagnosing his projection of negative characteristics onto his opponents while nonetheless buttressing their marginalization.

These issues of cultural projection are complicated by the series' rejection of heteronormative attraction, for the homosocial order of these boy fortune hunters' ship-bound lives depends on the continued refutation of heteroerotic courtship and marriage, and thus desires are both projected onto the othered characters and reveal the protagonists' desire for these objectified men. As Judith Butler explains of the erotic construction of the Other: "sexual fantasies may express a longing for a scene outside the fantasy, but the fantasy always figures that outside within its own terms, that is, as a moment inside the scene, effecting its fulfillment through a staging and distributing of the subject in every possible position. The consequence is that although it may well be some Other that I fantasize about, the fantasizing recasts that Other within the orbit of my scene, for fantasy is self-reflexive in its structure, no matter how much it enacts a longing for that which is outside its reach."[7] Such a complex dynamic unfolds in Baum's novels: heteroerotic desire is attributed primarily to the Other, as it is also marginalized when these American protagonists themselves express a fleeting, yet rarely pursued, interest in female characters. In her reading of G. A. Henty's and George Manville Fenn's boys' adventure fictions of the late nineteenth and early twentieth century, Amanda Chapman proposes that the male protagonists display a gender and erotic identity characterized by "queer elasticity," in that their narrative circumstances "promote or at least entertain fluid and non-normative masculine behavior . . . that we might expect would have been understood . . . as deviant in most other contexts."[8] By endorsing homosociality and downplaying heteroeroticism, and by addressing these themes through the American boys' interactions with various Native Others, Baum establishes American boyhood and adventuring as inherently queer experiences. In each of the novels' conclusions, the greatest threat that the boys confront is not posed by an Indigenous character but by heteroerotic desire, which necessitates some of their wiliest maneuvers to evade.

AMERICAN BOYS VERSUS INDIGENOUS ADULTS: CONSTRUCTING AND PROJECTING THE OTHER IN CHILDREN'S LITERATURE

In countless specimens of children's literature, youth stands as a preeminent and nearly unquestionable virtue, and within the Western genre of children's adventure novels of the late nineteenth and early twentieth centuries, laden as they are with imperialistic and jingoistic themes, plucky boy protagonists typically evince additional key traits, primarily their whiteness, cleverness, and bravery. In contrast, the Indigenous peoples against whom they combat are construed as nonwhite, adult, unintelligent, and either savagely aggressive or cowardly. In sum, Western children are superior in virtually all ways to Indigenous adults in these fictions. J. A. Mangan summarizes depictions of masculine virtue in this era's schoolboy literature: "Imperial manliness was developed differently in the various circumstances of geographical and climatic diversity, but in substance demanded everywhere a physical toughness, a 'tribal' loyalty, a superior confidence, a forceful will, and above all, subscription to a clearly defined moral code."[9] Any such moral code, however, devolves into a pliable device for the elevation of whiteness and the suppression of Indigenous peoples.

Whiteness tacitly defines American virtue throughout these series, as evident in the treatment of Bryonia and Nux, who are simultaneously esteemed as essential members of the fortune-hunting crew yet othered owing to their race and ethnicity, particularly because their darker skin tones render them slavelike in their characterization. The men play important roles in the adventures, especially Bryonia, whom Sam praises as "almost as skillful in surgery as in cooking." Indeed, Sam compares Bryonia's skills favorably to those of a white character, Capstan Bob, whom he ironically mocks as "a poor doctor before he became a good sailor" (*South Seas*, ch. 10). Sam refers to Bryonia and Nux as "my blacks" (*Panama*, ch. 8) and "our blacks" (*China*, ch. 23). Like Aunt Hyacinth in Baum's Daring Family series and Aunt Sally and Uncle Eben in his Mary Louise series, Bryonia and Nux are not enslaved—in response to Sam's query on the matter, Uncle Naboth replies, "Mercy, no! . . . They're as free as any of us, an' draw their wages reg'lar" (*Alaska*, ch. 5)—but Baum again envisions his darker-skinned characters as voluntarily forgoing payment for their services. At the conclusion of *The Boy Fortune Hunters in Panama*, after Sam, Ned Britton, and Uncle Naboth steal a fortune in diamonds from the Indigenous peoples, they share their wealth among their many fellow adventurers, but Bryonia and Nux refuse payment: "We had selected three good specimens of the 'white pebbles' to sell for the benefit of our faithful seamen, and the amount of prize money they received from this source greatly delighted them. Nux and Bryonia would never accept anything in the way of money at all. They said that they belonged to Uncle Naboth and 'Mars Sam,' and they knew very well that whatever we had they were welcome to" (*Panama*, ch. 24). Even these characters' names are insults: Nux's original name is Ketaha, and Bryonia's is Louiki, but the Americans rename them after herbal remedies, as Uncle Naboth explains: "brought out the medicine box, an' found that all the stuff he had left was two bottles of pills, one of 'em Nux Vomica, an' the other Bryonia" (*Alaska*, ch. 5). Like the Tottenhots in *The Patchwork Girl of Oz* who are less physically evolved than Oz's human characters, Bryonia and Nux are less morally evolved than Sam and the other white characters. After the death of the antagonists of their Alaskan adventure, Sam reports that he "ignored the fact that these men were wicked, and grieved that four human beings had suddenly been cut off in the prime of their manhood," whereas he records of Bryonia's and Nux's reactions: "To their simple minds Daggett and his gang of cut-throats had been properly punished for their wickedness" (*Alaska*, ch. 14).

Corresponding to his oblivious naivete concerning his racist attitudes, Sam Steele's presumption of his moral values is evident in his self-assessments of youthful virtue. "For I was a boy still full of a youthful energy and enthusiasm that needed a safety valve" (*Panama*, ch. 3), he chirps, as he also asserts that it is his longing for adventure, rather than riches, that motivates his actions: "After all, it was the adventure that charmed us, more than the longing for gain. We had been set a difficult task, and boylike we determined to accomplish it" (*China*, ch. 20). Baum portrays his protagonists as typical yet extraordinary American boys by stressing their uniqueness. Sam reports that "we were boys of more than ordinary experience, our adventures on many voyages having taught us to think quickly, act coolly and carefully consider every motive presented to us" (*South Seas*, ch. 2). American boys, hungry for fortune and ready for battle, await any adventure that might come their way. Moreover, as Baum's Boy Fortune Hunters novels stress the virtue of American boyhood, they simultaneously contrast the ingenuity of these youths to the traditional ways of Native adults. The young Americans inevitably triumph in these encounters, as they concurrently project a range of unappealing characteristics onto their foes, often depicting them as brutally violent, sexually voracious, and doggedly uncivilized—even while they themselves undertake brutally violent actions that undercut their self-assessment as civilized. These dynamics unfold throughout the series, particularly as they circulate around conceptions of gender, masculinity, and sexuality. As Joseph Bristow explains of boys' adventure stories, "these fictions devised extraordinary techniques to cover over their many inconsistencies. It was the duty of boys' narratives to suture those discrete elements that, for example, made the hero an agent of moral restraint, on the one hand, and the embodiment of intrepid exploration, on the other," proposing further that such novels underscore the paradox of masculinity, in that "male identity is something that can never be fully gained."[10] As Baum's protagonists pursue treasure, they simultaneously pursue an ideal version of masculinity as inherently white and American, while continually exposing the fault lines undercutting this vision.

But a telling set of contradictions reveal that, while Baum insists on his protagonist's youth, they could equally be considered adults, with this tension disrupting the clear distinction between youths and adults so central to his series' themes. Sam is sixteen years old when the series commences, and he confirms that he completed the "public school course" (*Alaska*, ch. 3); he is eighteen years old at the commencement of his third adventure (*Egypt*, ch. 1). By either of these two measures—having completed his education or by reaching the age of eighteen—Sam could reasonably be considered an adult according to the cultural mores of the era, but he insists on his boyhood: "I can't well object to being called a boy, because I am a boy in years, and experience hasn't made my beard grow or added an inch to my height" (*Yucatan*, ch. 1). The fuzzy lines between childhood, adolescence, and adulthood generated debate in the early twentieth century, as they continue to do today. The publication of G. Stanley Hall's *Adolescence* (1915) marked a pivotal moment in youth studies, and in this work Hall describes adolescence ending and adulthood beginning "after the maturity which comes at eighteen or twenty has been achieved."[11] More so, in a notable blunder, Baum allows eleven years to elapse without Sam aging: the adventurers set sail on May 7, 1897, for their journey to Alaska (*Alaska*, ch. 5), and their adventure in China commences with the "sinking of the first-class passenger steamship *Karamata Maru* in the neighborhood of Hawaii on June 17, 1908" (*China*, ch. 1). Baum maintains the youth of his protagonists over a decade's worth of seafaring, for youth stands as a malleable but persistent ideal. Despite their improbable youthfulness, these boys are accorded undue and outsized respect by the men around them, as Sam reports when assuming the role of captain: "I was, in reality, a mere boy, and the only wonder is that they consented to sail under my command" (*Panama*, ch. 1). Baum insists on the relative youth of his protagonists while according them the respect typically reserved for elder and thus more experienced men. Indeed, when their adversary Mai Lo praises a physician as "old and wise," Sam takes umbrage at the implied contrast—"And that means that we boys are young and foolish"—as he then segues into a chilling threat: "Some who decided to oppose us are lying buried in Alaska, Panama, and Egypt" (*China*, ch. 12).

Along with their youth, the boy fortune hunters view their whiteness as one of their defining virtues. More than simply a skin tone, whiteness symbolizes hierarchically in Western imperialist fictions, but, as Kathryn McInally notes, it represents an ideal that can uphold neither its virtuous claims nor its permanence, in that "whiteness is embodied in a *desire* for whiteness, an aspirational positioning involving a slippage between, and conflation of, 'whiteness' and cultural capital."[12] These young white American boys desire the company of other young white American boys, which is evident when the boys' ally Paul Allerton joins the fortune hunters for their Yucatan adventure along with his close but nonwhite friend Chaka. Apparently overlooking his deep friendship with Chaka, Allerton views whiteness as a marker of essential virtues: "I need more assistance than Chaka can render, and more intelligent comrades than the fierce native Itzaex. The chances of success would be much greater, I am sure, if I had half a dozen white comrades, brave and trustworthy, willing to follow me anywhere" (*Yucatan*, ch. 3). Whiteness here is aligned with valor in contrast to Indigenous cowardice, and Sam believes that whiteness trumps other characteristics of physical attractiveness and personal merit, evident in his rationale for hoping that the lovely Ama will select Allerton, rather than Chaka, in marriage: "While [Paul Allerton] lacked the personal beauty of the Maya chieftain, Paul was white, and therefore to my mind a more fitting mate for the beautiful Ama" (*Yucatan*, ch. 20). Simply put, within Sam's worldview an unattractive white man is ironically more attractive for marriage than a handsome person of color. One might well counterargue that one's personal features matter more for a successful marriage, but in this passage Sam focuses solely on physical attractiveness and its role in mate selection.

Further congruent with McInally's observations concerning the desirability of whiteness in imperialist fictions, several Indigenous people encountered by Sam and his allies extol its virtues. The princess Ilalah affirms the inherent goodness associated with whiteness—"Because the white man is beautiful as a spirit, and he is good and kind" (*Panama*, ch. 11)—and Ama endorses a longstanding prophecy concerning a white savior: "How many of you have heard your mothers say that whenever a white stranger finds a way to enter this valley he will become the savior of our people and the master of our race?" (*Yucatan*, ch. 26). The young ruler Attero similarly believes whiteness indicates virtue and declares, "What I like in the pale-skins . . . is the truth-tongue. You do not try to deceive me." In one of his notable moments of candor in which he pierces the veil of cultural projection, Sam admits the error of Attero's viewpoint and inwardly contradicts this naive conviction in white goodness: "I have said before that this boy was remarkably intelligent for a savage. . . . I am no more truthful than the average American, but it was not easy to try to deceive one of so simple and frank a character. . . . Had the pale-skins always been honest in their dealings with the dark-skinned races many national tragedies would have been averted" (*South Seas*, ch. 12). Here lamenting the violence associated with whiteness but more often benefiting from the values accorded to it, Sam's variability of opinion accords with the mutability of whiteness, in its adaptability to a range of narrative circumstances that continually posit its superiority. Further along these lines, Sam appears on occasion to perceive the limitations of Western arrogance, evidenced when he reads the diary of his deceased friend Kai Lun Pu: "Many of the passages were sarcastic comparisons between the customs of his own people and those of Europeans, and I must admit that, from Prince Kai's point of view, the Europeans did not always come out best" (*China*, ch. 24). Whiteness need not always be associated with virtue and morality, and thus its deeper resilience emerges in its ability to withstand, and thus transcend, any lasting critiques, with the white fortune hunters claiming victory by the novels' conclusions and even sympathetic and likable characters like Attero left dead in their aftermath.

Whereas many intercultural adventure novels depict race as a fixed quality, with white Westerners representing values of civilization and rationality contrasted with the superstitious ignorance of the ethnic Other, some correspondingly depict the ways in which cultural values transcend skin tone, notably in two complementary yet contrasting tropes: the non-Western characters who travel in the United States or Western Europe and adopt the customs of these lands, and the Western characters who "go native" amidst their disorienting experiences in an unfamiliar setting. Kai Lun Pu, who dies in a naval disaster at the beginning of *The Boy Fortune Hunters in China* and who, in his last bequest, encourages Sam, Joe, and Archie to plunder the riches of his ancestral funeral halls, aspires to westernize China, as Dr. Gaylord explains: "The redemption of China, gentlemen, must come through these young scions of the nobility who are being educated at the colleges of England and America. They'll imbibe modern, progressive ideas, and in time upset the old prejudices of the Flowery Kingdom altogether" (*China*, ch. 2). Dr. Gaylord also accuses Chinese people of savagery, claiming that they "have a disagreeable way of running amuck and slicing a few people into mincemeat before they can be overcome" (*China*, ch. 6). Dr. Gaylord foresees the mass enculturation of China as an extension of the West, and Sam, while in other instances insisting on the immutability of race, simultaneously believes that Kai Lun Pu transcends it intellectually: "In my recollections of him I have never thought of Prince Kai Lun Pu as a Chinaman. His features bore certain characteristics of his race, assuredly; but he was so thoroughly Europeanized, so cultured, frank and agreeable in demeanor, that no one could possibly think of him otherwise than as a royal good fellow whom it was a privilege to know" (*China*, ch. 3). In this passage race is permanently etched on the body yet surpassable through one's intellect and exposure to the West, with whiteness and Western culture ineradicably positioned above all other races and civilizations.

Along with whiteness, Americanness stands as an unquestioned virtue for the boy fortune hunters, notwithstanding its many contradictions, and this theme appears in many of Baum's other fictions as well. For instance, in *The Master Key* the protagonist Rob explains his impressive feats to the admiring French president Émile Loubet in a telling formulation: "That's true, Mr. President . . . but [I am] an American boy, you must remember. That makes a big difference, I assure you" (*Key*, ch. 12). In a similar example of the ways in which American virtue is constructed in the Boy Fortune Hunter series, their adversary Hashim asks, "Are you Americans true men?," to which Sam replies, "True as steel" (*Egypt*, ch. 12). The pun on his last name links the United States and truth with the hardness of steel, and thus with Sam himself. The superiority of American whiteness is often expressed in exponential terms, such as when Sam muses, "For my part I pinned my faith to our stalwart escort of American soldiers, thinking in my pride and ignorance that any one of them would be worth six Bega or Arabs if it came to a fight" (*Egypt*, ch. 8). Sounding a similar jingoistic note, Archie asks, "What can one miserable Chinaman do, opposed to three Americans?" (*China*, ch. 6). Sam also claims his status as an American renders him the social equivalent of any Indigenous person. "I'm not common, Joe . . . and I've a notion a decent American is the social equal of an Indian chief. It's social equality I'm talking about, not rank," he states, with his ally Chaka, an Indigenous man, agreeing: "'Cap'n Sam is right,' observed Chaka, with a smile that would have fascinated a woman. 'Equality among men is found only in heart and brain'" (*Yucatan*, ch. 4). Such dizzying contradictions accrue throughout their journeys, in which Americans demand equality that is rarely reciprocated to the Indigenous peoples whom they encounter. Furthermore, as much as Americanness is linked to truth, strength, and cultural superiority, it is also connected to violence and plunder, such as when Ned Britton proposes, "these Indians don't have firearms; but we've got a plenty, so I perpose as we march in, pepper 'em good if they show fight, an' then march out agin with the di'monds" (*Panama*, ch. 7). Sam warns Ned that these Indigenous people successfully warded off prior assaults, noting that a "company of carefully drilled soldiers got wiped off the earth," but Ned simply reaffirms the superiority of Americans: "Colombian sodgers don't count.... Our men is the right stuff 'cause they're all Americans" (*Panama*, ch. 7). Although Baum primarily upholds white Americans as avatars of youthful bravery and honor, Sam acknowledges the cultural bigotry implicit in this viewpoint when he criticizes Archie because his friend's "idea of being a 'free-born American citizen' was to be able to override the rights and privileges of others" (*Egypt*, ch. 3).

In light of the above scenes, "American" as a blanket adjective of democratic virtue means very little, particularly when Sam expresses royalist and oligarchic inclinations. In one such instance, he waxes eloquent over American freedom—"I was born and bred in a democratic republic, and believe that all men are free and equal"—only then to segue into a paean to noble birth lines: "nevertheless there was a serene dignity in this boy's countenance that plainly marked him as royal" (*South Seas*, ch. 11). When discussing his Colombian allies' plan for rebellion, Sam first advocates democracy: "In our own republic . . . the votes of the majority rule. Why do you not resort to the ballot instead of to arms?" (*South Seas*, ch. 3). His interlocutor Alfonso counterargues that the vast majority of Colombians are unworthy of franchise, "In Colombia we have a small class of wealthy and influential people and a horde of vulgar laborers who are little more than slaves" (*South Seas*, ch. 3). Instead of insisting on the necessity of democratic reforms, Sam reassesses his beliefs: "This seemed to put a new aspect on the revolution. I began to approve the action of the De Jiminez party and to sympathize with their 'cause'" (*South Seas*, ch. 3). This encounter concludes with a characteristically jingoistic dismissal, in which Sam insults all of Colombia as unworthy of his concern: "Their assumed importance was of course amusing to me, who looked upon their seven by nine country with tolerant disdain" (*South*

Seas, ch. 3). *The Boy Fortune Hunters in Egypt* begins with cabin boy Joe Herring escaping from the captain of the *Gonzales*, with protagonist Sam Steele commenting, "He was so abused by the dirty Mexican that he would rather die than return to his slavery" (*Egypt*, ch. 2). Even when complimenting Pedro, the boy fortune hunters' companion in their Yucatan adventure, Sam Steele insults Hispanic men in general: "We lost a man on the way back from China a while ago, and replaced him in San Francisco with a stalwart, brown-skinned Mexican, Pedro by name. He wasn't one of the lazy, 'greaser' sort, but an active fellow with an intelligent face and keen eyes" (*Yucatan*, ch. 1). Baum ridicules wealthy Latino men by emphasizing the cliché of their penchant for diamonds. Upon meeting Senhor De Jiminez, Sam Steele first notes that "his skin [is] of the dusky olive hue peculiar to natives of southern climes" and then perceives him as an exaggerated, caricatured figure: "At once I began speculating whether he was a vaudeville actor or a circus barker; but either idea was dispelled when I noticed his diamonds. These were enormous, and had a luster that defied imitation" (*South Seas*, ch. 1). "The poor man never knew we callous Americans were laughing at him," Sam adds (*South Seas*, ch. 4).[13]

If Sam's proclamations of American virtue cannot uphold the United States' democratic aspirations, any concept of American virtue in the series crumbles, which runs parallel to Sam's acknowledgments, often grudgingly expressed, of the accomplishments of other cultures. Among several derogatory passages assailing the Chinese people, Sam concedes their notable achievements: "It is a mistake to think that the Chinese are half civilized, or wholly uncivilized, as I myself had carelessly considered them until I visited their Empire. They boast a civilization older than any other existent nation; they were cultured, artistic and learned thousands of years before the Christian Era, and while the inventions and clever utilities of our modern Western civilization give us advantages in many ways over the Chinese, we cannot withhold our respect and admiration for the accomplishments of this ancient and substantial race" (*China*, ch. 18). Moreover, Sam recognizes the interchangeability of the terms "native" and "foreign" when one travels, in that when he perceives a person as an Other, this person likely perceives him as an Other as well. On arriving in Egypt, Sam recalls his sense of alienation: "It was a queer sensation to find ourselves moving amidst a throng of long-robed turbaned Arabs; fez-topped Turks, with Frenchmen, and Syrians; gray-bearded stooping Jews; blind beggars; red-coated English soldiers, and shrinking, veiled Moslem women." Archie agrees and cries, "What a mess of foreigners," but Sam concludes this passage: "Uncle Naboth, with a laugh, reminded him that we were the foreigners and this curiously mixed crowd, the natives" (*Egypt*, ch. 4). Sam's recognition of the variability of othering, as it may depend on something as simple as the land on which one currently stands, bespeaks his recognition of the folly of American singularity, while he more often reinforces it.

But in yet another contradiction, Sam appears indifferent to his hollow proclamations of American honor and the ways in which he disproves the virtue ostensibly at its core. Sam's blatant hypocrisy exposes the double bind placed upon the Indigenous Other throughout so many episodes of the series, as they are castigated and often killed for appreciating the allure of gems and other treasures in equal measure to the boy fortune hunters themselves. In a striking example of these dynamics, Sam condemns Native people for actions he undertakes himself. While the boys are questing for diamonds in Panama, Tcharn declares, "The chiefs who rule the islands and the coast, all of whom trade with the whites, have told me they are all alike. They are never satisfied, but always want something that belongs to others." One might expect Sam to deny such an accusation, but he readily admits to his readers, "I laughed at his shrewd observation, for that was our case, just then. We wanted the diamonds" (*Panama*, ch. 16). Tcharn has collected a large supply of the gems, despite his culture's prohibition against them, and explains, "I love the pebbles; so I took them, and they are mine." Sam narrates inwardly, "This was exasperating to a degree." He then upbraids Tcharn—"You had no right to do that.... Your king has forbidden you to gather the pebbles" (*Panama*, ch. 16)—thus chastising the Indigenous man for breaking the cultural taboo he aspires to ignore.

Similarly, in *The Boy Fortune Hunters in Egypt*, Sam avouches the values represented by his ship the *Seagull*—"we were a simple, honest American merchant ship, lying in home waters and without an element of mystery in our entire outfit" (*Egypt*, ch. 1)—yet soon discloses that their mission is little more than a scam: "Uncle Naboth . . . contracted with a big Germantown manufacturer of 'Oriental' rugs to carry a load of bales to Syria, consigned to merchants there who would distribute them throughout Persia, Turkey and Egypt, to be sold to American and European tourists and carried to their homes as treasures of Oriental looms" (*Egypt*, ch. 2). In a telling formulation, Uncle Naboth discusses an international scheme for selling fake merchandise: "If it wasn't for Yankee ingenooity an' Oriental trickery the supply 'd been exhausted years ago, an' our people 'd hev to carpet their floors with honest, fresh rugs instead o' these machine worn imitations. That would break their hearts, wouldn't it?" (*Egypt*, ch. 2). The line between the virtue of ingenuity and the vice of trickery is a breathtakingly slight one, yet Uncle Naboth employs it to denigrate a continent of peoples. In another such scene, Captain Steele chastises the villainous Van Dorn over his fortune-hunting—"This treasure . . . belongs to the Egyptian government, accordin' to your own say-so"—and Sam upholds his father's viewpoint: "This is an Egyptian treasure. . . . The laws seem to me to be just. What right have you, a foreigner, to remove this great wealth from the country?" (*Egypt*, ch. 6). Merely a few pages later, Sam reassesses his viewpoint and upholds the right of "free Americans" to liberate the Egyptian people of their treasures: "That the Khedive had made laws forbidding anyone to remove ancient treasure from Egypt did not affect us in the least. We were free Americans and in no way under the dominion of the Turks who had conquered Egypt" (*Egypt*, ch. 6).[14] Indeed, Sam often trades with the Indigenous people he encounters, offering them trifles in exchange for their great wealth. Evaluating his exchange of a watch with Tcharn, he muses, "It was little enough, indeed, for the transfer of the diamonds, which were worth a fortune; but the gems were valueless to him, even had he been able to own them without the risk of forfeiting his life" (*Panama*, ch. 17). In a subsequent adventure, a similar exchange is effected: "I thought it good policy to make him a present of the watch, which was a cheap affair, and he accepted it with evidences of joy and gave me in return a necklace of pearls worth a fortune" (*South Seas*, ch. 12). Like Peter Minuit purchasing Manhattan from the Lenape Native Americans for sixty guilders, Sam is always ready to bargain with Indigenous peoples, as long as the terms are exorbitantly in his favor.

As is too well attested by the history of imperialism, violence frequently erupts as the result of cross-cultural conflicts. Although Sam avows his peaceful inclinations—"No one likes to kill a human being when it can be avoided" (*Yucatan*, ch. 6)—he also asserts the need to "civilize" Indigenous peoples. "The trouble seems to be that no one has taken pains to civilize them" (*Yucatan*, ch. 7), he states, and his ready turns to violence are illustrated by his quick trigger finger: "Before I realized what I was doing I had pulled a revolver and sent a bullet into the fellow's skull" (*Yucatan*, ch. 9). Scores of Indigenous people are massacred throughout the series. In a particularly gruesome episode when escaping their adversaries, Sam and his ally Duncan Moit detonate bombs: "The explosion was instantaneous . . . and the air was filled with earth, wood and Indians. I do not know how many San Blas suffered in this catastrophy [sic], but those were left were thrown into such dire confusion that they fled in all directions and many leaped into the river in an endeavor to escape" (*Panama*, ch. 15). Soon after, Sam and Duncan run over their foes in a car: "He increased our rate of speed until we were fairly flying, and a moment more we bumped into the solid ranks of the Indians and sent them tumbling in every direction" (*Panama*, ch. 17). As this adventure winds down, Sam dismisses his vanquished foes—"The dead were unimportant savages" (*Panama*, ch. 23)—with similar feats achieved in stunningly violent or baroque fashion in the other novels, including the entombment of pirates in *The Boy Fortune Hunters in Alaska*; the violent deaths of Abdul Hashim, Gege-Merak, and Van Dorn in *The Boy Fortune Hunters in Egypt*; and the decapitation of antagonist Mai Lo by a gorilla in *The Boy Fortune Hunters in China*. *The Boy Fortune Hunters in Yucatan* includes countless deaths—"The slaughter must have been terrible, for not only did the fragment completely fill the vast space, but the rubble of loose rocks following it killed many on both sides" (*Yucatan*, ch. 26)—as does *The Boy Fortune Hunters in the South Seas*: "I shuddered to think of the wholesale destruction we must have caused. They were doggedly determined, however, to get the 'pale-skins' at any cost, and if we destroyed hundreds there were hundreds more to take their places" (*South Seas*, ch. 18). Amidst these massacres, the fortune hunters rarely lose sight of their objectives. "We stripped all the pearl ornaments from the dead natives that cluttered the deck, and afterward threw the bodies overboard" (*South Seas*, ch. 19), Sam coolly records, and in an odd statement mixing sentimentality with greed, he says: "Tiffany has since valued [the pearls] at forty thousand dollars, but I will not part with them. I liked Attero and have always regretted that Joe had to kill him" (*South Seas*, ch. 19). The value of the pearls is secondary to the memory of Attero, yet the looting of the pearls required Attero's death, in an aptly confused summary of Sam's hopelessly chaotic value system that questions whiteness and Americanness only to reinstate their supremacy in bloody fashion when treasure is on the line.

The savagery in the Boy Fortune Hunters novels reflects the ugliest parts of Baum's worldviews, in the ready dismissal of the humanity of various peoples, both literary and real. The violence of the books hinges on the rejection of these peoples variously coded as the Other to white Americanness, yet in a striking irony, these peoples, particularly their male characters, are repeatedly described as rapturously attractive. In constructing the Other, so too can be constructed the desire for the Other, as Baum's boy fortune hunters so frequently reveal.

HOMOSOCIAL ADVENTURING AND THE HANDSOME OTHER

Along with the various ways in which Indigenous peoples are viewed as the Others in their own lands, their sexualities are figured as rapacious and dangerous. On the other hand, the civilized white Americans supposedly represent temperance and sexual restraint, and their imperial adventures thus highlight oppositional cultural enactments of erotic desire. In a telling passage, Bryonia cautions Sam, "I wish, Mars Sam, . . . that the lady passengers had not showed themselves" (*South Seas*, ch. 9). Sam wonders in response, "Are the natives partial to white women, Bry?" Bryonia replies, "I know other chiefs . . . and I know they like to take women of other nations for wives" (*South Seas*, ch. 9). In deploying the long-standing and brutally racist trope of Indigenous men as the rapists of white women, Baum associates whiteness with erotic virtue and darker skin tones with sexual savagery, but the stunning paradox of the Boy Fortune Hunter series arises in the observation that heterosexuality itself is othered in the books' treatment of sexuality as a whole. For Sam, Joe, and Archie, heterosexual attraction stands as nearly as alien a feature of their white identities as the range of unappealing characteristics foisted upon Indigenous peoples.

For in contrast to the violently heteroerotic desires of the Indigenous men in the above passage, Baum imagines adventuring and fortune hunting as the activities of men united in homosocial bonds, and often in couples. The series introduces several men paired in close friendships, including Captain Gay and "Doc" Acker, who "were close friends and cronies, and lived together in perfect harmony" (*Alaska*, ch. 5). Bryonia and Nux are similarly coupled throughout the six volumes, and Paul Allerton, recounting his earlier rescue of his friend Chaka, avows the enduring strength of their bond, "We have been together nine years, and we are better friends than at first" (*Yucatan*, ch. 2). Sam observes the reciprocity of their relationship, "I noticed [Chaka] now spoke of Allerton as 'my brother Paul,' when mentioning him to us; and there was a world of affection in the way he said it" (*Yucatan*, ch. 4). Also, in a touching scene their homosocial friendship is compared to a heteroerotic relationship: "We looked at one another wonderingly as Allerton knelt down, took his friend's head in his lap and stroked the dark hair as tenderly as a woman might have done" (*Yucatan*, ch. 9).

Additional hints of queerness emerge in Baum's depictions of other deep male bonds. For example, when Sam inquires of his newly discovered Uncle Naboth, "Were you my father's friend?" Naboth replies enigmatically: "'That's as may be,' said Mr. Perkins, evasively. 'Friends is all kinds, from acquaintances to lovers. But the Cap'n an' me wasn't enemies, by a long shot, an' I've been his partner these ten years back'" (*Alaska*, 35). "Partner" here refers to their business partnership, but with his evident misogyny Uncle Naboth rejects the possibility of any type of partnership with women, and thus it is clear that homosocial relationships are the only ones available to him. Speaking of the aptly if misogynistically named Mrs. Ranck, Uncle Naboth exclaims: "'The woman!' he said, in a low voice. 'I jest can't abide women.'" In a sign of his own preference for homosocial companionship, Sam agrees with Uncle Naboth: "I sympathized with him, and said so" (*Alaska*, 36). Several details further hint that Uncle Naboth's misogyny camouflages his queerness, with Sam reporting that "Uncle Naboth seemed especially pleased to reach San Francisco again" (*Alaska*, 57). This city's status as a queer metropolis was well established by the early twentieth century: as Susan Stryker and Jim van Buskirk document, "because of the Gold Rush, the population of San Francisco was roughly 90 percent male throughout the 1850s and remained disproportionately high for years afterward." They further note that "activities in the Barbary Coast, old San Francisco's infamous saloon and brothel district, earned the city one of its earliest nicknames—Sodom by the Sea."[15] Considering the citizens of another great metropolis, New York City, Naboth dismisses them as "all smug-faced men an' painted-faced women" (*Panama*, ch. 2), yet it is unclear why he would disparage women wearing makeup when he struts about as a dandy: "Uncle Naboth was gorgeous in appearance. He was dressed in a vividly checked suit and wore a tourist cap perched jauntily atop his iron-gray locks" (*Panama*, ch. 3). By concentrating on Uncle Naboth's distaste for women and his preference for male companionship, and by foregrounding homosociality and marginalizing heterosociality throughout the series, Baum gently adumbrates the queerness of male-male friendships and partnerships, even if this queerness remains hazily undefined within the protocols of a children's series.

Among the series' numerous homosocial pairings with queer undertones, the friendship between Sam and his fellow boy fortune hunter Joe Herring stands preeminent. Sam frequently paints Joe with feminine terms, which heightens the intimacy of their relationship and frames homoerotic attraction under a veneer of heteroeroticism. Upon meeting Joe, Sam observes, "His brown hair, now wet and clinging about his face, curled naturally and was thick and of fine texture, while his dark eyes were handsome enough to be set in the face of a girl" (*Egypt*, ch. 1). Baum's pairing of Sam and Joe conflicts with the series's premise of three boy fortune hunters who should presumably be equals in friendship, in line with Sam's assertion that they share a jointly strong bond: "We three boys were inseparable comrades at the time of which I am writing." He nonetheless concedes that he prefers Joe over Archie, admitting that he and Joe "were a little closer to each other than we were to Archie" (*China*, ch. 1). Notably, both Joe and Archie are characterized with feminine traits, with Sam praising Joe as "modest and retiring as a girl" (*China*, ch. 4). Like Uncle Naboth, Archie struts around in dandy fashion, bedecked in "a style of dress gay enough to rival the plumage of a bird-of-paradise" (*Egypt*, ch. 2). In a frank assessment of Archie's character,

Sam details the intriguing intersection of his aggressive and gentle qualities: "Archie was stubborn as a mule, conceited as a peacock, reckless of all conventionalities, and inclined to quarrel and fight on the slightest provocation. But I should hasten to add that he was brave as a lion and tender as a woman to those he loved" (*China*, ch. 1). Given these converging queer characteristics, Archie could conceivably serve as an appropriate best friend for Sam, but despite these overlaps, Sam chooses Joe over Archie, and so, like the other homosocially coupled men of the series mentioned previously, they are united as a pair, with Sam rhapsodizing over their closeness. "Joe I found a treasure in many ways, and always a faithful friend" (*Egypt*, ch. 4), he asserts, and states his belief that his feelings are reciprocated: "Joe . . . was so devoted to me personally" (*Egypt*, ch. 8). It is clear that the two boys admire each other mutually, for when Alfonso wonders why Joe sails as second mate in a ship despite his great wealth, Joe replies: "Mainly because I love the life, and secondly because I love Sam, here" (*South Seas*, ch. 4).

Heightening the latent erotic tension surrounding these many homosocial relationships, Baum consistently registers the physical attractiveness of the boy fortune hunters' Indigenous male antagonists, limning the desirability of these many men as a key and consistent feature of their portrayals. As numerous scholars have noted, Western constructions of non-Western peoples are often built on latent or blatant sexual stereotyping. Edward Said's pioneering work in *Orientalism* details the ways in which "the Orient was almost a European invention," as he dissects the dehumanizing assumptions behind this and related hoary biases.[16] Baum includes disparaging assessments of the residents of Middle East and Asia throughout much of his fiction, such as when, in *The Master Key*, the protagonist Rob faces dangers when he moves away from the "European countries and approach[es] the lawless and dangerous dominions of the Orient" (*Key*, ch. 13). "The oriental mind is intricate. It seldom leads directly to a desired object or accomplishment, but prefers to plot cunningly and with involute complexity," Baum writes in *The Last Egyptian* (*Egyptian*, ch. 11), as he also extrapolates from one female character to all Asian peoples: "[Nephthys] was luxury-loving by nature, as are all Orientals, and accepted the comforts of her surroundings without questioning why they were bestowed upon her" (*Egyptian*, ch. 13).

Moreover, as Joseph Allen Boone discerns in his magisterial study *The Homoerotics of Orientalism*, desires and attractions cannot be divorced from their concomitant disavowal in many accounts of East-West encounters. Samir Dayal succinctly summarizes this dynamic: "Heterosexuality itself is rendered unstable in the non-West and especially in the 'Orient.'"[17] Within the Boy Fortune Hunter books, evidence of homoerotic desire for non-Western, nonwhite men extends beyond "the Orient" and spans the globe. Sam often comments on his adversaries' handsomeness, both individually and collectively, such as when he states, "Without question the San Blas were the best looking Indians I have ever seen. They resembled somewhat the best of the North American tribes, but among them was a larger proportion of intelligence and shrewdness" (*Panama*, ch. 9). By implying that a significant proportion of Native North Americans lack "intelligence and shrewdness," Sam reveals that he has assessed the attractiveness of various Indigenous Americans. During their Egyptian adventures, the boys employ guides through the desert, whom Sam praises as "handsome, well-formed fellows, with good features and dark, bronze hued complexions" (*Egypt*, ch. 8); among these men, Sam rhapsodizes over Ketti as "by far the handsomest and most intelligent of our escort, and his dignified and straightforward expression attracted me toward him" (*Egypt*, ch. 9). Ketti plays the role of a valued ally in this volume, and so his physical magnetism could be aligned with his virtuous character, yet Baum likewise accentuates the allure of the nefarious Abdul Hashim, sketching him as "tall and stately, with a calm, handsome face and steady eyes" (*Egypt*, ch. 11). Sam later extols Hashim: "Never have I seen more handsome features on any man, but they were as immobile as if carved from marble" (*Egypt*, ch. 12). He also mentions Hashim's "handsome bronzed features" and, with a particularly telling phrase, refers to him as "this big and handsome bandit" (*Egypt*, ch. 13). Evaluating the Faytans of the South Seas, Sam underscores their attractiveness: "They were handsome, stalwart fellows, averaging fully six feet in height I judged" (*South Seas*, ch. 8). In sum, Sam encounters a range of strikingly handsome men throughout the Boy Fortune Hunters series, many of whom he then confronts violently.

In contrast, and thus contributing powerfully to the novels' homoerotic undercurrents, Sam praises female beauty less frequently, and when he does, it is within the context of commenting on the attractiveness of an entire race. For example, while traveling in the lost kingdom of Tcha, he declares: "Having remarked upon the fine physique of the men of Tcha, I may as well state here that their women were the handsomest females I have ever seen. It would not have been possible to find an unattractive maid or matron in the hidden city" (*Yucatan*, ch. 17). Notably, Sam only mentions the beauty of these women after stressing the handsomeness of the men, with remarks in which he appears less personally invested; the introductory phrase "I may as well state here" indicates his attention is more focused on male beauty. Whereas the Tcha women merit his approval, Sam disparages the attractiveness of entire populations of women while praising their handsome male counterparts: "I have remarked upon the beauty of the male Itzaex, but I must confess their women are not up to the standard. Nearly all are short and dumpish in form, with dull eyes and apathetic countenances. I never saw a pretty Itzaex girl while I was there" (*Yucatan*, ch. 12). Not even one? an incredulous reader might be tempted to ask. In a passage marked by contradiction, presumption, and projection, Sam acknowledges the attractiveness of the Bega women of Egypt but insists that the Bega men reject them: "The Bega women were numerous in the village, were generally good looking and bold in their demeanor, yet the warriors seemed to make a point of disregarding them altogether, as if the sex was wholly unworthy of masculine attention" (*Egypt*, ch. 9). While one could interpret this passage as stressing the masculinist and misogynistic bias of Bega culture rather than as a comment on the men's sexual attraction to the women, Sam calls attention to the women's physical attractiveness, and thus posits, tacitly but persuasively, the men's erotic apathy toward them. Yet were this erotic indifference truly to characterize Bega culture, reproduction both in it and of it would cease, and so Sam's words represent more his projection of antieroticism onto the Bega men than their own reaction to the women. Certainly, at no point during the novel does a Bega man denigrate Bega women in the manner that Sam does.

In line with his mostly dismissive appraisals of women's beauty among nonwhite populations, Sam occasionally notes the attractiveness of individual female characters, with such passages suturing over his latent revelations of homoerotic desire. "But I think every well regulated young fellow is fond of chatting with a nice girl" (*China*, ch. 21), he states, clearly including himself among the members of the "well regulated"—a phrase that, while predating queer theory by numerous decades, demarcates heteronormativity. Certainly, he looks favorably upon the lovely Princess Ilalah: "Leaning over the side of the machine, her chin resting upon her hands at the edge of the car, was the most beautiful girl I had ever seen. Her form was tall and slender, her features exquisitely regular in contour. . . . I noticed that her skin was almost white in the sunshine, the bronze hue being so soft as to be scarcely observable" (*Panama*, ch. 11). Ilalah's skin tone—simultaneously bronze and white—marks her as foreign yet potentially assimilable to American culture, and one can envision a romantic plotline featuring the series's protagonist and this comely woman. Tellingly, however, Sam disparages the other characters' appreciation of Ilalah's attractiveness. He reports that "Uncle Naboth admired Ilalah more and more as he came to know her, and he told Duncan with great seriousness that she was worth more than all the diamonds in the world, to which absurd proposition the inventor gravely agreed" (*Panama*, ch. 18). First in awe of Ilalah's beauty, Sam's words now evince his greater passion for another fortune than for a beautiful woman. In considering another female character, Ama, Sam waxes poetic: "How shall I describe Ama to you? Shall I say she was the embodiment of grace and beauty, that her figure was tall and supple, her hair a golden bronze, her eyes turquoise and her lips budded like a rose? All that seems stale and flat in depicting Ama" (*Yucatan*, ch. 18). Despite these nods to heteroerotic attraction expressed in the lexicon of a sonneteer, Sam again prioritizes material gain over romantic conquest, and he also favors his homosocial partnerships to the extent of refusing to rescue maidens in distress. When he is selected to fly away to safety with Ama, he insists that he "had not the slightest intention of deserting my comrades for the sake of a girl" (*Yucatan*, ch. 26). The adventurers then locate the gas jackets that will allow them to escape, and Sam muses, "I'm almost sure that was the happiest moment of my life. I felt like kissing everybody all around—even including Ama and her maidens" (*Yucatan*, ch. 27). With this striking statement of homosocial desire, Sam admits his preference for kissing his male friends over the lovely women surrounding him. Even when noting a woman's attractiveness, Sam often conjoins an appreciation of her beauty with a disparaging remark on her ethnicity, such as in his appraisal of Iva. He first lauds her stunning beauty—"The girl was undeniably handsome. She would have been conspicuous by reason of her beauty in any civilized community. Here, surrounded by a barbaric desert tribe, she seemed a veritable daughter of Venus" (*Egypt*, ch. 8)—but then qualifies his evaluation: "It occurred to me I had been right in guessing that the young man entertained a tender feeling toward Iva. But I could scarcely blame him. She was very attractive—for a Bega" (*Egypt*, ch. 9). In this instance Sam's racism coincides with yet fails to cloak his misogyny, as he assumes his readers will join him in dismissing the possibility of finding a Bega woman attractive.

Within this homosocial world of boy adventurers where women's attractiveness is only grudgingly recognized, Baum writes little of erotic desire leading to sexual activity, yet the series's greater investment in overwriting heteroerotic desire should not eclipse its interest in male conflict involving male nudity, for Sam's adversaries frequently strip him and his compatriots of their clothing. A pirate orders him and his fellows, "Strip, my boys.... We want your togs," and following this theft, the pirates parade like dandies: "They seemed very proud of their acquisition, and strutted around like so many vain peacocks" (*Alaska*, ch. 7). Strenuous physical conditions necessitate that men remove their clothing—"Most of the men had stripped themselves naked, to work more comfortably, for the heat was well-nigh unbearable" (*Alaska*, ch. 13)—and Sam reports in another adventure, "We had been stripped naked while we slept and all our equipment and outfit, defensive and aggressive, including the four chests, had been taken from us" (*Yucatan*, ch. 16). In a particularly intriguing passage, Baum potentially refers to a character's erection: "Fully two hours had passed before we observed Chaka's naked body come bounding through the clearing without any attempt at concealment. Evidently he was in a state of excitement" (*Yucatan*, ch. 9). Chaka has apparently lost the loincloth he wore earlier, and while it is unlikely that any man could sustain an erection while running from his adversaries, the evidence of his "excitement" in this scene admits, even if it does not perhaps solicit, an erotic interpretation. Regardless of such an interpretive quibble, the boys are soon stripped again when they are informed, "You must go before the Tribunal naked, save for these robes I have brought" (*Yucatan*, ch. 16). Baum's insistence on the characters' nudity—they are not just "stripped" but "stripped naked" or some such variant phrasing—heightens the latent homoeroticism behind the series's celebration of homosocial adventuring. Of course, men who are stripped naked do not necessarily engage in sexual acts with one another, but as the conclusions of the six novels collectively demonstrate, nor are these boy fortune hunters likely to have sex with women in any of their narrative futures.

ANTI-EROTICISM, QUEER DESIRE, AND NARRATIVE CLOSURE

Despite the homosocial focus of the imperialist adventure genre as a whole, the conclusions of such novels frequently feature the heroes' return to "civilization" and thus affirm their heterosexuality as well, as they reunite with long-suffering wives, fiancées, or girlfriends, or possibly bring back with them maidens rescued from the villainous Indigenous people they recently defeated. The conclusions of each of the Boy Fortune Hunters novels nod to but then evade these erotically normative narrative pressures. *The Boy Fortune Hunters in Alaska* and *The Boy Fortune Hunters in China* evade heteroeroticism altogether, whereas the other four volumes, featuring adventures in Panama, Egypt, Yucatan, and the South Seas, end with the union of a male/female couple. Notably, however, none of these volumes celebrates the triumph of heteroerotic passion but instead quells the erotic energies that such endings typically solicit. Whereas most adventure novels ultimately endorse heteroerotic attraction, Sam marginalizes its desirability, even to the point of questioning the sanity of men who love women.

With the pirates defeated and great wealth at hand as *The Boy Fortune Hunters in Alaska* nears its resolution, Sam, his father Dick Steele, and his Uncle Naboth enter into a new partnership that cements the homosocial foundations of their family. Sam's mother died in the story's prehistory, and neither widower Dick Steele nor confirmed bachelor Uncle Naboth ever seeks female companionship. The men's new partnership, "Steele, Perkins and Steele," promises their future prosperity, and Uncle Naboth assures Dick Steele that, even if their "business ventures prove unsuccessful," he will always have "something to fall back on in [his] old age." Any worries about future financial problems are unwarranted, it appears, with Sam as narrator confirming the family's fortunes: "But success seemed to follow in the wake of the new firm, and the *Cleopatra*, as our ship is named, has made voyage after voyage with unvarying good fortune" (*Alaska*, ch. 20). This all-male family requires no assistance from women, nor does it look forward to a future in which women might join them as wives, stepmothers, or daughters-in-law. The *Cleopatra*, it appears, will be the predominant "female" figure in their lives, and even she is later replaced by the gender-neutral *Seagull*.

In the conclusion of *The Boy Fortune Hunters in Panama*, Sam's companion Duncan Moit marries Princess Ilalah, yet the heteroeroticism on display in their union is counterbalanced by racial othering, as it coincides with Duncan's rejection of Western culture and embrace of hers. As Sam reports, "We all assisted greatly to lend dignity to the day's ceremonies, which included the formal acknowledgment of Ilalah as ruler and lawgiver of the nation and her subsequent marriage—a most primitive rite—to the inventor Duncan Moit. Ilalah's husband was next adopted as a Techla" (*Panama*, ch. 23). Notably, Sam's dismissal of marriage as "a most primitive rite" appears to condemn it universally, not specifically to this Panamanian culture. Still, whether Sam indicts all marriages or only this particular intercultural marriage, it is clear that Duncan Moit "goes native" and abandons the purportedly civilizing influence of the West by adopting the traditions of the Indigenous people whom he initially sought to exploit. Shari Huhndorf argues that the "going native" trope in narratives of American Indians serves as "a means of constructing white identities, naturalizing the conquest, and inscribing various power relations within American culture," with these patterns in place as this American man assumes a position of authority in his new society.[18] Duncan then warns Sam, "You must never come back, you know. . . . We permit you to go freely now, as a return for your kindness to our queen; but should you be daring enough to return at any time I warn you that you will be received as enemies, and opposed to the death" (*Panama*, ch. 23). He further adds, "In the future, as in the past, the demoralizing influences of the whites and their false civilization will be excluded from the dominions of the San Blas" (*Panama*, ch. 23). While Sam has participated in just this sort of imperialistic resource usurpation, which then necessitates that these

Indigenous people protect themselves from white Americans like him, he diagnoses Duncan's rejection of Western culture as an act of insanity: "Yes, I had always suspected a streak of madness in Moit. Perhaps the destruction of his marvelous invention had served to unbalance a mind already insecurely seated" (*Panama*, ch. 23). Notably, Sam projects onto Moit an unhealthy and obsessive interest in his land-sea automobile, overlooking his own passion for his ship and seafaring lifestyle. For Sam, love for a boat surpasses love for a woman, and he expresses disbelief that any man would prefer the latter to the former.

Like *The Boy Fortune Hunters in Panama*, *The Boy Fortune Hunters in Egypt* depicts a marriage toward its conclusion, but in this instance it is monocultural. The couple, Ketti and Iva, allied themselves to the fortune hunters, even to the extent that Iva killed her villainous grandfather. Baum includes a moment of heteroerotic tenderness in depicting their betrothal ceremony: "Coming to her side, Ketti raised her gently and . . . gravely placed one hand beneath Iva's chin, palm upward, and the other hand upon her head, palm down" (*Egypt*, ch. 18). Sam, however, appears wholly uninterested in their marriage: "I am sure Ketti and Iva had an elaborate wedding ceremony thereafter; but that is not a part of my story, from which I fear I have digressed" (*Egypt*, ch. 18). For these boys adventuring in a predominantly homosocial landscape, Ketti and Iva's marriage distracts their attentions from their fortune-seeking exploits and their male friendships. The book's final chapters leave Ketti and Iva, and indeed all of Egypt, behind, allowing Sam additional opportunities of derring-do and adventuring, with heteroeroticism abandoned in a land construed as barbaric and uncivilized. In so doing, Baum envisions his adolescent male readers as similarly uninterested in romance, although it seems quite plausible that many of them would have found such story lines of heightened appeal.

Notwithstanding the series's primary depiction of Sam as homosocially and antierotically inclined, *The Boy Fortune Hunters in China* features him rakishly flirting with female characters, with his behavior offering insight into his expressions of desire and their limits. Upon encountering three young women in China, he proclaims his relief: "Really I was hungry for the sight of a girl, merely to relieve the monotony of our intercourse with the harsh-featured eunuchs; but more than all I was curious" (*China*, ch. 20). Sam frequently expresses bigoted sentiments when appraising the beauty of non-white women, yet he now chides any racists among his readers who would deny the allure of these young women: "Seated at the table were three young and pretty Chinese girls—and if you think a Chinese girl cannot be pretty you should have seen this group as I saw it" (*China*, ch. 20). Assuming the role of a dashing and brash American, Sam interrupts their meeting—"Pardon us, ladies, for intruding.... We are the foreign devils, and we're glad to make your acquaintance" (*China*, ch. 20)—and jauntily flirts: "'Will you come here again tomorrow?' I asked Nor Ghai, taking her little hand in mine—a liberty she did not resent" (*China*, ch. 21). After presuming this liberty with Nor Ghai and denying the heteroerotic attraction it apparently exposes, Sam insists that his actions should not be construed as flirtatious: "I don't say that little Nor Ghai was averse to a bit of flirtation, but none of us encouraged her because we had no thought of flirting with our new friends. We talked in boyish fashion and treated them exactly as if we were brothers and sisters" (*China*, ch. 22). Although Sam earlier upbraided any readers so biased by Western beauty standards that they would not concede the possibility of an attractive Chinese woman, he soundly rejects intercultural romance: "You must not think we had fallen in love with these Chinese beauties, for that was not the case. I don't say that I shall never fall in love; but when I do it will be with an American girl, and it won't matter much whether she is beautiful or not, so long as I love her" (*China*, ch. 21). One should not overlook the racist reasoning behind Sam's rejection of these young women, but it is additionally ironic that he pledges to love an American girl in the future, for the bulk of Sam's life is spent adventuring in lands other than the United States. With this declaration Sam foresees heteroerotic pursuits such as love and marriage in an undefined future but one that by necessity cannot unfold within the pages of Baum's series, in which the end of one overseas adventure simply promises the beginning of a new one.

The Boy Fortune Hunters in Yucatan features a marriage that straddles the borders both between the interracial and the monoracial and between the erotic and the antierotic. Throughout the novel Chaka and Paul Allerton vie for Ama's affections; the latter eventually triumphs. In deference to his deep affection for Allerton, Chaka accepts defeat gracefully: "Do not grieve for me, Brother Paul.... I am sure to be happier in my own country, ruling my people, than in your stiff and luxurious civilization. It's the call of the wild, I suppose, and I am wise to heed it" (*Yucatan*, ch. 28). Here the character marked as an ethnic Other abandons any interest in Western culture and opts to remain in his ostensibly uncivilized land. Similar to his brief nods to the marriages of Ilalah and Duncan Moit and of Iva and Ketti, Sam records that "Paul and Ama were quietly married," with the brevity of this account communicating his dispassionate view of heteroerotic bonds. Despite this marriage in its concluding pages, the book's last sentence evades detailing the couple's newfound domestic bliss: "The bride and groom started at once for a trip to the New Hampshire homestead, where, after paying off the mortgages, Paul intended to visit his family until obliged to rejoin his ship at San Diego" (*Yucatan*, ch. 28). A sailor's life belongs on the sea, and the closing words of *The Boy Fortune Hunters in Yucatan* point to the groom's return to the homosocial realm of the US Navy, much as Sam consistently returns to his homosocial adventuring even though he has already earned the fortune he seeks several times over.

The series's final book, *The Boy Fortune Hunters in the South* Seas, depicts the greatest threat to Sam's homosocial community but also his triumph over an interloping woman. Joe falls in love with the charming Lucia de Alcantara, which challenges the preeminence given to Sam and Joe's homosocial bond. After meeting her the boys ponder a business proposition to transport arms for Colombian revolutionaries, and Sam inquires of his friend, "Well, Joe, . . . what do you think now?" to which Joe replies, "Mighty pretty girl." Sam attempts to divert Joe's attention back to gunrunning: "But about the business deal?" (*South Seas*, ch. 3). Smitten, Joe speaks again of Lucia and the prospect of enjoying her companionship. "Usually, Sam, girls are dubs; but this Spanish creature has lots of 'go' to her and won't make bad company on the voyage," he declares. Sam quickly grows exasperated by his friend's ardor: "If I had let him ramble on about this girl I am sure he'd have kept me awake half the night. It didn't strike me there was anything remarkable about her either" (*South Seas*, ch. 3). Lucia jeopardizes the sanctity of Sam's male homosocial community, but Sam refuses to see the incipient heteroerotic attraction before his eyes and decides that Lucia remains uninterested romantically in Joe: "This girl . . . was always bright and cheery and the life of the party. . . . Joe pleased her better; but she was not the least bit a flirt and had no thought as yet of falling in love with anyone. Her feeling for Joe was one of good comradeship" (*South Seas*, ch. 4). For Sam, women do not belong on ships sailing for adventure, and he reports the general distaste for female company expressed by the seamen: "I think none of us—except perhaps our erratic second mate, Joe—was greatly delighted at the prospect of female passengers on a long voyage; but we had made our bargain and must abide by it" (*South Seas*, ch. 4). Much like his earlier suspicion that Duncan Moit's love for Ilalah proves the man's insanity, Sam perceives in Joe's attraction to Lucia a previously undetected erraticism that calls into question his rationality. Notwithstanding Sam's animus, Joe and Lucia grow closer over the ensuing adventure, particularly when she daringly rescues him in a biplane. This volume ends with their engagement, as Sam reports: "I noticed that Joe and Lucia exchanged rings, and overheard him promise to see her again. I wonder if he ever will?" (*South Seas*, ch. 20). With these intriguing, perhaps even taunting, words this entry in the Boy Fortune Hunters series closes, as does the series as a whole, and its simultaneous acknowledgment and evasion of heteroerotic attraction reinforces Sam and Joe's homosocial bond that might be threatened by the latter's engagement to Lucia. With his "promise to see her again," it would appear that Joe plans another seafaring voyage prior to their marriage, and thus he prioritizes more fortune-hunting with Sam over erotic consummation with the lovely Lucia.

And so the Boy Fortune Hunter series concludes with Sam and Joe together, with any heteroerotic hazards to their friendship once again left ashore. Homosociality does not necessitate homosexuality, of course, and so Sam's desires—alternating between recognizing and denigrating female attractiveness—remain erotically cryptic while nonetheless clear in his preference for homosocial adventuring. In one moment among his many adventures, Sam considers, "Being a boy and less stolid than my elders, I caught myself wondering if I should ever behold the handsome ship my father was building, and sighed at the thought that I might never stand upon its deck after all the ambitious plans we had laid for the future" (*Panama*, ch. 20). Contrasted with his diverging but frequently disparaging viewpoints of women and eroticism, Sam's fetishization of his boat and his affection for his fellow boy adventure hunters never falter. In sum, Sam desires a boat populated with men, sailing off to foreign countries for a fortune of which he has no use; in the endless repetitions of these journeys, he and Joe might flirt with occasional female characters but will never fall for any bond deeper than the homosocial one they share. For Baum's adventurous protagonists, there's always another journey to begin, another fortune to find, and thus another woman to leave behind in favor of your best boy-fortune-hunting friend.

Chapter 7

GENDER, GENRES, AND THE QUEER FAMILY ROMANCE OF EDITH VAN DYNE'S AUNT JANE'S NIECES SERIES

There is no doubt that John Merrick was eccentric. It is generally conceded that a rich man may indulge in eccentricities, provided he maintains a useful position in society . . . so it is not to be wondered at that the queer little man's nieces had imbibed some of his queerness. (*West*, ch. 1)

In L. Frank Baum's Aunt Jane's Nieces novels, a series of ten books penned under his aristocratic pseudonym of Edith Van Dyne, it is sharply ironic that wealthy Aunt Jane Merrick dies in the first novel—and is replaced by Jane's brother, the young women's even wealthier Uncle John. Aunt Jane's early demise aptly indicates the limits of female agency in this series, as the nieces—Patricia Doyle, Elizabeth DeGraf, and Louise Merrick—undertake a range of exciting adventures yet remain constrained by the genre conventions guiding the series. As with many female-oriented narratives of the early twentieth-century era, written as the women's rights movement successfully pursued enfranchisement with the 1920 ratification of the US Constitution's Nineteenth Amendment, readers see evidence of increased agency and independence for female characters that is counterbalanced by long-standing gendered biases and patriarchal prerogatives. In a scene illustrative of these dynamics, Uncle John advocates that women should be allowed greater opportunities for employment—"I wish more girls could be trained for nursing, as it is a more useful and admirable accomplishment than most of them now acquire"—a sentiment that Patsy endorses by deriding the shallow interests of most women as "Fox-Trots and Bunny-Hugs, for instance" (*Cross*, ch. 2). Consistent with prevailing mores of the day, no character counterbalances this viewpoint by advocating that women should be allowed to train and practice as doctors or that a young woman who fox-trots and bunny-hugs might yet merit the respect of all. Many of today's readers rightfully grate at these limitations on female agency yet recognize that they are prevalent throughout the corpus of American children's literature of this period. Given these conditions, it is hardly unique that Baum's Aunt Jane's Nieces novels grant their protagonists surprising freedoms in some contexts and impose rigid constraints in others.

Congruent with these parameters, each novel of the series features a primary plot with branching subplots, which collectively depict one or more of the nieces participating in an engaging and sometimes endangering adventure. In *Aunt Jane's Nieces* (1906), the dying, eponymous aunt summons Patsy, Beth, and Louise to her estate to determine which niece will inherit her fortune, only for her deceased fiancé's nephew, Kenneth Forbes, to be determined the true heir. *Aunt Jane's Nieces Abroad* (1906) depicts the young women, Uncle John, and Kenneth Forbes traveling to Italy, where Uncle John is kidnapped by bandits; readers also meet Arthur Weldon, Louise's future husband. *Aunt Jane's Nieces at Millville* (1908) involves a trip to Uncle John's newly acquired farm, where the nieces attempt to solve the mystery of the previous owner's death under suspicious circumstances, and *Aunt Jane's Nieces at Work* (1909) portrays them assisting Kenneth in his political campaign. Louise's mother encourages Uncle John to facilitate the nieces' debut among New York City's social elite in *Aunt Jane's Nieces in Society* (1910), despite the depraved and mercenary characters they subsequently encounter. *Aunt Jane's Nieces and Uncle John* (1911) features a westward journey, during which the young women assist a young orphan to reunite with her uncle. With their entrepreneurial spirit on display, the nieces establish a newspaper in *Aunt Jane's Nieces on Vacation* (1912), and in *Aunt Jane's Nieces on the Ranch* (1913), Patsy, Beth, and Uncle John visit newlyweds Louise and Arthur in their California abode. The nieces plan their future as movie studio moguls in *Aunt Jane's Nieces Out West* (1914), during which they encounter a second Aunt Jane, a screenplay reader surnamed Montrose, and her two nieces, actresses Maud and Flo Stanton. (Baum was apparently unconcerned with confusing readers by introducing a second Aunt Jane so many episodes after the first one's demise.) In *Aunt Jane's Nieces in the Red Cross* (1915), the series's final installment set during World War I, Patsy and Beth leave Louise behind and journey with Maud to Europe to tend to wounded soldiers. Inquisitive investigators of puzzling events, enterprising entrepreneurs in the journalism and film industries, sympathetic nurses to the wounded in war, amid a range of other such roles, Patsy, Beth, and Louise enjoy a refreshing freedom of motion and agency designed to appeal to the era's young female readers but, significantly, to appeal to their brothers as well, as made clear in accompanying promotional material: "Distinctly girls' books and yet stories that will appeal to *brother* as well—and to older folk. Real and vital—rousing stories of the experiences and exploits of three real girls who do things. Without being sensational, Mrs. Van Dyne has succeeded in writing a series of stories that have the tug and stir of fresh young blood in them" (*Millville* front matter). In sum, Baum conceived his *Aunt Jane's Nieces* novels as juvenile and gendered works for girls that simultaneously transcend the specificity of this target audience by challenging long-standing protocols, to the extent that boys, such as the readers of his Boy Fortune Hunters series, might find them engrossing as well.

In building his Aunt Jane's Nieces series, Baum integrates three typically distinct genres into a unique hybrid: his Americanized genre of fairy tale, the nascent genre of detective fiction, and the protean and female-centered genre of romance. Each of these genres offers potential models of agency for women characters in an era of rapidly shifting gendered norms, yet each genre's innovations are counterbalanced by time-worn narrative conventions, structures, and themes. Briefly, in Baum's vision of his Aunt Jane's Nieces series as American fairy tales, virtue is rewarded not with marriages to handsome princes but with the financial largesse of a wealthy uncle, which points to the larger fairy tale of capitalism's economic potential for unemployed women. The story lines in the series indebted to detective fiction rely on deus ex machina conclusions that strip the nieces of their role as the genre's logical and clearheaded protagonists, thereby depriving readers of a new model of women's intellectual acumen and adventurous derring-do. Finally, Baum's reformulation of romance, a genre that has long prized women's agency owing to female characters' prominent roles in courtship rituals, reenvisions it more as a queer family affair than as the formation of a heterosexual couple. These genres and their gendered themes overlap with one another, and any arbitrary dividing lines between them would unnecessarily simplify Baum's multigeneric vision. Notwithstanding this caveat, the remainder of this chapter examines these combinations of gender and genre first from the perspective of fairy tale, then of detective fiction, and finally of romance, teasing out the implications of gender and genre in a world where women can master their destiny only as far as Baum's pen and Uncle John's fortune allow.

A FAIRY GODFATHER WITH DEEP POCKETS: AMERICAN FAIRY TALES OF ECONOMICS AND WOMEN'S AGENCY

Set in the contemporary period of their production in the early twentieth century, the Aunt Jane's Nieces series, while not overtly political, acknowledges women's shifting roles in society in myriad ways. While the suffragists' struggle for enfranchisement won the headlines, Juliette Gordon Low achieved a similarly noteworthy shift in the realm of girls' culture by founding the Girl Scouts on March 12, 1912. Fostering a new vision of femininity as physically active and engaged in outdoor pursuits, the Girl Scouts upended many traditional stereotypes of girls' childhoods while retaining others. As Rebekah Revzin explains of this contradiction, "The original Girl Scouts ... participated in activities that stressed accomplishment of personal goals and individual independence while maintaining strains of traditional feminine activity."[1] Such a bifurcated vision of girlhood permeates much children's literature of the period, as Ellen Singleton demonstrates of Jessie Graham Flower's Grace Harlowe series (1910–24): "Although the adventures of ... Grace may be interpreted, on the one hand, as symbols of resistance to cultural assumptions of masculine superiority in sport and physical activity, these highly active and physically competent female characters support, through their continuous iterations of femininity, the ideological attribution of maleness to physical skill, risk-taking, and adventure."[2] Congruent with these cultural shifts, the three nieces share a refreshingly feminist viewpoint that women should participate equally with men in the civic sphere. When planning their futures in journalism, Patsy declares, "The daily newspaper is an established factor in civilization, and 'whatever man has done, man can do'—an adage that applies equally to girls" (*Vacation*, ch. 3). Exploring women's role in journalism at the turn of the twentieth century, Paige Gray posits that Baum's Aunt Jane's Nieces series "suggests the power of journalism to effect 'social revolution'" and more so, that "through the newspaper, adolescent girls and young women can transform American society."[3] The unconventionality of Patsy, Beth, and Louise marks them as appealing protagonists and, moreover, as attractive to their millionaire benefactor, with the narrator noting that Uncle John's "nieces had endeared themselves to him more by their native originality and frank disregard of ordinary feminine limitations than in any other way" (*Vacation*, ch. 3). At the same time, Uncle John, in his role in loco parentis and in loco fairy godmother, asserts his authority, and more importantly, spends his fortune as the necessary gateway to their adventures.

Although set in the modern-day United States, the Aunt Jane's Nieces novels are bedecked with fairy-tale tropes that treat the young women's adventures as extraordinary, bordering on the marvelous. While fairy-tale elements could be seen as undermining the tenuous verisimilitude otherwise on display, for the most part Baum integrates fairy-tale tropes to stress the exciting adventures and delightful pleasures that the nieces share with Uncle John rather than to handicap their overarching sense of gentle realism. *Realism*, in this sense, does not refer to one of the prevailing literary modes of the period, a genre that sought to reflect life accurately with fully drawn characters facing challenging but never fantastic circumstances, or to its contemporary offshoot of naturalism, evident in the gritty works of such authors as Stephen Crane, Jack London, and Theodore Dreiser. Yet even in this hybrid world of fairy tales and gentle realism, readers can discern strict limitations to female agency, for Baum's fairy-tale themes and plotlines depend not as much on the actions and agency of the nieces as simply on the financial largesse of their wealthy benefactor.

Baum frequently characterizes fairy tales as rejuvenating and refreshing, as well as a means of establishing deeper ties among friends and family. As *Aunt Jane's Nieces* draws to a close and Uncle John prepares to relocate to join Patsy and her father, Major Doyle, in their home, she invites him to dinner and promises, "The Major and I have some wonderful fairy tales to tell you" (*Nieces*, ch. 28). Sicily, the Nieces' destination in *Aunt Jane's Nieces Abroad*, is described as a "glorious fairyland" (*Abroad*, ch. 12), despite the dangers encountered there, and Louise's newborn daughter, Jane, is extolled as a "fairy" (*Ranch*, ch. 5), thus connecting infancy and childhood with fairy-tale themes. The various characters whom the nieces encounter are drawn into the fairy-tale wonder of their lives, as is the orphan Myrtle. "Why, these hours since I met you have seemed like a fairyland" (*Uncle*, ch. 3), she exclaims, and the narrator similarly comments: "It seemed like a fairy tale to [Myrtle], and she imagined herself a Cinderella with two fairy godmothers, who were young and pretty girls possessing the purse of Fortunatus and the generosity of Glinda the Good" (*Uncle*, ch. 4). Never shy to cross-promote his works, Baum's nod to Glinda testifies to his prevailing interest in fairy tales across the broad range of his publications. The nieces, mulling their ambition to open a film studio, plan to adapt fairy tales for the screen, as Patsy affirms: "We will order some fairy tales, such as the children like. They would be splendid in motion pictures." Notably, in another moment of metacommentary, Baum endorses his own works through the words of Mrs. Montrose: "The various manufacturers have made films of the fairy tales of Hans

Andersen, Frank Baum, Lewis Carroll and other well-known writers" (*West*, ch. 12). With such nods to fairy tales, both Baum's own and those of others, the Aunt Jane's Nieces series flirts with magic and enchantment, although containing these tropes within its overarching gentle realism.

In an intriguing twist of narrative gender roles, Uncle John assumes the fairy-tale role of fairy godmother. First baffled by his clandestine maneuvers to share his fortune, Patsy wonders about her secret benefactor, and Uncle John teases her, "You must have a fairy godmother, Patsy" (*Nieces*, ch. 26). Distinctions of gender and sex are unrecognized for this key role of the fairy-tale tradition, and this fairy godmother is also referred to in paternal terms, such as when the narrator notes that Uncle John extends his largesse to Beth and Louise as well: "It was now that Uncle John proved a modern fairy godfather to Aunt Jane's nieces" (*Abroad*, ch. 2). Despite the gendered lability of the fairy godmother role, such freedoms are not uniformly extended to the nieces. That is to say, these fairy tales liberate Uncle John from the constraints of traditional masculinity while reinforcing the control that the godmother/godfather characters wield over their wards. Within this Americanized version of the fairy tale, the role of a fairy godmother or godfather is stripped to its economic essence of disbursing funds. "The girls had not been rich when their fairy godfather first found them" (*West*, ch. 1), the narrator states, thereby underscoring the economic benefits of a "fairy godmother" with ample financial resources. Uncle John's fortune paves the way for the nieces' many adventures, such as when they establish an unprofitable newspaper. Arthur calculates their eye-popping losses—"Every paper we send out—for one cent—costs us eighty-eight cents to manufacture"; Louise, however, rebuts his economic argument for one focusing on personal growth: "We did not undertake this publication to make money, and it does not cost us more than we are willing to pay for the exceptional experiences we are gaining" (*Vacation*, ch. 17). Here emerges another notable paradox in Baum's depiction of women's agency: the financial underwriting of a wealthy male benefactor is necessary for the nieces to pursue their business plans, with these aspirations (such as for their newspaper and film studio) both demonstrating their independence and accomplishment and their utter disregard to the financial necessity of earning a profit.

Traditional fairy tales offer at best a conflicted model of female agency, for in many instances their heroines wield little control over their story lines, with an expectation, as Catherine Tosenberger outlines, that they conform to the "the demands for women to be obedient, subservient, beautiful, and, especially, silent."[4] Such a blanket statement cannot cover the field of fairy tales in their entirety, but in many instances the unquestioned virtue of the female protagonist positions her as worthy of reward, and so magic, fate, and fairies intervene without much effort on her part. Cinderella would not attend the ball without her Fairy Godmother's intervention; Snow White and Sleeping Beauty slumber until awakened by their princes. When "Fairy Godmother" Uncle John enters the nieces' orbit, he makes it clear that they will no longer control the direction of their lives by orchestrating Patsy's dismissal from her job. In a telling passage, Patsy resents but then accepts her loss of agency: "[Patsy] felt that the conduct of her life had been taken out of her own hands entirely, and that she was now being guided and cared for by her unknown friend and benefactor. And although she was inclined to resent her loss of her independence, at first, her judgment told her it would not only be wise but to her great advantage to submit" (*Nieces*, ch. 28). Swept away by her fairy-tale fate, Patsy need not worry about employment, despite that she earlier proclaimed her indifference to wealth, evident in her words to Major Doyle: "We're millionaires now . . . because we've health, and love, and contentment" (*Nieces*, ch. 3). First millionaires in health, love, and contentment, and then millionaires in money, the nieces acquiesce to a fairy-tale story line that requires them to abandon themselves to the currents set in motion by Uncle John, with his control over the purse strings impeding their achievement of the "happily ever after" ending typical of romance (as will be discussed subsequently).

Uncle John's largesse is perhaps most apparent in his shepherding his nieces to a variety of new locales: they travel abroad to Sicily in *Aunt Jane's Nieces Abroad* and summer in a charming farm and village in *Aunt Jane's Nieces at Millville*. As the title explains, they enjoy a sumptuous vacation— *Aunt Jane's Nieces on Vacation*—and enjoy living in California in *Aunt Jane's Nieces on the Ranch* and *Aunt Jane's Nieces Out West*. During their travels in the US West, the fairy-tale virtue of Aunt Jane's nieces is often tacitly registered through their whiteness. Certainly they and Uncle John, while crossing the nation, indulge in cultural tourism and record their distaste for many of their nonwhite hosts: "the Navajos proved uninteresting people, not even occupying themselves in weaving the famous Navajo blankets, which are now mostly made in Philadelphia. Even Patsy, who had longed to 'see the Indians in their native haunt,' was disgusted by their filth and laziness" (*Uncle John*, ch. 8). In a related moment from the Mary Louise series, Baum compares Indigenous Americans to the United States' adversaries in World War I, painting both as rapists of young women, in the words of Mr. Jones: "Back of the Austrians are the Germans, and those Prussians are worse than wild American Indians. . . . If they got their clutches on my daughter it would be more horrible than death and I don't propose to leave her in danger a single minute" (*Mystery*, ch. 11). Disparaging the multicultural population of California, Arthur Weldon, Louise's husband, speaks of his hiring practices at their ranch, where he openly discriminates against Japanese Americans: "Only Mexicans, except for the Chinese cook.... It is impossible to get American help and the Japs I won't have" (*Ranch*, ch. 3).[5] In various moments such as these, the whiteness of the nieces and their associates is inextricably linked to their virtue, and to the assumed justness of Uncle John lavishing his fortune upon them.

As much as Uncle John's status as "fairy godmother" depends on his vast financial reserves, it is striking how wealth is concomitantly depicted as an enervating element in one's life that should be strenuously avoided. In an early example of this theme, the narrator reports that Aunt Jane "became a crabbed, disagreeable woman, old before her time and friendless because she suspected everyone of trying to rob her of her money" (*Nieces*, ch. 2). Beth fears that a fortune would undermine her integrity and ethics: "It's in my nature to be dreadfully wicked and cruel and selfish, and perhaps the money isn't worth the risk I run of becoming depraved" (*Nieces*, ch. 1). Moreover, one of Uncle John's financial associates denigrates families who benefit from the generational accumulation of wealth: "Von Taer ... is an aristocrat with an independent fortune, who clings to the brokerage business because he inherited it from his father and grandfather. I hold that such a man has no moral right to continue in business. He should retire and give the other fellow a chance" (*Society*, ch. 2). As part of the series's fairy-tale narrative arc, Uncle John is primarily portrayed as uninterested in his fortune and as actively attempting to divest himself of it: "[Uncle John] had been so busily occupied in industry that he never noticed how his wealth was piling up until he discovered it by accident. Then he promptly retired, 'to give the other fellows a chance,' and he now devoted his life to simple acts of charity and the welfare and entertainment of his three nieces" (*Millville*, ch. 1). Endorsing the nouveau riche who exemplify enterprise and endeavor over old-money families who idle in decadence and decay, Baum celebrates American values of the Protestant work ethic and personal independence yet then undercuts any meaningful distinction between the two as they apply to the nieces. For as much as Uncle John represents self-made American success, the many depictions of his generosity are counterbalanced by examples of his ruthless and monopolistic practices. As Uncle John explains of the great wealth he accumulated in the tin can industry, "The shop grew to be a great factory, employing hundreds of men. Then I bought up the factories of my competitors, so as to control the market" (*Nieces*, ch. 29). Also undercutting his image as a man of the people, Uncle John, speaking of Kenneth Forbes's political aspirations, believes that the government should be populated by wealthy men: "Kenneth, especially, who has such large landed interests, ought to direct the political affairs of his district" (*Work*, ch. 1). In his support of these oligarchic principles, Uncle John bribes a local newspaperman: "I'll give you two hundred and fifty to support Mr. Forbes in this campaign, and if he's elected I'll give you five hundred extra" (*Work*, ch. 6). As Ramona Caponegro observes, "Most of Uncle John's unconventionality stems from his contradictory relationship toward his fortune, revealing Baum's own uncertainty about creating such a wealthy character."[6]

In another such contradiction to the series's fairy-tale economics, Uncle John appears sympathetic to the working class and the working poor yet benefits from their exploitation, which becomes evident when he negotiates with the mill manager Skeelty about subscriptions for the nieces' newspaper. The mill operates a predatory company store, and Skeelty sees an opportunity for more exploitative profit: "I'll solicit the subscriptions myself, and deduct the price from the man's wages, as I do the cost of their other supplies. But the Company gets a commission for that, of course" (*Vacation*, ch. 6). Considering this proposal, Uncle John expresses concern for the workers: "It occurs to me that he is hiring these poor workmen at low wages and making a profit on all their living necessities, which he reserves the right of supplying from his own store. No wonder the poor fellows get dissatisfied" (*Vacation*, ch. 6). Uncle John does not extend this concern to any action on the workers' behalf, instead accepting the deal offered by Skeelty.

The fairy-tale economics of the Aunt Jane's Nieces novels promises young women agency through money and consumer consumption, yet their actions are constrained because their "Fairy Godmother" controls the purse strings. Joe Sutliff Sanders observes of women's spending practices during this period, "Consumption at the turn of the century thus promised girls a sense of self, a confirmed subjectivity. Girls of this period could partake of that promise because they played an important role in the earning and spending cycle of bourgeois life at the turn of the century."[7] Patsy, Beth, and Louise express themselves through their newfound fortunes, particularly by pursuing (a)vocational interests in journalism and film, yet the ultimate fairy tale that Baum's novels project is that young women could do so without a rich "Fairy Godmother" behind them.

SLEUTHS WITHOUT A CLUE

Before the Hardy Boys and Nancy Drew mystery series firmly established detective fiction as a key subgenre of children's literature in the late 1920s and early 1930s, the genre's roots in literary fiction began with Edgar Allan Poe's groundbreaking short stories, notably "The Murders in the Rue Morgue" (1841) and "The Purloined Letter" (1844), featuring investigator C. Auguste Dupin. Over the ensuing decades, various authors contributed to this burgeoning genre, which exploded in popularity and profit with Arthur Conan Doyle's *A Study in Scarlet* (1887), his first novel featuring Sherlock Holmes, to which franchise he added numerous novels and short-story collections over the next forty years. Poe's and Doyle's fictions established key features of the genre prevailing over countless specimens from its inception to the current day. According to George Dove, detective stories feature four essential elements: "First, the main character is a detective.... Second, the main plot of the story is the account of the investigation and resolution.... Third, the mystery is no ordinary problem but a complex secret that appears impossible of solution. Finally, the mystery is solved."[8] Building on Dove's first and third points, the detective is frequently characterized as a person (and commonly a man) of superior insight and intelligence. For example, in "The Murders in the Rue Morgue," Poe's Dupin explains his reasoning: "In investigations such as we are now pursuing, it should not be so much asked 'what has occurred,' as 'what has occurred that has never occurred before.'"[9] Doyle's Sherlock Holmes famously cautions, "How often have I said to you that when you have eliminated the impossible, whatever remains, *however improbable*, must be the truth?"[10] The most appealing detectives of the mystery tradition—including such notable figures as Agatha Christie's Miss Jane Marple, P. D. James's Adam Dalgleish, and Barbara Neely's Blanche White—display unparalleled perspicacity and deductive reasoning skills, piecing together the clues of the puzzles that leave the other characters (and most readers) befuddled. Mystery novels are often conceived as a game between author and reader, with the author having the upper hand in constructing it to confuse his audience. As Baum's narrator wryly proposes, "That's the way with mysteries; they're often hard to understand" (*Millville*, ch. 11).

Baum played a significant role in redefining the scope of detective fiction to include female protagonists, for in addition to the Aunt Jane's Nieces novels, his Mary Louise series and his Daring Twins series respectively showcase the efforts of teen sleuths Josie O'Gorman and Phoebe Daring to solve local enigmas. Collectively these works contribute to new visions of women's agency, as these girl detectives inhabit a masculine narrative role that constructs them, to varying degrees, as tomboys, or at least tomboyish. Each of the Aunt Jane's Nieces novels includes a mystery, with the first addressing the conundrum of the lost will that will reinstate Kenneth Forbes to his rightful fortune. *Aunt Jane's Nieces Abroad* involves the kidnapping and rescue of Uncle John, and *Aunt Jane's Nieces at Millville* concerns the mysterious circumstances surrounding Captain Wegg's fortune, with this novel's strong interest in the mystery genre indicated by several chapter titles: chapter 7, "Louise Scents a Mystery"; chapter 10, "The Mystery Deepens"; and chapter 11, "Three Amateur Detectives." The nieces expose shenanigans in a local political campaign and discover the true identity of a mysterious maid in *Aunt Jane's Nieces at Work*, and Louise is kidnapped by a society roué in *Aunt Jane's Nieces in Society*. This novel introduces a new recurring character, teen detective Quintus Fogerty. In *Aunt Jane's Nieces and Uncle John*, the nieces reunite a young orphan with her lost uncle, and *Aunt Jane's Nieces on Vacation* features the baffling circumstances surrounding Thursday Smith, a young man suffering from amnesia with a possible past as a flimflam artist. Louise's infant is apparently kidnapped in *Aunt Jane's Nieces on the Ranch* (only to be discovered safely hidden in the house's secret rooms), and in *Aunt Jane's Nieces Out West*, their new friend Ajo Jones is mistaken for a European jewel thief. *Aunt Jane's Nieces in the Red Cross* is more focused on the nieces' efforts on behalf of soldiers wounded on the battlefield, yet it also contains the suspicious affairs of the spy Maurie. These ten mysteries differ in scope and complexity, but they all include enigmas for the nieces, and thus for the readers, to solve.

At the same time that Baum is indebted to the emerging genre of detective fiction, he derides its merits with several telling snubs. When Louise plans to investigate the puzzling backstory of Captain Wegg, the narrator ascribes this desire as arising from her penchant for denigrated literary forms: "An extensive course of light literature, not void of 'detective stories,' had at this moment primed Louise with its influence to the extent of inducing her to scent a mystery in the history of Captain Wegg" (*Millville*, ch. 7). In a digressionary thread in which nearby residents aspire to write fiction for the nieces' newspaper, Baum mocks the local yokels, as evident in Skim's first foray in the literary arts: "What folks want now is a detective story. Feller sees a hole in a fence an' says, 'Ha! there's ben a murder!'" (*Vacation*, ch. 16). Baum frequently alludes to Sherlock Holmes, such as when Skim's mother suggests the name "Sherholmes Locke" for her son's protagonist (*Vacation*, ch. 16). Also, when Uncle John turns his attention to the mystery that has piqued his nieces' attention, Major Doyle replies, "You're no Sherlock Holmes" (*Millville*, ch. 18). Baum refers to Sherlock Holmes in many other works, including

Phoebe Daring's mention of Doyle's detective and Émile Gaboriau's detective Monsieur Lecoq (*Phoebe*, ch. 8). Orissa Kane's companion H. Chesterton Radley-Todd compares himself to the famed sleuth: "This is my first experience as an imitator of the late lamented Sherlock Holmes, and I may point with pride to the fact that I've unraveled the supposed plot to murder Miss Orissa Kane" (*Flying*, ch. 24). While comparing Baum to Doyle represents a conspicuous example of the dangers of comparing "apples to oranges," Baum's allusions to Sherlock Holmes indicate that he noted the popularity of Doyle's fiction and sought to capitalize on it, even if his interest in the genre remained mostly superficial.[11]

The mysteries of the Aunt Jane's Nieces novels allow Baum to individualize his protagonists, because as they jointly pursue justice, they evince differing motivations: "Louise longed to solve the mystery. Beth wanted to punish the wrongdoers. Patsy yearned to exonerate the friends whom she imagined unjustly accused. Therefore the triple alliance for detective purposes was a strong one" (*Millville*, ch. 12). An intellectual puzzle to Louise, a quest for justice to Beth, and an act of mercy to Patsy, the mysteries that the nieces confront allow Baum to consider the strengths and weaknesses of these female characters, and thus to depict them in ways that liberate or constrain the agency typically associated with women during the early twentieth century. Facing the rigors of investigative work, the nieces routinely exhibit their sharp brains and physical strength. Foremost, they view the mysteries that they encounter as intellectual exercises, as evident when Beth considers the strange connection between Kenneth's new housemaid and a missing local woman: "Somehow, [Beth] could not rid herself of the impression that whether or not she was mistaken in supposing Eliza to be the missing Lucy, she had stumbled upon a sphinx whose riddle was well worth solving" (*Work*, ch. 12). Louise understands that detectives rely on logic rather than emotion—"You'll never make a successful detective if you allow your personal feelings to influence you" (*Millville*, ch. 11). She further explains, "Detective stories . . . are only useful in teaching us to observe the evidences of crime. This crime, for example, is so intricate and unusual that only by careful thought, and following each thread of evidence to its end, can we hope to bring the criminal to justice" (*Millville*, ch. 16). When the nieces interview a ranch hand about Louise's missing daughter, Beth perceives that he has lied about recognizing the photo of a suspect, and Patsy confirms her cousin's suspicions: "I am sure of it . . . but that does not enlighten the mystery any" (*Ranch*, ch. 8). In one of the few cases that the nieces solve, Patsy realizes Louise's baby has not been kidnapped but that she and her babysitters are trapped in the walls of the ranch house: "Of course not. . . .

She's imprisoned" (*Ranch*, ch. 11), she exclaims and soon adds, "Oh . . . I told you the wall was hollow!" (*Ranch*, ch. 12).

Detective fiction often employs tropes of the adventure novel when protagonists face unexpected dangers, necessitating physical strength to complement their intellectual acuity, and the nieces are often called on to rescue others, including men. When Patsy rescues Kenneth from a tree, she tells him, "I'm very strong, and I'm sure I can save you," and the narrator agrees: "Patricia's strength was equal to her courage, and . . . she did what few other girls of her size could ever have accomplished" (*Nieces*, ch. 15). In an exciting passage involving a horse-drawn carriage pushed to the edge of a precipice, Beth rescues the driver: "'Hold fast,' she called calmly to the driver, and began dragging him upward, inch by inch," a feat that amazes an onlooker who murmurs, "However could such a slip of a girl do so great a deed?" Beth replies modestly: "Why, it's nothing at all . . . we're trained to do such things in the gymnasium at Cloverton, and I'm much stronger than I appear to be" (*Abroad*, ch. 10). Moreover, Beth's marksmanship enables her to intimidate criminals, yet Baum then undercuts this image of a female sharpshooter, as Kenneth Forbes explains, "She had to go and faint, like a ninny, and she cried all the way home, because she had hurt the brigand's finger." Beth then resolves, "I'll never touch a revolver again as long as I live" (*Abroad*, ch. 26).

In view of the intellectual acumen and physical strength displayed by the nieces on numerous occasions, it is striking that Baum, other than in *Aunt Jane's Nieces on the Ranch*, does not depict them actually solving the mysteries, which are instead resolved by a string of deus ex machina conclusions. Uncle John declares, "the chief business of detectives is to make mistakes" (*Work*, ch. 16), which might initially appear to indicate that detectives must engage in positing and investigating a range of hypotheses before solving a crime but instead points to the fact that the nieces' gaffes do not lead to greater insights. As the narrator summarizes of their adventure in *Aunt Jane's Nieces at Millville*, "The band of self-constituted girl detectives had been 'put out of business,' as Patsy said, because the plain fact had developed that there was nothing to detect, and never had been. There had been no murder, no robbery, no flight or hiding on the part of the Weggs to escape an injured enemy; nothing even mysterious, in the light of the story they had just heard" (*Millville*, ch. 18). Thus, what appeared to be a mystery is better understood as a collective flight of women's fancy, and, moreover, Uncle John correctly attributed this imbroglio to their overactive imaginations: "Mystery! . . . Lordy, no, Louise. You've been readin' too many novels" (*Millville*, ch. 6). Rather than a portrayal of a new model of women's agency and action, the novel reverts to the trope of feminine whimsy. Further along these lines, despite their extensive experience attempting to solve perplexing mysteries, the nieces do not always see themselves as capable of investigating and instead request assistance from professional detectives, such as when Patsy suggests to Arthur: "I think you ought to telegraph for detectives. If ever a mystery existed, here is one, and only a clever detective could know how to tackle such a problem" (*Ranch*, ch. 10).

Baum further limits the nieces' role as the novels' primary investigating agents by introducing the detective Quintus Fogerty. Adhering to the protocols of children's literature, Baum casts Fogerty as an adolescent male on the cusp between his teen years and early adulthood. He has a "boyish voice," and the narrator records, "His face attested to but eighteen or nineteen years, in spite of its deep lines and serious expression" (*Society*, ch. 12). Fogerty plays a key role in tracking down Louise and her abductor in *Aunt Jane's Nieces in Society*, and Uncle John again hires "the clever detective" to solve the mystery of Thursday Smith, who explains his enigmatic backstory: "Two years ago last May, on the morning of Thursday, the twenty-second, I awoke to find myself lying in a ditch beside a road. Of my life previous to that time I have no knowledge whatever" (*Vacation*, ch. 10). Whereas the resolution of a mystery stands as the primary plotline for most detective fiction, Thursday's romantic interest Hetty doubts any benefits will accrue by resolving this conundrum: "What will you gain if you unmask the past of Thursday Smith? You uncover a rogue or a man of affairs, and in either case you will lose your pressman. Better leave the curtain drawn, Miss Doyle, and accept Thursday Smith as he is" (*Vacation*, ch. 21). Fogerty's training as a private investigator proves fruitless when he fails to solve this mystery, at first believing Thursday to be the swindler Harold Melville, one of the "cleverest pair of confidence men who ever undertook to fleece the wealthy lambs of the metropolis" (*Vacation*, ch. 22). In this novel's deus ex machina conclusion, Fogerty admits his error in a telegram: "Harold Melville just arrested here for passing a bogus check under an assumed name. Have interviewed him and find he is really Melville, so Thursday Smith must be some one else, and doubtless a more respectable character. Shall I undertake to discover his real identity?" To this query, the narrator reports, "Uncle John let Thursday and Hetty answer this question, and their reply was a positive 'no!'" (*Vacation*, ch. 24). A mystery novel that ends without its mystery solved, *Aunt Jane's Nieces on Vacation* defies the foremost protocol of the genre.

In *Aunt Jane's Nieces Out West*, Baum includes a female detective squarely based on the Sherlock Holmes model of deductive logic—Maud Stanton, a Hollywood actress who joins the primary cast of characters in the penultimate and final entries of the series.[12] When the nieces' friend Ajo is arrested and tried for the crimes of a European jewel thief, Maud correctly deduces that Ajo could not have bought a controlling interest in a film studio with only the proceeds from such crimes. Her sister Flo comments, "Maud's a wonder when she wakes up. She ought to have been a 'lady detective'" (*West*, ch. 18). Further examining the evidence, Maud also determines that Ajo could not have committed the crime, owing to his documented presence far from its location. As Arthur Weldon explains, Maud's logical deductions should clear Ajo of any suspicion: "You win, Maud. . . . That clew of yours was an inspiration. [Jack Andrews, the real thief] arrived in America on January twenty-seventh, just one day after Jones had a motion picture of himself taken at the stockholders' meeting of the Continental Film Company." Patsy agrees: "With this evidence . . . the most stupid judge on earth would declare the boy innocent" (*West*, ch. 23). Rather than a dénouement celebrating women's ingenuity and intelligence, Ajo is subjected to a gross miscarriage of justice and sentenced to extradition for trial and is saved only by the arrival of an unexpected telegram: "Jack Andrews arrested here in New York to-day by Burns detectives. Countess Ahmberg's collection of pearls was found in his possession, intact" (*West*, ch. 26). Thus the paradox of feminine agency in the Aunt Jane's Nieces series as detective fiction: the nieces are equally likely to create a mystery from their vivid imaginations as they are to confront an actual mystery, and Baum devises additional methods to constrain their agency when a real mystery is at hand.

As a whole the Aunt Jane's Nieces novels engage in yet then shy away from the enigmas at their foundation, which are dismissed as flights of fancy, explained by telegrams, or otherwise resolved by means other than women's intelligence. Deus ex machina conclusions inevitably disappoint, for they remove characters' fates from their own hands. As Alan Pickrell argues, "While [Baum's] imagination and creativity may have been incomparable and his gifts of humor and word play remarkable, he had trouble with plotting, so his books are frequently marred by a lack of focus and anti-climaxes."[13] Indeed, Patsy dismisses the ways in which authors can simply abandon the need for intricate plotting in their mystery novels: "Detective stories don't have to stick to facts; or, rather, they can make the facts to be whatever they please. So I don't consider them as useful as they are ornamental" (*Millville*, ch. 16). "Ornamental" rather than "useful" aptly characterizes the role of Patsy, Beth, and Louise in solving the many mysteries they confront, as Baum circumvents his heroines from emancipating themselves from the strictures of genre. Furthermore, as much as Baum returns to the trope of the girl detective in his Mary Louise and Daring Twins series, these detectives also fail to solve the crimes before them. Plucky girl detective Josie O'Gorman of the Mary Louise books, whose father's ambition is "that his daughter might become a highly proficient female detective" (*Country*, ch. 14), finds herself victim to her own overactive imagination, as she realizes: "'Well,' said Josie with a sigh, 'you've pricked my bubble, Daddy, and made me ashamed. With all my professed scorn of theories, and my endeavors to avoid them, I walked straight into the theoretic mire and stuck there'" (*Country*, ch. 26).[14] Phoebe Daring endorses women's innate strength for detective work—"Many girls develop a native talent for unraveling mysteries and, both in modern journalism and in secret service, women have proved themselves more intelligent investigators than men" (*Phoebe*, ch. 17)—but she fails to solve the conundrum before her. This puzzle remains unresolved until the state governor arrives to explain her errors: "It doesn't take much of a detective to figure that out, Phoebe. It's the science of deduction. . . . You had all the pieces of the puzzle, but could not fit them together" (*Phoebe*, ch. 22).[15] Perhaps readers can find room for optimism in these young women's failures, for as J. Halberstam proposes, "Failure preserves some of the wondrous anarchy of childhood and disturbs the supposedly clean boundaries between adults and children, winners and losers."[16] A more pessimistic view would counter that for Aunt Jane's nieces and his other female detectives, Baum curtails women's agency and intellect to the point that the mysteries portrayed in these novels prove unsolvable by their protagonists and only resolvable by external forces, resulting in the deeper mystery of the genre's allure for Baum.

HETEROEROTIC COURTSHIP AND THE QUEER FAMILY ROMANCE

From its roots in the Middle Ages to its primary classification as genre fiction today, romance eludes easy definitions yet foremost prioritizes the protagonists' mutual quest for love. Its medieval incarnations, as Derek Pearsall explains, center on a knight's pursuit of love, chivalry, and questing: "The hero . . . chooses to go out from a secure bastion of wealth and privilege . . . to seek adventures in which the values of chivalry and service to ladies (not only being in love but 'being a lover,' a social grace as much as a private emotion) will be submitted to test and proved."[17] Cervantes pilloried romance in *Don Quixote*, yet the genre simply adapted to new social circumstances by forgoing many of its more fantastical elements and reached storied heights in American literature with Nathaniel Hawthorne's works, particularly *The House of the Seven Gables* and *The Marble Faun*. Straddling high and low literary culture, the romance also developed as a key mode of genre fiction, and many of its story lines focus on the romantic relationship of a couple and the often Machiavellians forces prohibiting their union. Although best known for *Little Women*, Louisa May Alcott also penned the torridly titled *A Long Fatal Love Chase*, a novel that exemplifies the type of suspenseful romance popular in mid- to late-nineteenth-century America. As R. B. Gill suggests, "Romance often is characterized in terms of its ability to affect the reader, to operate as wish fulfillment and a (often questionable) substitute for engagement with the issues of real life."[18] Over its long history, a determinate feature of romance has not shifted: the centrality of women's agency in amatory pursuits, with women wooed by men and sometimes wooing these male protagonists as well. Virtually by definition, romance necessitates that the protagonists leave behind the kinship ties of childhood in favor of marriage, concluding with an undepicted narrative future of procreation and the growth of their own families. In this light, romances tacitly posit the psychosexual maturation of their protagonists. Romance thus stands as an apt yet provocative genre for children's literature, in that these stories must feature the social and emotional maturation of their protagonists while many concurrently hesitate to depict the full complexities of human sexuality and emotional relationships.

For Baum, romance requires thrilling events characterized by unexpected twists and turns, with its lead couple facing nefarious forces opposing them until they unite in a novel's final pages. His anonymously published *The Last Egyptian*, subtitled A *Romance of the Nile*, illustrates his conception of the genre's possibilities and its baroque potential, in the thrilling tale of its eponymous antagonist, Kara, who plots an elaborate revenge against Charles Consinor, the ninth earl of Roane, and his family, to punish him for jilting his grandmother decades ago. Kara's plans entail forcing Consinor's granddaughter Aneth to marry him. Notably, this romance ends, as do so many, with the female lead marrying the male lead, as Aneth and Gerald Winston travel to Luxor to marry; their confederate Tadros asserts his masterful role in outwitting Kara and assisting the lovers: "With Tadros for dragoman ... all things are possible" (*Egyptian*, ch. 26). Given the subtitle of this novel, it is evident that Baum perceived it as adhering to the tropes of the romance tradition, and moreover, that he was deeply familiar with these tropes. For the Aunt Jane's Nieces novels, however, Baum jettisons key elements of romance, particularly by leaving the pursuit of love unfulfilled.

In an early example of the series's investment in romance, Louise's mother informs her daughter about Aunt Jane's past, explaining that "Jane was rich, having inherited a fortune and a handsome country place from a young man whom she was engaged to marry, but who died on the eve of his wedding day," to which Louise exclaims, "How romantic!" (*Nieces*, ch. 2). The fifteenth chapter of *Aunt Jane's Nieces and Uncle John* is titled "The Romance of Dan'l," and in this short romance readers learn the backstory of this mysterious musician conscripted to serve a rowdy band of ranchers, in which his nemesis Herr Gabert stole his opera score and his wife, until Dan'l avenged himself by killing Gabert in a duel.[19] Minor characters with romantic backstories populate the Aunt Jane's Nieces novels, as evident in Beth's assessment of a mysterious housemaid: "I now think I was wrong in suspecting her to be the lost Lucy Rogers; but there is surely some romance connected with her, and she is not what she seems to be" (*Work*, ch. 13). Another character comments similarly on the nurse hired to tend to Louise's baby: "The poor thing has had a sad history and there's a bit of romance and tragedy connected with it; but she has been quite blameless" (*Ranch*, ch. 18). Patsy appears to be a romantic at heart, as she envisions her new friends Maud Stanton and Ajo Jones whisking themselves away to paradise: "I've a romance all plotted, of which A. Jones is to be the hero. He will fall in love with Maud and carry her away to his island." Uncle John, however, disputes Ajo's ability to serve as a romantic lead: "Could Maud—could any girl—be attracted by a lean, dismal boy with a weak stomach, such as A. Jones?" (*West*, ch. 6). Romances, similar to detective fiction, often depict thrilling scenes of danger, and the primary characters of the Aunt Jane's Nieces novels enjoy the thrills of romantic adventure, evident when Uncle John is kidnapped in Sicily and the narrator reports: "Uncle John was greatly interested in the adventure. It was such a sharp contrast to the hum-drum, unromantic American life he had latterly known that he derived a certain enjoyment from the novel experience" (*Abroad*, ch. 17). Beyond simple thrills, Baum theorizes the moral and pedagogical value of romance, evident in the words of his filmmaking character Otis Werner: "We try ... to give to our pictures an educational value, as well as to render them entertaining.... Underlying many of our romances and tragedies are moral injunctions which are involuntarily absorbed by the observers, yet of so subtle a nature that they are not suspected" (*West*, ch. 2). Baum also saw the need for at least a hint of verisimilitude in romance, evident when Uncle John explains the parallels between art and real life: "I believe in A. Jones, and I see no reason to doubt his story.... If real life was not full of romance and surprises, the novelists would be unable to interest us in their books" (*West*, ch. 10). As evident from these varying scenes, Baum envisions romance as a genre involving courtship, adventure, and a moral lesson, with the path of true love endangered by elements beyond the protagonists' control.

At the same time that these and other scenes point to the series's interest in the romance tradition, the Aunt Jane's Nieces books—similar to the Oz and Boy Fortune Hunter series in this regard—present few examples of happily married couples, thus undermining the goal of heterosexual romance to which the genre ostensibly aspires. Beth's parents model not marital bliss but domestic bickering, evident when Julia DeGraf derides her husband, Adolph, as a "fool" and a "doddering old imbecile" (*Nieces*, ch. 1) and when the narrator divulges Beth's opinion of them: "To be frank, [Beth] cared little for her gross and selfish parents, and they in turn cared little for her beyond the value she afforded them in the way of dollars and cents" (*Society*, ch. 4). Beth is the only of the nieces with both parents alive; Louise's father and Patsy's mother died prior to the series's commencement. In *Aunt Jane's Nieces on the Ranch*, a supporting character, Bulwer Runyon, is encouraged to marry Mildred Travers, for whom his amatory feelings appear startlingly ambivalent: "Well, perhaps a little; but it's nothing like that currant-jelly, chocolate bonbon, glucose-like feeling which I've observed is the outward demonstration of love" (*Ranch*, ch. 20). Influenced by her readings in romance, Patsy lightheartedly agrees that Runyon does not love Travers—"No regulation lover . . . ever had an appetite. The novels all say so. Therefore you can't love Mildred a bit"—but she nevertheless encourages the bride-to-be to pursue marriage: "Runyon is a big baby, and needs a nurse more than little Jane" (*Ranch*, ch. 22). Exceptions to this general pattern exist, such as the union of Ethel Thompson and Joe Wegg in *Aunt Jane's Nieces at Millville* and Hetty Hewitt and Thursday Smith in *Aunt Jane's Nieces on Vacation*, but on the whole, the Aunt Jane's Nieces series marginalizes heteroerotic attraction, courtship, and marriage in its story lines.

In many series of children's books, characters mature emotionally and, to some degree, sexually, yet the Aunt Jane's Nieces novels often abrogate any such evidence of psychosexual development. In the series's first installment, while Aunt Jane evaluates Patsy, Beth, and Louise as potential heirs, they meet Kenneth Forbes, the rightful heir to her fortune. Although readers might expect one of the nieces to become romantically attached to Kenneth and thus to unite their fortunes, Baum denies him the role of romantic lead and instead paints him as terrified of the female characters he encounters: "'Girls! Girls at Elmhurst?' cried the boy, shrinking back with a look of terror in his eyes" (*Nieces*, ch. 6). Kenneth later frets, "It isn't that I'm afraid of girls, you know; but they may want to insult me, just as their aunt does" (*Nieces*, ch. 6). He doth perhaps protest too much, as the scene is soon repeated when he cries, "'Girls?' with an accent of horror." Upon learning of Beth's and Louise's arrival, he flees: "With a cry that was almost a scream, he . . . flew out the door as if crazed" (*Nieces*, ch. 10). Louise flirts with Kenneth—"You needn't be afraid of me. . . . I'm very fond of boys, and you must be nearly my own age" (*Nieces*, ch. 14)—but he pushes her away. Still, when Uncle John tells Aunt Jane, "these girls are just the sort of companions he needs, to soften him and make him a man. I've no doubt he'll come out all right, in the end" (*Nieces*, ch. 16), Baum is apparently laying the foundations for a romance between Kenneth and one of the nieces, yet love never blossoms for him in the remaining novels. Indeed, as much as he appears to stand as one of the series's major characters, with a primary role in *Aunt Jane's Nieces, Aunt Jane's Nieces Abroad*, and *Aunt Jane's Nieces at Work*, he is merely mentioned in *Aunt Jane's Nieces in Society* and is then dropped from the series entirely, presumably a bachelor to the end.

Whereas Kenneth Forbes is ultimately dismissed as an appropriate suitor in line with his aversion to women, another set of "suitors" is situated as too aggressive, with their "courtships" masking their intentions of rape. Of course, within the protocols of turn-of-the-century children's literature, rape is never named as such, but suggestive phrasings leave little doubt concerning the dangers posed to Patsy, Beth, and Louise. When the dastardly roué Charles Connoldy Mershone schemes for Louise's hand in marriage to win her fortune, he arranges for her abduction. The detective investigating her disappearance asks, "Tell me, could he have any object in spiriting away that young lady—in abducting her?" to which Arthur Weldon replies with a telling phrase: "Could he? . . . He had every object known to villainy" (*Society*, ch. 11). Uncle John similarly worries, "It may be his idea to compromise her, and break her heart!" (*Society*, ch. 12). Mershone admits of his nefarious plans: "Before [Louise] again rejoins her family and friends she will either be my wife or Arthur Weldon will prefer not to marry her" (*Society*, ch. 13). Although Baum never uses the word *rape*, Mershone's intentions are evident through these euphemistic phrases. In *Aunt Jane's Nieces and Uncle John*, the extended family travels throughout the US West and encounters a small community of English "remittance men," which the narrator defines as "the 'black sheep' or outcasts of titled families, who having got into trouble of some sort at home, are sent to America to isolate themselves on western ranches, where they receive monthly or quarterly remittances of money to support them" (*Uncle*, ch. 10). With words both baroque and menacing, the leader of these men, Algernon Tobey, insists the nieces provide the pleasure of their companionship: "Beauteous visions, since you have willfully invaded the territory of Hades Ranch, of which diabolical domain I, Algernon Tobey, am by grace of his Satanic majesty the master, I invite you to become my guests and participate in a grand ball which I shall give this evening in your honor." Tobey adds pointedly, "They cannot refuse us the pleasure of their society" (*Uncle*, ch. 11). The image of the nieces being shared among these many men in an enforced dance carries undertones of gang rape, and so Baum tempers the threat posed, with the narrator stating that "their faces betokened reckless good humor rather than desperate evil" and recording Uncle John's reaction as "neither frightened nor unduly angry, but rather annoyed by the provoking audacity of the fellows" (*Uncle*, ch. 12). Baum then re-escalates the threat, as Tobey warns them: "But if you oppose us and act ugly about this fête, gentlemen, we shall be obliged to put a few bullets into you, and decide afterward what disposition to make of the girls" (*Uncle*, ch. 12). From an enforced dance to murder to an unspecified "disposition to make of the girls," the threat of sexual violation reemerges, and Patsy coolly replies: "You are arbitrary and not inclined to respect womanhood. Therefore but one course is open to us—to submit under protest to the unwelcome attentions you desire to thrust upon us" (*Uncle*, ch. 12). They turn the tables on their aggressors and escape unmolested, with the scene nonetheless portraying sexuality as menacing.

Developing such antiromance sentiments of the series further, Uncle John is depicted as an inveterate bachelor who expresses disparaging views about women and marriage. He praises himself as an objective evaluator of women's worth—"So good a judge that I've kep' single all my life" (*Nieces*, ch. 12)—and explains his reasons for eschewing courtship: "I never married, for all my heart was in the business, and I thought of nothing else" (*Nieces*, ch. 29). Akin to Kenneth Forbes, Uncle John is depicted as perpetually boyish, such that maturation into adult sexuality appears unlikely: "[Uncle John] strove to enjoy life in a shy and boyish fashion that was unusual in a man of his wealth as it was admirable. He had never married" (*Millville*, ch. 1). Also along these lines, Uncle John appears hostile to married couples, such as when he contemplates whether to retain an employee attached to his recently purchased summer estate: "If Old Hucks is a farm hand and a bachelor . . . let him stay till I come and look him over. If he's a married man and has a family, chuck him out at once" (*Millville*, ch. 2). When the series's second Aunt Jane enters its story line, Uncle John initially appears romantically interested in her, much to Patsy's delight: "Mrs. Montrose and Uncle John sat on the sands to watch the merry scene, while the young people swam and splashed about, and they seemed—as Miss Patsy slyly observed—to 'get on very well together'" (*West*, ch. 5). No romance develops, and this hint of a blossoming love affair is left to wither on the vine, although Uncle John enjoys the company of Patsy's father, Major Doyle, throughout the series. The two men "loved and respected one another with manly cordiality" (*Society*, ch. 5).

Emulating her uncle, Patsy embraces a strict chastity and readily brushes off the possibility of romance. As the nieces and Maud Stanton prepare to join the Red Cross, Ajo foresees romance rather than nursing in their future:

"You're both too pretty, my dears, to undertake such an adventure. Why, the wounded men would all fall in love with their nurses and follow you back to America in a flock; and that might put a stop to the war for lack of men to fight it." In Ajo's admittedly exaggerated vision, romance ends war, but Patsy curtly dismisses his words: "Don't be silly, Ajo. . . . I've decided to go with Maud and Beth, and you know very well that the sight of my freckled face would certainly chill any romance that might arise" (*Cross*, ch. 2). Patsy's self-assessment counters the series' continual description of her affability, such that all who meet her fall to her unfailing charisma: "Patsy Doyle was a universal favorite and won friends without a particle of effort" (*Vacation*, ch. 2). Although the narrator also comments frankly on her relative lack of physical attractiveness—"Patsy had no 'figure' to speak of, being somewhat dumpy in build, nor were her piquant features at all beautiful" (*Vacation*, ch. 2)—many readers would likely see this passage as presaging the "ugly duckling" trope and assume that she will mature into marriage with an appropriately attractive mate. Baum portrays Beth as the most beautiful of the nieces—she "was as beautiful in form and feature as Patsy Doyle was plain" (*Ranch*, ch. 1)—yet she rarely attracts suitors. In one notable exception to this pattern, Tom Horton expresses interest in her: "Tom secretly hoped they were [in danger from a volcanic eruption], and laid brave plans for rescuing Beth or perishing at her side" (*Abroad*, ch. 5). He is not a recurring character.

With heteroerotic romances rarely developing in the series, Baum focuses instead on the extended family as the key scene of libidinal investment. As Sigmund Freud explains of a child's social development: "The liberation of an individual, as he grows up, from the authority of his parents is one of the most necessary though one of the most painful results brought about by the course of his development. It is quite essential that the liberation should occur and it may be presumed that it has been to some extent achieved by everyone who has reached a normal state. Indeed, the whole progress of society rests upon the opposition between successive generations."[20] Maria Tatar situates this Freudian concept within the realm of fairy tales and children's literature: "The family romance first takes shape at the time when a child is beginning to liberate himself from parental authority. A growing sense of dissatisfaction with his own parents, stemming from a sense of being slighted or neglected, leads the child to seek relief in the idea that he must be a stepchild or an adopted child."[21] Yet other than with Louise's story line of marrying Arthur Weldon, the Aunt Jane's Nieces novels concentrate instead on the characters' preference to rechannel any errant desires back to the extended family and on Louise's narrative ostracism as an apparent punishment for her successful pursuit of heteroerotic attachment. A queer family, one disinvested from procreation and heteroerotic impulses, stands as the preferred site of desire.

As the sole consummated romance among the primary characters of the ten novels, Louise's courtship and marriage to Arthur Weldon highlights the narrative potential of romance as well as its limitations in a children's literature series. Readers first meet Arthur disguised as Count Ferralti in *Aunt Jane's Nieces Abroad*, with this ploy designed to assist the courtship despite the reservations of Louise's mother, who disapproves of his presumed penury. Arthur lacks the dashing bravery typical of male protagonists of romance, which is evident in the narrator's assessment of him: "Arthur Weldon's nature was a queer combination of weakness and strength. He was physically brave but a moral coward" (*Society*, ch. 6). Opinions change when Arthur inherits a fortune, and readers later learn that the romance is proceeding: "There was a rumor that [Louise] was engaged to be married to Arthur Weldon, a young man of position in the city; but Uncle John ignored the possibility of losing one of his cherished nieces and declared that Louise was still too young to think of marriage" (*Millville*, ch. 7). Viewing his nieces as too immature for courtship, Uncle John attempts to constrain their amatory decisions, but Louise's feelings for Arthur continue to grow: "No one now suspected that at last [Louise's] deepest, truest womanly affections were seriously involved. The love for Arthur that had lain dormant in her heart was aroused at a time when she was more mature and capable of recognizing truly her feelings" (*Society*, ch. 8). Moreover, Louise asserts her independence through her marriage, ignoring Uncle John's objections: "These three nieces of Mr. Merrick were well worth looking at. Louise, the eldest, was now twenty—entirely too young to be a bride; but having decided to marry Arthur Weldon, the girl would brook no interference and, having a will of her own, overcame all opposition" (*Vacation*, ch. 2). Alone among the nieces, Louise shakes off the shackles of the extended family romance and begins a family of her own.

Subsequent to these acts establishing her erotic independence, Louise suffers a narrative penalty for her marriage and drifts to the background in several subsequent titles. The early pages of *Aunt Jane's Nieces and Uncle John* announce that, following her harrowing ordeal in *Aunt Jane's Nieces in Society*, Louise has married Arthur: "At the period when this story opens the eldest niece, Louise Merrick, had just been married to Arthur Weldon, a prosperous young business man" (*Uncle*, ch. 1). As a result of her marriage, Louise does not join them on this adventure, and she is similarly banished in *Aunt Jane's Nieces in the Red Cross*. As Alexander Doty theorizes, many plotlines that focus on "the activities and relationships of women . . . situate most male characters as potential threats to the spectator's narrative pleasure."[22]

That is to say, male characters threaten to shift the focus of female-centered narratives from a group of women to one man's pursuit of one woman, and the converse of this axiom is that the women who embrace male characters are sometimes then ostracized from further story lines. Even in the novels in which she continues to appear, Louise misses out on various jaunts and adventures, such as when her cousins travel to Ajo's yacht but Louise remains behind: "Louise couldn't leave the baby, who was cutting teeth" (*West*, ch. 22). Further emphasizing the preeminence of the extended family over romance, the narrator reports that Uncle John grows closer to Patsy and Beth following Louise's marriage: "All of Mr. Merrick's present interest in life centered on his three nieces, and because Louise was happily married and had now an establishment of her own—including a rather new but very remarkable baby—Uncle John was drawn closer to the two younger nieces and devoted himself wholly to their welfare" (*West*, ch. 1). By extricating herself from her extended family unit, Louise wins a family of her own but is then excluded from the extended family that stands as the novels' central focus, thus proving the alienating narrative effects of erotic attraction in this series of books envisioned for young readers. In contrast to the protagonists of Baum's Boy Fortune Hunters series, who evade heteroerotic attachments and continue adventuring, Louise's marriage marks the tail end of her narrative line.

Although heteroerotic romances are marginalized in these novels, attraction and devotion are portrayed as abundantly and fervently expressed within this queer extended family. These themes are first featured as a grotesque family courtship, in which the nieces vie for Aunt Jane's fortunes by disingenuously soliciting her affections. As the narrator recounts, "[Louise] sighed and kissed [Aunt Jane] again, stroking the gray hair softly with her white hand.... 'You are my father's eldest sister, and I mean to make you love me, if you will give me the least chance to do so.'" She adds flirtatiously of their next encounter, "I shall count the minutes" (*Nieces*, ch. 8). Beth reports her willingness to sacrifice her principles while courting Aunt Jane: "I even kissed her, when she asked me to, and it sent a shiver all down my back" (*Nieces*, ch. 9). To win a fortune in these books, the nieces must first vie for their aunt's affections, with Aunt Jane fully cognizant of these dynamics: "I'll wait and see which girl is the most desirable, and give them each an equal chance" (*Nieces*, ch. 8), she avows, assessing Patsy, Beth, and Louise for their individual merits and their attention to her whims. The opening novel of the series thus introduces its theme of interfamilial romance, in which relatives seek to win the affections of one another for personal gain. In this instance, however, money perverts the family romance, and following Aunt Jane's death and Kenneth Forbes's reinstatement as rightful heir, Baum turns his attention to another queer family romance but one in which financial desire has been excised entirely owing to Uncle John's largesse.

For if romance is discouraged outside the family unit (as apparent in Louise's fate), and if romance can be perverted within the family (as evident in Beth's and Louise's "courtships" of Aunt Jane), Baum nevertheless envisions beneficially queer family romances among the other characters. As evidence of these dynamics, Patsy inspires the utter devotion of her father and uncle. Baum writes that Major Doyle "fairly worshipped his daughter" (*Society*, ch. 5), and this sentiment is echoed verbatim when readers learn that "these two old men—the stately Major and the round little Uncle John—fairly worshiped Patsy" (*Uncle*, ch. 1). Uncle John cements his authority over the nieces' marital prospects through the implicit threat of withholding their inheritances, as the narrator explains: "Patricia was recognized as Uncle John's favorite niece and it was understood that she was to inherit the bulk of his property, although some millions might be divided between Beth and Louise 'if they married wisely.' Neither Uncle John nor the Major ever seemed to consider Patsy's marrying; she was such a child that wedlock for her seemed a remote possibility" (*Society*, ch. 5). It soon becomes apparent that, whereas Patsy's relative youth is deemed a prohibitive factor in her marital prospects, such constraints are not applied to a range of other characters. As mentioned previously, Louise is the only one of the three nieces to marry, but the narrator establishes the unsuitability of marriage for her because she "was, in fact, only twenty years of age—quite too young to be a wife and mother" (*Ranch*, ch. 2). Notwithstanding this injunction, both Baum's narrator and his paternal characters view the nieces' relative youth differently than the youthfulness of other young women. In *Aunt Jane's Nieces at Work*, the mother of a missing daughter describes her as eighteen years old and as a "well-developed young woman" (*Work*, ch. 11), and in *Aunt Jane's Nieces Out West*, the nieces encounter a young married couple: "[Hahn] had eloped, at seventeen years of age, with his father's stenographer, a charming girl of eighteen who belonged to one of the best families in Washington" (*Ranch*, ch. 6). Age functions as a malleable concept throughout the series, employed to prohibit Patsy from marriage but not to do so for a range of ancillary characters. In sum, she stands as the center of this queer family romance, and the series therefore requires her to inspire asexually familial, rather than erotically romantic, devotion.

Complementing Uncle John's long-standing commitment to bachelorhood, his story line involves his emotional maturation into his newfound family romance. In the series's first novel, he disparagingly assesses all women to Aunt Jane: "I've always noticed that girls are just girls—and nothing more.

Jane, your sex is a puzzle that ain't worth the trouble solving. You're all alike, and what little I've seen of my nieces convinces me they're regulation females—no better nor worse than their kind" (*Nieces*, ch. 12). By the series's second novel, he has reassessed his views. Patsy gently reprimands him, "You are too severe, Uncle John. . . . The trouble with you is that you've never been in love yourself." He corrects her by emphasizing that, for him, familial affection trumps romantic love: "'Never been in love!' He beamed upon the three girls with devotion written all over his round, jolly face" (*Abroad*, ch. 26). After a lifetime of rejecting courtship, Uncle John succumbs to the pleasures of the extended family romance, and further to this end, he and Major Doyle are figured as a homosocial couple who jointly tend to the girls' upbringing and to each other's needs, which the narrator acknowledges: "In the days when Major Doyle had thought [Uncle John] a poor man and in need of a helping hand, the grizzled old Irishman had been as tender toward him as a woman" (*Abroad*, ch. 1). When Patsy introduces Uncle John into her and her father's household—"Uncle John is my dear mother's brother, and he's to come live with the Major and me, as long as he cares to" (*Nieces*, ch. 23)—her father Major Doyle graciously accepts him without question: "I'll love Uncle John like my own brother" (*Nieces*, ch. 24).

One of the greatest ironies of the Aunt Jane's Nieces series arises in the realization that Uncle John emerges as its most dynamic character. Whereas Patsy and Beth never pursue love, and whereas Louise marries but is then marginalized from key story lines, Uncle John achieves the most notable transformation in the series, from a committed bachelor to a devoted family man. Reading the novels as a queer family romance illuminates these tensions, in that erotic attractions must be dampened to refocus attention on a sixty-year-old man who functions as both benefactor of the girls' fates and regulator of their sexual maturations. By foregrounding an extended family romance, Baum leaves Patsy and Beth in a state of eternal adolescence, stripped of the necessary agency to determine their futures as wives and mothers, or simply as young women no longer living under the shadow of their rich uncle.[23] Moreover, such a limited vision of women's agency troublingly aligns with Baum's ostensibly comic accounts of domestic abuse in other entries of his canon, such as in Jarrod's description of his marital woes in *Tamawaca Folks*: "I'm not as bad as I used to be. Ask my wife. She'll tell you I haven't knocked her down and stamped on her in over a month" (*Tamawaca*, ch. 10). Mr. Cumberford, a reformed scoundrel who assists "Flying Girl" Orissa Kane in her aviating adventures, recalls his horrifically violent domestic conflicts: "I pounded her two or three times. Once I choked her until it's a wonder she ever revived. . . . Only a brute would lift his hand against a woman. But Burthon's sister—my wife—had a fiendish temper, and her tantrums aroused all the evil in my nature" (*Flying*, ch. 13). Likewise, accounts of child abuse arouse the heartfelt concern of some characters, such as when, in *Mary Louise in the Country*, the young girl Ingua says to Mary Jane: "It's a'most a pity Gran'dad can't see it . . . He'd be so crazy he'd hev them claws o' his'n 'round my throat in a jiffy." Baum captures Mary Louise's shocked response, as she "drew back, startled" and queries, "Did he ever do that?" Ingua's response transposes the scene from the horrors of child abuse into the ostensible comedy of the child's wily ways: "Only once; but that time near ended me. It were a long time ago, an' he was sorry, I guess, 'cause he bought me a new dress nex' day—an' new shoes! I ain't had any since . . . so the other day I asked him wasn't it about time he choked me ag'in" (*Country*, ch. 4). In light of these scenes, one of the strongest "fairy tale" tropes of the Aunt Jane's Nieces series might simply be the possibility of women living their lives untouched by violence.

Intermingling the conventions of fairy tales, detective fiction, and romance, Baum experiments with a range of forms for his female protagonists throughout the Aunt Jane's Nieces series, offering them opportunities for surprising independence that concurrently curtail expressions of women's agency. While this pattern holds true for much fiction of the era, Baum's deployment of multiple genres, and more so, his innovations of them as forms both distinctly American and girl-oriented, offered a variety of ways to reimagine, rather than to reinstate, long-standing gendered norms. Of course, possibilities always emerge for resistant readings, a prospect that Barbara Creed raises in her study of tomboy fictions: "The narrative of the tomboy functions as a liminal journey of discovery in which feminine sexuality is put into crisis and finally recuperated into the dominant patriarchal order—although not without first offering the female spectator a series of contradictory messages which may well work against their overtly ideological purpose of guiding the young girl into taking up her proper destiny."[24] One can look to the margins of these texts for signs of unconstrained female agency—Patsy's editorial aspirations, Beth's steel-eyed marksmanship, Louise's defiant marriage—but for the most part, the series's fairy godmother controls the possibilities available to the nieces, most evident in the fact that this godmother is a man—as is their author.

Conclusion

QUEER ETHICS AND BAUM'S PREJUDICES

This project began, as is the case for many scholars of children's literature, as a labor of love. In returning to Baum's stories that I devoured ravenously as a child, I found the double pleasure of "then and now": seeing anew what drew me into his fictional worlds then, and realizing the deeper complexities and contradictions of his works now. So much of Baum's work remains almost startlingly fresh in its continued appeal, including his sharp humor, such as when the Scarecrow expresses his gratitude toward the Tin Woodman, "Thank you, friend Nick . . . Nothing can resist your kind heart and your sharp axe" (*Marvelous*, ch. 15), or in the patently obvious insight of the clown Flippityflop: "You certainly can't expect wisdom in a country of Clowns" (*Merryland*, ch. 7). And who wouldn't appreciate a dragon who defends himself with the line, "I'm a dragon and a gentleman!" (*Yew*, ch. 9)? Moreover, Baum realized that children's literature, while typically expected to be morally didactic, could jettison suffocating themes, such as when the narrator of one his short stories confesses that it lacks a deeper meaning: "I suppose [the glass dog] is there yet, and am rather sorry, for I should like to consult the wizard about the moral to this story" (*American*, "The Glass Dog"). Less accomplished authors of children's literature have difficulty capturing the ephemeral and mercurial qualities of childhood itself, but Baum's child characters express an appealing genuineness, evident in a minor character's evaluation of her doll: "It must have been a pretty toy when new, but the doll had never won Gladys's whole heart so long as it remained immaculate and respectable" (*Annabel*, ch. 1). He also understands children's transactional sense of morality, such as when the former Boolooroo promises to rehabilitate himself: "I'll not be wicked any more. . . . I'll reform. It's always best to reform when it is no longer safe to remain wicked" (*Sky*, ch. 26). Surely many children caught pilfering from cookie jars recognized their nascent and still undeveloped moral code in Baum's Boolooroo. On so many pages of his fiction, Baum captures those ephemeral and mercurial qualities that characterize the very best of children's literature.

Even as a child, though, I took exception to some aspects of Baum's stories. He promised that his stories would not scare children—"That's why you'll never find anything in my fairy tales which frightens a child. I remember my own feelings well enough to determine that I would never be responsible for a child's nightmare" (*Visitors*, 46)—yet both then and now I find the following image rather terrifying: "His teeth were in his ears, and he ate with them and heard with his mouth" (*Mo*, ch. 10). Occasional puns enliven the style and variety of a narrative's humor, but Baum frequently overindulges, such as in the threefold bear puns in a dialogue between the chimpanzee Miss Chim and the Woggle-Bug:

"We call this the bearier," said Miss Chim, pointing to the soldiers, "because they oblige all strangers to paws."
"I should think it was a bearicade," remarked the Woggle-Bug. (*Woggle-Bug*, 40)

Such an onslaught of puns become taxing, and Baum apparently realized that some readers might find them tiresome, and so the Woggle-Bug defends their intellectual sophistication: "our language contains many words having a double meaning; and that to pronounce a joke that allows both meanings of a certain word, proves the joker a person of culture and refinement, who has, moreover, a thorough command of the language" (*Marvelous*, ch. 14). Baum's puns on nationalities in *The Sea Fairies*—"Turks eating turkey," "the Prince of Whales," "hungry for Hungary," "Russian so fast toward the Poles," among others (*Fairies*, ch. 20)—quickly become grating. It does not require a particularly precocious child to grow weary of the humor behind knock-knock jokes.

Moreover, reading Baum's fictions as an adult allows one to notice some flaws that were likely missed during childhood, including their blatant contradictions, repetitions, and typographical gaffes. Baum writes of his utopia, "There were no poor people in the Land of Oz, because there was no such thing as money, and all property of every sort belonged to the Ruler. Each person was given freely by his neighbors whatever he required for his use, which is as much as anyone may reasonably desire" (*Emerald*, ch. 3), but the next book in the series begins with Ojo asking Unc Nunkie why they are so poor (*Patchwork*, ch. 1). For an author who produced an average of three to four books annually from 1900 until his death in 1919, it is perhaps not surprising that Baum repeats odd plotlines—the opening of *Dot and Tot in Merryland* mirrors that of his "Little Miss Muffet" from *Mother Goose in Prose*, as he also returns to such baroque plot devices as lace smuggling and camel tramplings.[1] Indeed, Baum either simply forgot or otherwise abandoned major characters and their story lines. The joint protagonist of *The Daring Twins* with his sister Phoebe, Phil Daring departs for college with barely a mention in the novel's sequel *Phoebe Daring*. Boy fortune hunter Archie Ackley disappears for the final volume of the Boy Fortune Hunters series. Among the Aunt Jane's Nieces books, the first chapter of *Aunt Jane's Nieces and Uncle John* is titled, "Introducing 'Mumbles,'" and readers soon meet Patsy's winsome pet dog; unlike Toto in the Oz series, Mumbles is then forgotten for all subsequent titles. As a likely consequence of his frenetic rate of production, some books do not appear to have been carefully proofread. John Estes Cook's *Tamawaca Folks: A Summer Comedy* satirizes the leisurely lifestyle of vacation resort Macatawa, Michigan—one of Baum's preferred vacationing spots, as evident from the "Author's Note" of *Ozma of Oz*, which he signed there—but the joke is lost when he typed in Macatawa instead of Tamawaca (*Tamawaca*, ch. 8) and simply misspelled it as Tamacawa (*Tamawaca*, ch. 11). In a wonderfully queer misspelling, the Tin Woodman, Nick Chopper by name, is renamed Dick Chopper (*Visitors*, October 16, 1904).

Such flubs could well be found endearing, yet even one of Baum's earliest advocates, Edward Wagenknecht, conceded of his fictions, "In distinction of style they are utterly lacking and often in imaginative distinction as well."[2] His best narratives convey a sense of motion and purpose as his characters proceed on their quests, but David L. Greene rightly notes, "Baum's central flaw as a writer [is] his inability to delete irrelevant material or to revise material that weakens rather than strengthens his focus" (*Bluejay*, xii). In his best works, Baum matches his imaginative strengths with memorable characters and a purposeful story line, and in his lesser works, readers find less colorful characters better described as meandering than as questing. By definition, not all of an author's works can be the best, and the varying quality of Baum's fiction simultaneously attests to the sheer range and scope of his productivity. Certainly as well, Baum's critical fortunes have waxed and waned over the decades since their publication, as Suzanne Rahn documents, with readers finding a range of reasons for cherishing or for denigrating his works, and expressing their hopes or doubts that generations of young readers will rediscover his stories.[3]

The reputations of virtually all esteemed authors undergo the vagaries of reception, with peaks and valleys of acclaim, yet even when leveling searing indictments, literary criticism can never be divorced from canon formation—even as the very concept of canons has been rightly challenged. By the simple yet deliberative act of discussing authors and their works, scholars designate them as worthy of examination, and often worthy of teaching and sharing with the wider culture. Again referring to my personal history as a child reader, I initially found the idea of a canon wonderfully appealing. It was almost like a magic pill from a fairy tale: read these works, and you will know this field! Pick up a Norton anthology, and many, many hours later you will emerge sufficiently suffused in literature to know its traditions, history, and luminaries. Moreover, virtually all artistic and academic disciplines benefit from a canon or variation thereof, even such fields as gender and queer studies that seek to reframe prevailing modes of expression and inquiry, evident in Gabriele Dietze, Elahe Haschemi Yekani, and Beatrice Michaelis's assertion that gender studies is "becoming a discipline that is unable to avoid canonizing knowledge and, in the process ... proclaim[ing] discourses of truth in more and more places in the (Western) academy."[4] The line between literary scholar and enthusiastic fan is a tenuous one that wavers as one performs multiple roles: individual reader at home, member of an avid community of similar devotees, and teacher (and thus authority) at school. In light of these factors, I realize the inherent ethical paradox of this volume: in presenting Baum as a foundational author of queer and trans fictions of children's literature, I tacitly argue for his inclusion in the queer canon broadly and the queer children's literature canon specifically; at the same time, I must also acknowledge the inherent ugliness of much of his fiction in his too-frequent deployment of vicious stereotypes—as I have addressed throughout this volume.

As has been well documented, the history of the Western canon contains celebrated masterworks but normalizes troubling assumptions about what merits inclusion, often to the detriment of marginalized voices. Yet canons are not monolithic and can be adapted as times change, as Henry Louis Gates Jr. observed concerning his editorial work on an anthology: "A well-marked anthology functions in the academy to *create* a tradition, as well as to define and preserve it. A Norton anthology opens up a literary tradition as simply as opening the cover of a carefully edited and ample book."[5] Issues of inclusion and exclusion also circulate around queer canons, a particularly fraught subject given the marginalized status of queer people who found in reading both an oasis from heteronormative ideology and the possibility of a wider community. As Martin Joseph Ponce avows, "Gay and lesbian readers frequently attest to the pivotal role that reading for representations of same-sex desire has played in facilitating sexual self-understanding and alleviating a sense of isolation."[6] Reading queer fiction allows queer people to see ourselves represented in a world that for too long denied the validity of our lives and desires, but as Ponce further notes, the vision of a Western queer canon frequently defaults into one privileging whiteness: "At stake is not just racial exclusion from dominant canons of gay (and, to a lesser extent, lesbian) literature but the racial and colonial oppressions on which those 'grand narratives' are based and which they can, in turn, perpetuate."[7] Many Western queer classics focus on all-white settings and ignore the lives of people of color, and others unquestioningly reinforce ugly stereotypes of nonwhite people.

As the previous chapters of this volume document, Baum expressed derogatory views toward a wide range of nonwhite and other peoples, including Native Americans, Jews, Black people, Hispanics, Arabs, Asians, and Italians and Italian American immigrants. An apt adage asserts that sunlight is the best disinfectant, and thus it was important not to gloss over or obscure these passages but to look at them closely, thus to better see the complexity of his treatment of humanity as a whole and LGBTQ+ issues in particular. While Baum's prejudices are not pleasant to discuss, they must be confronted so that readers can see the man and his fiction in their full complexity. In a passage thematically relevant to these issues, the narrator of *The Life and Adventures of Santa Claus* regrets aspects of the story he must tell: "Now I will gladly have done with wicked spirits and with fighting and bloodshed. It was not from choice that I told of the Awgwas and their allies, and of their great battle with the immortals. They were part of this history, and could not be avoided" (*Santa*, ch. 7). I began this project with the aspiration of claiming Baum as a proto-queer writer, but this part of his history could not, and should not, have been avoided.

Baum's fans have long struggled to reconcile such passages with the pleasures of his texts. For example, Greene acknowledges but partially exonerates the litany of racial stereotypes in *The Woggle-Bug Book*: "At his best Baum rose above his age in emphasizing the importance of judging each person as an individual: why, then, did he fill *The Woggle-Bug Book* with racial and national stereotypes? . . . *The Woggle-Bug Book* is dominated by the kind of humor that Baum thought the public wanted" (*Woggle-Bug*, xvi–xvii). Here any bigotries Baum might have internalized are displaced onto his contemporary readers. Even when critics concede the racism and bigotries in Baum's fiction, one often sees a corresponding effort to contextualize them, and thus to minimize them, as part of his cultural milieu. To excuse such prejudicial viewpoints as simply reflective of their time feels callow, and to envision any sort of queer literary canon that valorizes white identities at the expense of other races and ethnicities feels horrific. Certainly, today's readers can contextualize these sentiments, and an apt comparison can be made to Baum's views of radium, which he believed to be a miracle cure. In *The Patchwork Girl of*

Oz, the Chief of the Horners proclaims its wonders: "We Horners spend all our time digging radium from the mines under this mountain, and we use it to decorate our homes and make them pretty and cosy. It is a medicine, too, and no one can ever be sick who lives near radium" (*Patchwork*, ch. 23). Glinda the Good agrees and compares a magical substance to it: "It is more wonderful than even radium, for I recognize it as a rare mineral power called Gaulau by the sorcerers" (*Glinda*, ch. 23). If Baum acted in accordance with his belief in radium's healing powers, he would have poisoned himself, and in imbibing and disseminating perniciously noxious attitudes toward humans of various races and ethnicities, he poisoned his fiction for countless readers. In a telling moment from his corpus, Uncle John dismisses soldiers dying on World War I battlefields as "foreigners," but Ajo corrects him: "Human beings" (*Red Cross*, 33). Baum created both characters, the one who derides wounded men as unworthy of his concern and the one who speaks to the commonality of all humanity, with Baum figuring himself as a split voice endorsing both views. In sum, Baum's fantasylands abound with such leaps of imagination and wonder, yet his unimaginative deployment of crude stereotypes hobbles the otherwise illimitable pleasures of his fiction. Aware of this irresolvable tension, readers must ascertain for themselves whether the rich play of Baum's imagination offers sufficient remittance for the taxing burden of his prejudices. It is not an easy issue to resolve but one that stands as a defining question facing literary criticism today.

Perhaps, though, a queer canon that encourages readers to perceive that queerness most often reflects a desire rather than a virtue, and thus that queers are as susceptible to the moral and ethical failings of others, would paradoxically point us to a deeper understanding of the challenges of intersectionality. In her pioneering work on intersectionality, Kimberlé Crenshaw proposes, "Recognizing that identity politics takes place at the site where categories intersect . . . we can better acknowledge and ground the differences among us and negotiate the means by which these differences will find expression in constructing group politics."[8] Sounding a similar note, Gloria Anzaldúa proclaims, "It's about honoring people's otherness in ways that allow us to be changed by embracing that otherness rather than punishing others for having a different view, belief system, skin color, or spiritual practice. Diversity of perspectives expands and alters the dialogue, not in an add-on fashion but through a multiplicity that's transformational, such as in mestiza consciousness."[9] Furthermore, as Laura Jiménez eloquently explains, intersectionality hinges on its multiple enactments and embodiments, as these lived identities must then be expressed and respected, with her insights particularly relevant to the pedagogy of children's literature.[10]

Queer intersectionalities must push forward to a more inclusive future, while acknowledging the ways in which whiteness has historically disfigured this objective. There is no silver lining to Baum's prejudices unless his failings can help modern queer readers of varying backgrounds and identities to more energetically pursue an intersectional and ethical future inclusive of all.

NOTES

INTRODUCTION: A PRIMER ON L. FRANK BAUM'S QUEER LEXICON

1. *Clueless*, dir. Amy Heckerling.
2. In *The Life and Adventures of Santa Claus*, Baum's magical land of Burzee is populated by Fairies, Knooks, Ryls, and Nymphs; Ryls also appear in *American Fairy Tales* (in "The Dummy That Lived"), *The Enchanted Island of Yew*, and *The Road to Oz*.
3. *Oxford English Dictionary* [*OED*], s.v. "mince" 6a; https://www.oed.com.
4. *Green's Dictionary of Slang*, s.v. "lavender" 1 (www-oxfordreference-com).
5. For the definition of *horny* as "sexually excited, lecherous" and "in a state of sexual desire, in rut," see the *OED*, s.v. "horny" 2b. This usage is documented to 1889.
6. *OED*, s.v. "lesbian" 2.
7. *OED*, s.v. "dick" 4 (a); *Green's Dictionary of Slang*, s.v. "dick" 5.
8. *OED*, s.v. "faggot" 8 (c).
9. *Green's Dictionary of Slang*, s.v. "faggot" n¹.
10. *OED*, s.v. "gay" 4 (d).
11. *Green's Dictionary of Slang*, s.v. "gay" 6.
12. *OED*, s.v. "gay" 4 (b).
13. *Green's Dictionary of Slang*, s.v. "kiki" 1. It should also be noted that the meanings of words, and particularly of slang words, continue to evolve. *Kiki* now refers to a social gathering for queer men, particularly Black gay men and other queers of color. I have been unable to trace the evolution of the word from its earlier to its current queer meanings.
14. Michelle Ann Abate and Kenneth Kidd, eds., *Over the Rainbow: Queer Children's and Young Adult Literature*, 3–4.
15. According to the *OED*, the use of *fairy* to denote "An effeminate or homosexual man" is attested to as early as 1896; see *OED*, s.v. "fairy" 4(c). To argue that Uncle Henry is denying his homosexuality in this line exceeds the realm of Baum's likely meanings, yet it also underscores the promiscuity of words and the difficulty of curtailing their meanings from sexual implications.
16. *OED*, s.v. "queer" (2).
17. For an engrossing examination of Bunbury's multiple queer significations, see Christopher Craft, "Alias Bunbury: Desire and Termination in *The Importance of Being Earnest*."

18. *Green's Dictionary of Slang*, s.v. "Dorothy's friend, *also* friend of Dorothy." Although it is beyond the scope of this volume, the film *The Wizard of Oz* evinces its own queer sensibility in its technicolor Oz versus its monochromatic Kansas, in Margaret Hamilton's scene-stealing role as the Wicked Witch of the West, and in various lines of dialogue and song with queer undertones. When the Scarecrow directs Dorothy at a fork in the Yellow Brick Road, he advises, "That is a very nice way.... It's pleasant that way, too.... Of course, people do go both ways," which potentially hints at bisexuality. The Cowardly Lion refers to himself as a "dandy-lion" and ruefully sings, "Yes, it's sad, believe me, missy, / When you're born a sissy." In the final analysis, it is a bit ironic that the film version of *The Wizard of Oz* is the iconic touchstone of queer culture rather than the books, since the film depicts Dorothy's rejection of Oz and her return to Kansas. The book series, on the other hand, frees her forever from the "unromantic State of Kansas" (*Road*, ch. 1).

19. Another theory behind the phrase "friend of Dorothy" posits that it arose from celebrated wit Dorothy Parker and her New York City social circle in the 1920s, which included many gay men. While numerous trends trickle out from New York across the United States, Baum's books circulated more widely throughout the culture.

20. Judith Butler, "Doing Justice to Someone: Sex Reassignment and Allegories of Transsexuality," 622.

21. On Oz's queer appeal, see Dee Michel, *Friends of Dorothy*.

22. Lady Gaga, "Born This Way," Streamline, 2010.

CHAPTER 1. L. FRANK BAUM'S "PROGRESSIVE FAIRIES" AND THE QUEERNESS OF CHILDREN'S LITERATURE

1. This brief account of Baum's life is heavily indebted to Katharine M. Rogers, *L. Frank Baum: Creator of Oz*.

2. Mary Cadogan and Patricia Craig, *You're a Brick, Angela!*, 372.

3. Baum was keenly interested in the marketing of his books, a topic ably explored in Kent Drummond, Susan Aronstein, and Terri Rittenburg's *The Road to Wicked: The Marketing and Consumption of Oz from L. Frank Baum to Broadway*.

4. Paul Deane, *Mirrors of American Culture*, 4.

5. On Baum and questing narratives, see John Algeo, "Oz and Kansas: A Theosophical Quest"; Karla Walters, "Seeking Home: Secularizing the Quest for the Celestial City in *Little Women* and *The Wonderful Wizard of Oz*"; and Teresa Devroe, "Follow the Yellow Brick Road to Nirvana."

6. After Baum's death in 1919, the Oz books continued publication for decades under an array of authors, including Ruth Plumley Thompson, John R. Neill, Jack Snow, Rachel R. Cosgrove, and coauthors Eloise Jarvis McGraw and Lauren Lynn McGraw.

7. For studies of Baum's Oz novels as American fairy tales, see Laura Barrett, "From Wonderland to Wasteland: *The Wonderful Wizard of Oz*, *The Great Gatsby*, and the New American Fairy Tale"; Jack Zipes, "Oz as American Myth"; and Jordan Brotman, "A Late Wanderer in Oz."

8. One could argue that Baum's tales should not be construed as fairy tales because this genre develops from oral and folkloric traditions. As Andrew Teverson argues, fairy

tales are "stories that have survived in multiple versions, at different times, and in different regions, and have therefore, in the course of time, even if not originally, become communal property"; they are "not associated exclusively with the authorship of any one individual" (*Fairy Tale*, 14–15). Certainly, Baum envisioned these tales as fairy tales, and so I refer to them as such; the term "fairy-tale-like-tales" would be more accurate but suffers from an intolerable clunkiness in expression.

9. Alonzo Hamby, "Progressivism: A Century of Change and Rebirth," 43.

10. Michael McGerr, *A Fierce Discontent: The Rise and Fall of the Progressive Movement in America, 1870–1920*, xiv.

11. Katharine M. Rogers, *L. Frank Baum: Creator of Oz*, 170.

12. Henry Littlefield, "*The Wizard of Oz*: Parable on Populism," 58. For a detailed critique of Littlefield's thesis, see Michael Gessel, "Tale of a Parable."

13. McGerr, *A Fierce Discontent: The Rise and Fall of the Progressive Movement in America, 1870–1920*, xiv.

14. On Wilson's racist policies, see Eric Yellin, *Racism in the Nation's Service*, in which he identifies the methods of this president's appointees for "thread[ing] white supremacy into the federal bureaucracy" (3).

15. L. Frank Baum, quoted in Evan Schwartz, *Finding Oz: How L. Frank Baum Discovered the Great American Story*, 187.

16. Reneau H. Reneau, *Misanthropology: A Florilegium of Bahumbuggery*, 162.

17. Robert W. Venables, "Looking Back at Wounded Knee," 37.

18. Toni Morrison, *Playing in the Dark*, 14.

19. Ebony Elizabeth Thomas, *The Dark Fantastic*, 6–7.

20. Robin Bernstein, *Racial Innocence*, 18.

21. Philip Nel, *Was the Cat in the Hat Black?*, 41.

22. *Green's Dictionary of Slang* documents *jigaboo* and its many variants as denoting "a derog[atory] term for a black person" and dates this usage to 1924, in yet another instance of Baum either prefiguring slang terms or employing them before they were recognized as such.

23. Siobhan Somerville, *Queering the Color Line*, 39.

24. Scott Herring, ed., *Autobiography of an Androgyne* by Ralph Werther, xx.

25. Eric Tribunella, "Childhood Studies: Children's and Young Adult Literature," 697, 702.

26. Kenneth Kidd, *Freud in Oz*, 94.

27. Derritt Mason, *Queer Anxieties of Young Adult Literature and Culture*, 25.

28. For discussion of children's literature as a genre, see Beverly Lyon Clark, *Kiddie Lit: The Cultural Construction of Children's Literature in America*; Kimberley Reynolds, ed., *Modern Children's Literature: An Introduction*; and Gillian Avery and Julia Briggs, eds., *Children and Their Books*.

29. Steven Bruhm and Natasha Hurley, eds., *Curiouser: On the Queerness of Children*, xiii.

30. Alison Lurie, *Don't Tell the Grown-Ups: The Subversive Power of Children's Literature*, x. See also her *Boys and Girls Forever: Children's Classics from Cinderella to Harry Potter*.

31. For the foundational exploration of the carnivalesque, see Mikhail Bakhtin, *Rabelais and His World*, trans. Hélène Iswolsky. For a Bakhtinian reading of Oz, see Joel Chaston, "Baum, Bakhtin, and Broadway."

32. Umberto Eco, "The Frames of Comic Freedom," 6.

33. Roberta Seelinger Trites, "Queer Discourse and the Young Adult Novel," 143.

34. Jacqueline Rose, *The Case of Peter Pan, or the Impossibility of Children's Fiction*, 1–2.

35. Karin Lesnik-Oberstein, *Children's Literature: Criticism and the Fictional Child*; Perry Nodelman, *The Hidden Adult: Defining Children's Literature*; and Michelle Ann Abate, *No Kids Allowed: Children's Literature for Adults*.

36. On the variability of childhood as a cultural construction, see Kent Baxter, *The Modern Age: Turn-of-the-Century American Culture and the Invention of Adolescence*; and Gary Cross, *The Cute and the Cool: Wondrous Innocence and Modern American Children's Culture*.

37. Robin Bernstein, "Children's Books, Dolls, and the Performance of Race; or, The Possibility of Children's Literature."

38. Marah Gubar, "Risky Business: Talking about Children in Children's Literature Criticism," 454.

39. For a succinct overview of theoretical analyses of adults and their role in children's literature studies, see Victoria Ford Smith, "Adult."

40. Kathryn Bond Stockton, "Eve's Queer Child," 185; italics in original. See also her *The Queer Child, or Growing Sideways in the Twentieth Century*.

41. Kenneth Kidd, "Introduction: Lesbian/Gay Literature for Children and Young Adults," 114.

42. Kenneth Kidd, "Queer Theory's Child and Children's Literature Studies," 185.

CHAPTER 2. TRANS TALES OF OZ AND ELSEWHERE

1. Heather Love, "Queer," 175.

2. Yolanda Martínez-San Miguel and Sarah Tobias, "Trans Fantasizing: From Social Media to Collective Imagination," 238.

3. Susan Stryker and Paisley Currah, "Introduction," 1.

4. Derritt Mason, "Trans," 184.

5. Julian Gill-Peterson, *Histories of the Transgender Child*, 11.

6. On a related note, and of deep concern to this chapter, trans theories have alerted readers and writers to the challenges and presumptions of gendered language, particularly in the rather limited options of English pronouns. The use of *they/them/theirs* as singular constructions ameliorates many of these issues, yet I mostly refrain from employing them for the purpose of more accurately capturing the movement between genders depicted in Baum's fiction. For the purposes of this chapter, I hope that *he/him/his* and *she/her/hers* offer a more precise descriptive lexicon for analyzing gender shifts in these fictional landscapes, even as *they/them/theirs* better captures the identities of many transgender people.

7. Jody Norton, "Transchildren and the Discipline of Children's Literature," 294.

8. Examinations of gender in Oz include Charles Rzepka, "'If I Can Make It There': Oz's Emerald City and the New Woman"; Richard Tuerk, "Dorothy's Timeless Quest"; Yoshido Junko, "Uneasy Men in the Land of Oz"; and Stuart Culver, "Growing Up in Oz."

9. J. L. Bell, "Dorothy the Conqueror," 13–17.

10. Joel Chaston, "If I Ever Go Looking for My Heart's Desire: 'Home' in Baum's *Oz* Books," 209–19.

11. Edward W. Hudlin, "The Mythology of *Oz*: An Interpretation," 446. For Campbell's construction of the monomyth, see Joseph Campbell, *The Hero with a Thousand Faces*; for a critique of its gendered biases, see Maria Tatar, *The Heroine with 1001 Faces*.

12. Susan Crane, *Gender and Romance in Chaucer's* Canterbury Tales, 3.

13. Stuart Culver documents that, at the same time Baum was writing *The Wonderful Wizard of Oz*, he was also writing a treatise on window dressing for stores, which in many ways illuminates his emphasis on fashion in Oz; see Culver, "What Mannikins Want: *The Wonderful Wizard of Oz* and *The Art of Decorating Dry Goods Windows*."

14. In regard to Baum's view of women's rights, Nancy Tystad Koupal observes that Baum "championed . . . women's suffrage" (Michael Gessel, Nancy Tystad Koupal, and Fred Erisman, "The Politics of Oz: A Symposium," 156), and Raylyn Moore documents that Baum's mother-in-law was close friends with Susan B. Anthony and Elizabeth Cady Stanton (*Wonderful Wizard, Marvelous Land*, 50–51). See also Katharine M. Rogers's biography of Baum: *L. Frank Baum: Creator of Oz*, esp. 12, 28–29, 31–32.

15. Koupal suggests that the Aberdeen Guards of South Dakota, a group of twelve women formed as an auxiliary of the Grand Army of the Republic, inspired Baum to create the many female armies of Oz. She quotes Baum's reaction to the guard: "Much curiosity has been expended as to how well a body of young ladies can be taught to drill, but even their most confident friends were agreeably surprised at the precision of their manovuers [sic], the accuracy of their movements and their erect and soldier-like bearing" (*Landlady*, 72–74; see also the photograph of the guard on 116).

16. One might well wonder why a fairy requires a mortal character to effect such a transformation, but in this instance fairies rely on humans deploying their "powers as a mortal" (*Yew*, ch. 4). This would apparently make mortals fairies, but, as in so many other cases, it is best not to expect too much logic in Baum's fairylands.

17. On the intersection of clothing and trans life, see the documentary *Suited*, dir. Jason Benjamin (Casual Romance Productions, 2016).

18. One of John R. Neill's illustrations included among the novel's front matter broaches topics of gender, a topic explored in chapter 5.

19. For Baum's anti-Arab stereotyping of Ali Dubh, see chapter 4.

20. Chick's intriguing position of "Head Booleywag" is later reconceived as the more conventional role of Prime Minister in *The Magic of Oz* (ch. 2).

21. J. L. Bell, "Home-Made Bread by the Best Modern Machinery: An Appreciation of *John Dough and the Cherub*," 8. Baum's expertise with chickens is documented in his *The Book of the Hamburgs: A Brief Treatise on the Mating, Rearing, and Management of the Different Varieties of Hamburgs*, in which he discusses their breeding and sex characteristics.

22. Frank Joslyn Baum and Russell P. MacFall, *To Please a Child: A Biography of L. Frank Baum, Royal Historian of Oz*, 214–15. See also Sean P. Duffley, "Baum under Scrutiny: Early Reviews of *John Dough and the Cherub*," for the book review in the *Chicago Record-Herald*, for December 14, 1906. The son's biography of his father leans heavily toward hagiography, and one should question the accuracy of conversations cited in it. Despite these issues, ancillary evidence supports this quasi-historical account of the Chick the Cherub controversy.

23. Michelle Ann Abate, *Tomboys: A Literary and Cultural History*, xiii.

24. Jennifer Guglielmo and Salvatore Salerno, eds., *Are Italians White? How Race Is Made in America*.

CHAPTER 3. QUEER EROTICISMS IN OZ AND ELSEWHERE

1. L. Frank Baum, qtd. in James Thurber, "The Wizard of Chitenango," 141.

2. On the potential queerness of dandyism, see Dominic Janes, *Oscar Wilde Prefigured: Queer Fashioning and British Caricature, 1750–1900*.

3. Joe Lucchesi, "'The Dandy in Me': Romaine Brooks's 1923 Portraits," 163.

4. Richard Spears, *Slang and Euphemism*, 256.

5. For further discussion of Uncle Naboth and Sam Steele's misogyny, see chapter 6; for further discussion of Kenneth Forbes's fear of women and its impact on the romantic plotlines of the Aunt Jane's Nieces series, see chapter 7.

6. For analyses of Baum's engagement with history in his fictions, see Gretchen Ritter, "Silver Slippers and a Golden Cap: L. Frank Baum's *The Wonderful Wizard of Oz* and Historical Memory in American Politics"; Francis MacDonnell, "'The Emerald City Was the New Deal': E. Y. Harburg and *The Wonderful Wizard of Oz*"; and Michael Gessel, Nancy Tystad Koupal, and Fred Erisman, "The Politics of Oz: A Symposium."

7. Dorothy's parents are hardly mentioned in the Oz series. No explanation for her father's absence is given, and Uncle Henry's musings provide the only information about her mother: "As for Uncle Henry, he thought his little niece merely a dreamer, as her dead mother had been, for he could not quite believe all the curious stories Dorothy told them of the Land of Oz" (*Emerald*, ch. 2).

8. On Baum and the Persephone myth, see Richard Tuerk, *Oz in Perspective: Magic and Myth in the L. Frank Baum Books*, 171–78.

9. Lee Edelman, *No Future: Queer Theory and the Death Drive*, 13; italics in original.

10. See Adrienne Rich, "Compulsory Heterosexuality and Lesbian Existence" and "Reflections on 'Compulsory Heterosexuality.'"

11. René Girard, *Deceit, Desire, and the Novel: Self and Other in Literary Structure*; and Eve Kosofsky Sedgwick, *Between Men: English Literature and Male Homosocial Desire*, 21.

12. For a discussion of Denslow's illustration, see chapter 5.

13. The Latin *nimis* is an adverb meaning "very much"; Amee appears to be a variant of Amy, a name derived from the Latin *amo, amare*, to love.

14. This is the same witch whom Dorothy kills with her house in the film version of *The Wizard of Oz*. The shoes were changed from silver to ruby to highlight the film's Technicolor wonders.

15. Jacques Lacan, *The Seminar of Jacques Lacan, Book VII: The Ethics of Psychoanalysis, 1959–1960*, 151.

16. Plato, *The Symposium*, 22–25.

17. While in most instances men are patched to other men, Cap'n Bill is threatened with patching to a goat: "Cap'n Bill regarded the billygoat with distinct disfavor, and the billygoat glared evilly upon Cap'n Bill" (*Sky*, ch. 24). Homosocial union to a goat stands beyond the parameters of this study.

18. Dina Giovanelli and Natalie Peluso, "Feederism: A New Sexual Pleasure and Subculture," 331, 335.

19. On St. Sebastian as a queer and masochistic figure, see Robert Mills, "'Whatever you Do is a Delight to Me!' Masculinity, Masochism, and Queer Play in Representations of Male Martyrdom."

20. Gilles Deleuze, *Masochism: Coldness and Cruelty*, 114.

21. Examples of Baum's Orientalist themes in *Daughters of Destiny* include when railroad investor Dr. Warner, fretting over virtuous Janet, states, "These Orientals are equal to any villainy. Knowing Janet as we do, and believing in her modesty and truth, it is absurd to interpret her letter in any other light" (*Daughters*, ch. 17). Her brother Allison construes all Asian men as monstrous: "I can't understand . . . how any decent American girl can go into raptures over a brown-skinned Oriental, with treacherous eyes and a beastly temper" (*Daughters*, ch. 11). Prince Kasam, whom one might expect to defend his people, sees them as uncivilized—"We Baluchi are a wild race, as yet untamed by the influence of your western civilization" (*Daughters*, ch. 1)—and in wooing Janet, he justifies his rash actions by reinforcing the binary of the Western man of restraint and the Eastern man of unbridled desire: "We of the East are children of impulse, obeying the dictates of our hearts spontaneously and scorning that cold formality so much affected by your race. . . . But I love you; and, after all, that is enough for a man to say!" (*Daughters*, ch. 13).

22. *Mary Louise Adopts a Soldier* was published in 1919, the same year as Baum's death. Sampson finished this novel from Baum's notes, and then wrote five more books in the series: *Mary Louise at Dorfield*, *Mary Louise Stands the Test*, *Mary Louise and Josie O'Gorman*, *Josie O'Gorman*, and *Josie O'Gorman and the Meddlesome Major*.

CHAPTER 4. THE QUEER CREATURES OF OZ AND ELSEWHERE EAT ONE ANOTHER

1. Studies of Oz as a utopia include Andrew Karp, "Utopian Tension in L. Frank Baum's Oz"; Barry Bauska, "The Land of Oz and the American Dream"; S. J. Sackett, "The Utopia of Oz"; and Edward Wagenknecht, *Utopia Americana*.

2. Osmond Beckwith, "The Oddness of Oz," 91.

3. Kara Keeling and Scott Pollard, *Table Lands*, 6.

4. Claude Lévi-Strauss, *The Origin of Table Manners*, vol. 3 of *Mythologiques*, 489. See also Carol M. Counihan, *The Anthropology of Food and Body: Gender, Meaning, and Power*.

5. Peggy R. Sanday, *Divine Hunger: Cannibalism as a Cultural System*, 3. See also Gananath Obeyesekere, *Cannibal Talk: The Man-Eating Myth and Human Sacrifice in the South Seas*. For cannibalism in fairy tales, see Marina Warner, "Fee Fie Fo Fum: The Child in the Jaws of the Story."

6. William Arens, *The Man-Eating Myth: Anthropology and Anthropophagy*, 145.

7. Andrew Karp, "Utopian Tension in L. Frank Baum's Oz," 118.

8. Alison Lurie, *Boys and Girls Forever: Children's Classics from Cinderella to Harry Potter*, 39.

9. Carolyn Daniel, *Voracious Children: Who Eats Whom in Children's Literature*, 162.

10. Matthew Beaumont, "Heathcliff's Great Hunger: The Cannibal Other in *Wuthering Heights*," 139.

11. Michel de Montaigne, "Of Cannibals," *The Complete Works: Essays, Travel Journal, Letters*, 189.

12. Tess Cosslett, *Talking Animals in British Children's Fiction*, 1.

13. Susanne Skubal, *Word of Mouth: Food and Fiction after Freud*, 105.

14. Claude Lévi-Strauss, *The Origin of Table Manners*, 478.

15. For studies of the cultural work of shame, see Stephen Pattison, *Shame: Theory, Therapy, Theology*, and June Price Tangney and Ronda L. Dearing, *Shame and Guilt*.

16. Carolyn Daniel, *Voracious Children*, 25.

17. Of course, some meat dishes, such as steak tartare, are served raw. Nonetheless, one need only think of the popular trope of horror films in which a human infected with vampirism or lycanthropy starts eating raw meat (e.g., *The Hunger* [1983], *Wolf* [1994], *Cursed* [2005]) to see the ways in which the consumption of raw foods is culturally linked to primitivism and savagery.

18. It is somewhat ironic that this man is punished for making a bird-egg omelet, if Billina herself advocates eating chicken eggs. The man lists two other transgressions—cutting off a fox's tail and suffocating fish—but he labels all three of his actions as "wicked things" deserving punishment (*Lost*, 596). Here again readers are confronted with the arbitrary nature of dietary laws in Oz.

19. It should also be noted that Dorothy finds a ham sandwich in her lunchbox-tree meal, which muddies taxonomical distinctions between vegetarian and carnivorous appetites even more.

20. The fad dietician Horace Fletcher (1849–1919), known as "the Great Masticator," pithily advised, "Nature will castigate those who don't masticate." His publications include *Fletcherism: What It Is, or How I Became Young at Sixty* and *The New Glutton or Epicure*.

21. Roy C. Wood, *The Sociology of the Meal*, 47–48.

22. Arab characters are featured prominently in Baum's two novels set in Egypt—*The Boy Fortune Hunters in Egypt* and *The Last Egyptian*—and are frequently disparaged. Archie, one of the Boy Fortune Hunters, says of his family's business products, "They're shipped to a lot of dirty Arabs who can't be trusted" (*Egypt*, ch. 2). Gerald Winston, protagonist of *The Last Egyptian*, interacts with Arabs as his inherent inferiors. "The only way to manage an Arab is to make him believe you know what you are about," he opines, and later adds, "It is good for the Arab to be kicked at times" (*Egyptian*, ch. 1). Anti-Arab stereotypes also appear in Baum's fiction for young girls, such as when the tomboy Ingua promises to reform herself: "Ma says I've been a little Arab, but she means to make a lady of me. I hope she will" (*Country*, ch. 28).

CHAPTER 5. JOHN R. NEILL: ILLUSTRATOR (AND AUTHOR) OF
L. FRANK BAUM'S QUEER OZ AND ELSEWHERE

1. Michael Patrick Hearn, "Introduction to *The Annotated Wizard of Oz*," *The Annotated Wizard of Oz: Centennial Edition*, lii; see also his *W. W. Denslow: The Other Wizard of Oz*, 32–39; and Evan Schwartz, *Finding Oz: How L. Frank Baum Discovered the Great American Story*, 300.

2. Jack Snow, *Who's Who in Oz*, 274; Michael Patrick Hearn, "John R. Neill: The Royal Illustrator of Oz and More!," 8.

3. In this chapter I do not address Ruth Plumly Thompson's continuations of the Oz series, nor do I consider Neill's illustrations of her many Oz volumes.

4. Michael Riley, *Oz and Beyond: The Fantasy World of L. Frank Baum*, 234.

5. James Thurber, "The Wizard of Chitenango," 142.

6. Snow, *Who's Who in Oz*, 274.

7. H. Nichols B. Clark, "High Adventure and Fantasy: Art for All Ages," 148.

8. Rebecca Loncraine, *The Real Wizard of Oz: The Life and Times of L. Frank Baum*, 270.

9. Hearn, "Introduction to *The Annotated Wizard of Oz*," xliii. For Baum's disputes with Neill, see also Katharine M. Rogers, *L. Frank Baum: Creator of Oz*, 212–13.

10. Leo Steinberg, *The Sexuality of Christ in Renaissance Art and in Modern Oblivion*, 1.

11. Clifford Bishop and Cristina Moles Kaupp, "The Erotic Muse: Art and Artifice," 328.

12. Thomas King, "Performing 'Akimbo': Queer Pride and Epistemological Prejudice," 27.

13. In *The Road to Oz*, Neill alternates the general format of his chapter-opening vignettes between this genital image and a circular garland. In this latter image, a character placed in a centered circle rises above a circle of faces, mostly female, which is situated below the center. In *Rinkitink in Oz*, Neill uses the genital format for all chapter-opening vignettes.

14. On the many phallic and other symbolic connotations of the nose, see George R. Elder, *An Encyclopedia of Archetypal Symbolism*, 2.245–57.

15. Katharine M. Rogers, *L. Frank Baum*, 275n19.

16. Hearn, "John R. Neill," 11.

17. Lucia Impelluso, *Nature and Its Symbols*, 238.

18. Parenthetical citations of Neill's Oz books employ the respective shortened titles: *Wonder City*, *Scalawagons*, *Bucky*, and *Runaway*.

19. Hearn, "Introduction to *The Annotated Wizard of Oz*," lxxxvi.

20. See, for example, *Wonder City*, ch. 16, and *Runaway*, ch. 16; cf. Baum's *Marvelous*, ch. 10, and *Patchwork*, ch. 19.

21. In researching the materials discussed in this chapter, I consulted the original Reilly & Lee publications of the Oz books from the early 1900s, a collection of which is held in the Baldwin Library of Historical Children's Literature, Department of Special and Area Studies Collections, University of Florida Smathers Library. I thank Suzan Alteri and Michele Wilbanks for their invaluable assistance in researching Neill's illustrations of Oz, as well as for the Baldwin Library's assistance in securing images from the early editions of Baum's novels. I additionally consulted Reilly & Lee's 1956 reprint editions—which for the most part faithfully reconstruct the originals but delete some color plates and repaginate the volumes. I also thank John Venecek of the University of Central Florida Library for some timely advice.

CHAPTER 6. CULTURAL PROJECTION, HOMOSOCIAL ADVENTURING, AND THE QUEER CONCLUSIONS OF FLOYD AKERS'S BOY FORTUNE HUNTERS SERIES

1. This continuity error is explained by the fact that Baum earlier published *The Boy Fortune Hunters in Alaska* and *The Boy Fortune Hunters in Panama* under the pseudonym

Capt. Hugh Fitzgerald. These works were respectively titled *Sam Steele's Adventures on Land and Sea* (1906) and *Sam Steele's Adventures in Panama* (1907).

2. H. Alan Pickrell, "Recycled Steele: L. Frank Baum's Boys' Series Books," 24.

3. Ernest May, *American Imperialism*, 3. On US imperialism during the late nineteenth and early twentieth centuries, see also Colin Moore, *American Imperialism and the State, 1893–1921*; on the early roots of American imperialism, see Andy Doolen, *Fugitive Empire*.

4. It should be noted that Sam Steele's adversaries in *The Boy Fortune Hunters in Alaska* are white pirates. This book of the series is consequently less interested in issues of racial and ethnic othering, yet these antagonists are still marginalized owing to their social class.

5. Bill Thompson, "Bibliographia Pseudonymiana: Capt. Hugh Fitzgerald: *Sam Steele's Adventures on Land and Sea* and Floyd Aker's: *The Boy Fortune Hunters in Alaska*," 28.

6. Harold Anderson, "Human Behavior and Personality Growth," 3; italics in original.

7. Judith Butler, *The Judith Butler Reader*, 189.

8. Amanda Chapman, "Queer Elasticity: Imperial Boyhood in Late Nineteenth-Century Boys' Adventure Fiction," 57.

9. J. A. Mangan, "Noble Specimens of Manhood: Schoolboy Literature and the Creation of a Colonial Chivalric Code," 191.

10. Joseph Bristow, *Empire Boys: Adventures in a Man's World*, 226.

11. G. Stanley Hall, *Adolescence*, 617.

12. Kathryn McInally, "Not Quite White (Enough): Intersecting Ethnic and Gendered Identities in *Looking for Alibrandi*," 59; italics in original.

13. Such disparaging portraits also appear in the more genteel novels penned under Baum's Edith Van Dyne pseudonym, who similarly stereotypes Hispanic men as obsessed with jewelry, as in the description of antagonist Ramon Ganza in *The Flying Girl and Her Chum*: "His face was smeared with dust and grime and the whole aspect of the outlaw was ghastly and repulsive—perhaps rendered more acute by the jewelled rings that loaded his fingers" (*Chum*, ch. 28). In a particularly galling passage of the same novel, Captain Krell declares the exponential superiority of white men over Hispanics: "One white man is worth six Mexicans" (*Chum*, ch. 20). In the Aunt Jane's Nieces series, Uncle John states succinctly, "Mexicans are stupid creatures to have around" (*Ranch*, ch. 1). Collectively, Baum's Edith Van Dyne exposes herself as grossly prejudiced.

14. *Khedive* refers to the rulers of Egypt from 1867 to 1914 who served as the sultan of Turkey's viceroy. Sam justifies his actions by referring to Turkish rule over Egypt, yet the end result—absconding with artifacts that belong in the Cairo Museum—would remain the same.

15. Susan Stryker and Jim van Buskirk, *Gay by the Bay: A History of Queer Culture in the San Francisco Bay Area*, 18.

16. Edward Said, *Orientalism*, 1. See also Joseph Allen Boone, *The Homoerotics of Orientalism*.

17. Samir Dayal, "By Way of an Afterword," 310.

18. Shari Huhndorf, *Going Native: Indians in the American Cultural Imagination*, 6.

CHAPTER 7. GENDER, GENRES, AND THE QUEER FAMILY ROMANCE OF EDITH VAN DYNE'S AUNT JANE'S NIECES SERIES

1. Rebekah Revzin, "American Girlhood in the Early Twentieth Century: The Ideology of Girl Scout Literature, 1913–1930," 262.

2. Ellen Singleton, "Grace and Dorothy: Collisions of Femininity and Physical Activity in Two Early Twentieth-Century Book Series for Girls," 131.

3. Paige Gray, *Cub Reporters*, 59.

4. Catherine Tosenberger, "The True (False) Bride and the False (True) Bridegroom," 208.

5. In another such instance in Edith Van Dyne's Mary Louise series, readers encounter Jo, a Japanese American man, who is referred to as "the Jap" (*Soldier*, ch. 20); Baum further describes him "as silent and inscrutable as the race from which he sprang" (*Soldier*, ch. 26). In *The Master Key* the protagonist Rob uses the derogatory term *Jap* when flying over the landscape and observing giant birds: "It's no wonder the Japs draw ugly pictures of these monsters" (*Key*, ch. 15).

6. Ramona Caponegro, "The Accidental Sleuth: Investigating Mysteries and Class in Three Series for Girls," 15.

7. Joe Sutliff Sanders, "Spinning Sympathy: Orphan Girl Novels and the Sentimental Tradition," 56.

8. George Dove, *The Reader and the Detective Story*, 10. See also John Cawelti, *Adventure, Mystery, and Romance: Formula Stories as Art and Popular Culture*, 80–105.

9. Edgar Allan Poe, *The Portable Edgar Allan Poe*, 254.

10. Arthur Conan Doyle, *The Sign of the Four*, chap. 6, p. 41; italics in original.

11. For additional connections between Baum and Doyle, see Richard Rutter, "Cyclic Mysteries: Parallel Tracks in the Detective Fiction of L. Frank Baum and Arthur Conan Doyle," 2–3.

12. The name Maud Stanton unites Baum's wife's name of Maud Gage Baum with his mother's name of Cynthia Ann Stanton Baum.

13. Alan Pickrell, "L. Frank Baum's *Aunt Jane's Nieces*: Pseudonyms Can Pay Off," 168.

14. Of Baum's five Mary Louise novels, Mary Louise and Josie O'Gorman successfully solve only the intertwined puzzles of Alora Jones's mysterious father and Alora's kidnapping, which are depicted in the appropriately titled *Mary Louise Solves a Mystery*.

15. Oddly, the governor later contradicts himself: "I say 'we' have discovered this, but really it was Phoebe who solved the whole mystery" (*Phoebe*, ch. 24). This appears more a kind rhetorical gesture than an accurate assessment of the novel's events.

16. J. Halberstam, *The Queer Art of Failure*, 3

17. Derek Pearsall, *Arthurian Romance: A Short Introduction*, 21.

18. R. B. Gill, "*The Wind in the Willows* and the Style of Romance," 159.

19. Dan'l also appears as a character in Baum's poetry, in the eponymous poem included in *By the Candelabra's Glare* (*Glare*, 65).

20. Sigmund Freud, "Family Romances" (1909), *The Standard Edition of the Complete Psychological Works of Sigmund Freud*, vol. 9, p. 237.

21. Maria Tatar, "From Rags to Riches: Fairy Tales and the Family Romance," 32.

22. Alexander Doty, *Making Things Perfectly Queer: Interpreting Mass Culture*, 41. Doty's reference to a spectator highlights his interest in television and cinematic narratives, but his wider point concerning narrative structure holds for readers and novels.

23. This reading of the Aunt Jane's Nieces series is based on the original novels, but as Randolph Cox documents, Baum changed the ending *of Aunt Jane's Nieces in the Red Cross* significantly from its original 1915 text to its 1918 publication. In the new ending of this novel, Maud Stanton marries Charlie Holmes, a cameraman filming the battlefields of World War I, and beautiful Beth marries noble Dr. Gys. As Cox notes, "Patsy is left single, but it is likely she will marry Ajo as soon as the war is over. Uncle John is just as happy to have one niece to look after for the time being" (*"Aunt Jane's Nieces on Tour*: A Probably Phantom Title," 189–90). This variant ending complicates but does not overwrite the interpretations advanced in this chapter, for, as Cox notes, Uncle John remains with one niece still under his control, with Beth likely facing the same narrative constraints as Louise following her marriage.

24. Barbara Creed, "Lesbian Bodies: Tribades, Tomboys, and Tarts," 88.

CONCLUSION: QUEER ETHICS AND BAUM'S PREJUDICES

1. Joe Herring learns that his father, punningly named Lovelace, was a lace smuggler in *The Boy Fortune Hunters in Egypt* (*Egypt*, ch. 19). In *Aunt Jane's Nieces on the Ranch*, Mildred Travers divulges the circumstances of her mysterious background, including her father's crimes as a lace smuggler: "He . . . purchased laces and other goods in Mexico and brought them into the United States secretly, without paying the duty which the robbing government officials imposed" (*Ranch*, ch. 15). In *John Dough and the Cherub*, a "mad camel trampled the Sheik to death" (*Dough*, ch. 1); chapter 26 of *The Boy Fortune Hunters in Egypt* is titled "The Mad Camel."

2. Edward Wagenknecht, *Utopia Americana*, 37.

3. For an insightful overview of Baum's reception over the course of the twentieth century, see Suzanne Rahn, "Analyzing Oz: The First One Hundred Years," ix–xxxviii, as well as her *The Wizard of Oz: Shaping an Imaginary World*, 12–22.

4. Gabriele Dietze, Elahe Haschemi Yekani, and Beatrice Michaelis, "Modes of Being vs. Categories," 119.

5. Henry Louis Gates Jr., *Loose Canons: Notes on the Culture Wars*, 31–32; italics in original.

6. Martin Joseph Ponce, "Queers Read What Now?," 317.

7. Ponce, "Queers Read What Now?," 319.

8. Kimberlé Crenshaw, "Mapping the Margins," 1299.

9. Gloria Anzaldúa, "(Un)natural Bridges, (Un)safe Spaces," 4.

10. Laura Jiménez, "My Gay Agenda."

WORKS CITED

PRIMARY SOURCES

L. Frank Baum's Works (listed chronologically by series and/or subject matter)

The Oz Series

The Wonderful Wizard of Oz. Reilly & Lee, 1900.
The Marvelous Land of Oz. Reilly & Lee, 1904.
Queer Visitors from the Marvelous Land of Oz: The Complete Comic Strip Saga, 1904–1905. Sunday Press, 2009.
Ozma of Oz. Reilly & Lee, 1907.
Dorothy and the Wizard in Oz. Reilly & Lee, 1908.
The Road to Oz. Reilly & Lee, 1909.
The Emerald City of Oz. Reilly & Lee, 1910.
The Patchwork Girl of Oz. Reilly & Lee, 1913.
Tik-Tok of Oz. Reilly & Lee, 1914.
The Little Wizard Stories. Reilly & Britton, 1914.
The Scarecrow of Oz. Reilly & Lee, 1915.
Rinkitink in Oz. Reilly & Lee, 1916.
The Lost Princess of Oz. Reilly & Lee, 1917.
The Tin Woodman of Oz. Reilly, 1918.
The Magic of Oz. Reilly & Lee, 1919.
Glinda of Oz. Reilly & Lee, 1920.

Fairy Tales, Alphabets, and Miscellaneous Juvenile Texts

Mother Goose in Prose. Way & Williams, 1897.
By the Candelabra's Glare: Some Verse. Privately printed, 1898.
Father Goose: His Book. George M. Hill, 1899.
The Army Alphabet. George M. Hill, 1900.
The Navy Alphabet. George M. Hill, 1900.
A New Wonderland. R. H. Russell, 1900.
The Songs of Father Goose. George M. Hill, 1900.
American Fairy Tales. George M. Hill, 1901.

Dot and Tot of Merry Land. George M. Hill, 1901.
The Master Key: An Electrical Fairy Tale. Bowen-Merrill, 1901.
The Life and Adventures of Santa Claus. Bowen-Merrill, 1902.
The Enchanted Island of Yew. Bobbs-Merrill, 1903.
The Maid of Athens. Privately printed, 1903.
Prince Silverwings. A. C. McClurg, 1903.
The Surprising Adventures of the Magical Monarch of Mo and His People. Bobbs-Merrill, 1903.
The Woggle-Bug Book. Reilly & Britton, 1905.
Queen Zixi of Ix, or The Story of the Magic Cloak. Century, 1905.
John Dough and the Cherub. Reilly & Britton, 1906.
Father Goose's Year Book; Quaint Quacks and Feathered Shafts for Mature Children. Reilly & Britton, 1907.
Baum's American Fairy Tales: Stories of Astonishing Adventures of American Boys and Girls with the Fairies of Their Native Land. Bobbs-Merrill, 1908.
L. Frank Baum's Juvenile Speaker: Readings and Recitations in Prose and Verse, Humorous and Otherwise. Reilly & Britton, 1910.
Baum's Own Book for Children: Stories and Verses from the Famous Oz Books, Father Goose, His Book, Etc. Etc. Reilly & Britton, 1911.
The Sea Fairies. Reilly & Britton, 1911.
The Daring Twins: A Story for Young Folk. Reilly & Britton, 1911.
Phoebe Daring. Reilly & Britton, 1912.
Sky Island. Reilly & Britton, 1912.
The Snuggle Tales. Reilly & Britton, 1916.

Technical Manuals

The Book of the Hamburgs: A Brief Treatise upon the Mating, Rearing, and Management of the Different Varieties of Hamburgs. H. H. Stoddard, 1886.
The Art of Decorating Dry Goods Windows and Interiors. Show Window Publishing, 1900.

Miscellaneous Edited Texts

The Musical Fantasies of L. Frank Baum. Ed. Alla T. Ford and Dick Martin. The Wizard Press, 1958.
Our Landlady. Ed. Nancy Tystad Koupal. University of Nebraska Press, 1996.

Published Anonymously

The Last Egyptian: A Romance of the Nile. Edward Stern, 1907.

As Floyd Akers

The Boy Fortune Hunters in Alaska. Reilly & Britton, 1908.
The Boy Fortune Hunters in China. Reilly & Britton, 1909.
The Boy Fortune Hunters in Egypt. Reilly & Britton, 1909.
The Boy Fortune Hunters in Panama. Reilly & Britton, 1909.
The Boy Fortune Hunters in Yucatan. Reilly & Britton, 1910.
The Boy Fortune Hunters in the South Seas. Reilly & Britton, 1911.

As Laura Bancroft

The Twinkle Tales. Reilly & Britton, 1906.
Policeman Bluejay. Reilly & Britton, 1907.
Twinkle and Chubbins: Their Astonishing Adventures in Nature-Fairyland. Reilly & Britton, 1911.

As John Estes Cook

Tamawaca Folks: A Summer Comedy. Tamawaca Press, 1907.

As Capt. Hugh Fitzgerald

Sam Steele's Adventures on Land and Sea. Reilly & Britton, 1906.
Sam Steele's Adventures in Panama. Reilly & Britton, 1907.

As Suzanne Metcalf

Annabel: A Novel for Young Folks. Reilly & Britton, 1906.

As Schuyler Staunton

The Fate of a Crown. Reilly & Britton, 1905.
Daughters of Destiny. Reilly & Britton, 1906.

As Edith Van Dyne

Aunt Jane's Nieces. Reilly & Britton, 1906.
Aunt Jane's Nieces Abroad. Reilly & Britton, 1906.
Aunt Jane's Nieces at Millville. Reilly & Britton, 1908.
Aunt Jane's Nieces at Work. Reilly & Britton, 1909.
Aunt Jane's Nieces in Society. Reilly & Britton, 1910.
Aunt Jane's Nieces and Uncle John. Reilly & Britton, 1911.
The Flying Girl. Reilly & Britton, 1911.
Aunt Jane's Nieces on Vacation. Reilly & Britton, 1912.
The Flying Girl and Her Chum. Reilly & Britton, 1912.
Aunt Jane's Nieces on the Ranch. Reilly & Britton, 1913.
Aunt Jane's Nieces Out West. Reilly & Britton, 1914.
Aunt Jane's Nieces in the Red Cross. Reilly & Britton, 1915.
Mary Louise. Reilly & Britton, 1915.
Mary Louise in the Country. Reilly & Britton, 1916.
Mary Louise Solves a Mystery. Reilly & Britton, 1917.
Mary Louise and the Liberty Girls. Reilly & Britton, 1918.
Mary Louise Adopts a Soldier. Reilly & Britton, 1919.

SECONDARY SOURCES

Abate, Michelle Ann. *No Kids Allowed: Children's Literature for Adults*. Baltimore: Johns Hopkins University Press, 2020.
Abate, Michelle Ann. *Tomboys: A Literary and Cultural History*. Philadelphia: Temple University Press, 2008.

Abate, Michelle Ann, and Kenneth Kidd, eds. *Over the Rainbow: Queer Children's and Young Adult Literature*. Ann Arbor: University of Michigan Press, 2011.

Algeo, John. "Oz and Kansas: A Theosophical Quest." In *Proceedings of the Thirteenth Annual Conference of the Children's Literature Association*, edited by Susan R. Gannon and Ruth Anne Thompson, 135–39. Kansas City: University of Missouri, 1988.

Anderson, Harold. "Human Behavior and Personality Growth." In *An Introduction to Projective Techniques and Other Devices for Understanding the Dynamics of Human Behavior*, edited by Harold Anderson and Gladys Anderson, 3–25. Englewood Cliffs, NJ: Prentice-Hall, 1951.

Anzaldúa, Gloria. "(Un)natural Bridges, (Un)safe Spaces." In *This Bridge We Call Home: Radical Visions for Transformation*, edited by Gloria Anzaldúa and Analouise Keating, 1–5. New York: Routledge, 2002.

Arens, William. *The Man-Eating Myth: Anthropology and Anthropophagy*. Oxford: Oxford University Press, 1979.

Avery, Gillian, and Julia Briggs, eds. *Children and Their Books*. Oxford: Clarendon, 1989.

Bakhtin, Mikhail. *Rabelais and His World*. Translated by Hélène Iswolsky. Bloomington: Indiana University Press, 1984.

Barrett, Laura. "From Wonderland to Wasteland: *The Wonderful Wizard of Oz*, *The Great Gatsby*, and the New American Fairy Tale." *Papers on Language and Literature* 42, no. 2 (2006): 150–80.

Baum, Frank Joslyn, and Russell P. MacFall. *To Please a Child: A Biography of L. Frank Baum, Royal Historian of Oz*. Chicago: Reilly & Lee, 1961.

Bauska, Barry. "The Land of Oz and the American Dream." *Markham Review* 5 (1976): 21–24.

Baxter, Kent. *The Modern Age: Turn-of-the-Century American Culture and the Invention of Adolescence*. Tuscaloosa: University of Alabama Press, 2008.

Beaumont, Matthew. "Heathcliff's Great Hunger: The Cannibal Other in *Wuthering Heights*." *Journal of Victorian Culture* 9, no. 2 (2004): 137–63.

Beckwith, Osmond. "The Oddness of Oz." *Children's Literature* 5 (1976): 74–91.

Bell, J. L. "Dorothy the Conqueror." *Baum Bugle* 49, no. 1 (2005): 13–17.

Bell, J. L. "Home-Made Bread by the Best Modern Machinery: An Appreciation of *John Dough and the Cherub*." *Baum Bugle* 50, no. 3 (2006): 7–13.

Bernstein, Robin. "Children's Books, Dolls, and the Performance of Race; or, The Possibility of Children's Literature." *PMLA* 126, no. 1 (2011): 160–69.

Bernstein, Robin. *Racial Innocence: Performing American Childhood from Slavery to Civil Rights*. New York: New York University Press, 2011.

Bishop, Clifford, and Cristina Moles Kaupp. "The Erotic Muse: Art and Artifice." In *Sexualia: From Prehistory to Cyberspace*, edited by Clifford Bishop and Xenia Osthelder, 326–65. New York: Könemann, 2001.

Boone, Joseph Allen. *The Homoerotics of Orientalism*. New York: Columbia University Press, 2014.

Bristow, Joseph. *Empire Boys: Adventures in a Man's World*. New York: Routledge, 1991.

Brotman, Jordan. "A Late Wanderer in Oz." *Chicago Review* 18, no. 2 (1965): 63–73.

Bruhm, Steven, and Natasha Hurley, ed. *Curiouser: On the Queerness of Children*. Minneapolis: University of Minnesota Press, 2004.

Butler, Judith. "Doing Justice to Someone: Sex Reassignment and Allegories of Transsexuality." *GLQ* 7, no. 4 (2001): 621–36.

Butler, Judith. *The Judith Butler Reader*. Edited by Sara Salih. London: Blackwell, 2004.

Cadogan, Mary, and Patricia Craig. *You're a Brick, Angela! A New Look at Girls' Fiction from 1839 to 1975*. London: Victor Gollancz, 1976.

Campbell, Joseph. *The Hero with a Thousand Faces*. Princeton: Princeton University Press, 1949.

Caponegro, Ramona. "The Accidental Sleuth: Investigating Mysteries and Class in Three Series for Girls." *Clues: A Journal of Detection* 27, no. 1 (2009): 11–21.

Cawelti, John. *Adventure, Mystery, and Romance: Formula Stories as Art and Popular Culture*. Chicago: University of Chicago Press, 1976.

Chapman, Amanda. "Queer Elasticity: Imperial Boyhood in Late Nineteenth-Century Boys' Adventure Fiction." *Children's Literature* 46 (2018): 56–77.

Chaston, Joel. "Baum, Bakhtin, and Broadway: A Centennial Look at the Carnival of Oz." *Lion and the Unicorn* 25, no. 1 (2001): 128–49.

Chaston, Joel. "If I Ever Go Looking for My Heart's Desire: 'Home' in Baum's Oz Books." *Lion and the Unicorn* 18 (1994): 209–19.

Clark, Beverly Lyon. *Kiddie Lit: The Cultural Construction of Children's Literature in America*. Baltimore: Johns Hopkins University Press, 2003.

Clark, Beverly Lyon. *Regendering the School Story: Sassy Sissies and Tattling Tomboys*. New York: Garland, 1996.

Clark, H. Nichols B. "High Adventure and Fantasy: Art for All Ages." In *Myth, Magic, and Mystery: One Hundred Years of American Children's Book Illustrations*, edited by Trinkett Clark and H. Nichols B. Clark, 125–56. New York: Roberts Rinehart, 1996.

Clueless. Directed by Amy Heckerling. Paramount, 1995.

Cosslett, Tess. *Talking Animals in British Children's Fiction, 1786–1914*. Farnham: Ashgate, 2006.

Counihan, Carol M. *The Anthropology of Food and Body: Gender, Meaning, and Power*. New York: Routledge, 1999.

Cox, Randolph. "*Aunt Jane's Nieces on Tour*: A Probably Phantom Title." *Dime Novel Roundup* 74 (2005): 187–90.

Craft, Christopher. "Alias Bunbury: Desire and Termination in *The Importance of Being Earnest*." *Representations* 31 (1990): 19–46.

Crane, Susan. *Gender and Romance in Chaucer's* Canterbury Tales. Princeton: Princeton University Press, 1994.

Creed, Barbara. "Lesbian Bodies: Tribades, Tomboys, and Tarts." In *Sexy Bodies: The Strange Carnalities of Feminism*, edited by Elizabeth Grosz and Elspeth Probyn, 86–103. New York: Routledge, 1995.

Crenshaw, Kimberlé. "Mapping the Margins: Intersectionality, Identity Politics, and Violence against Women of Color." *Stanford Law Review* 43, no. 6 (1992): 1241–199.

Cross, Gary. *The Cute and the Cool: Wondrous Innocence and Modern American Children's Culture*. Oxford: Oxford University Press, 2004.

Culver, Stuart. "Growing Up in Oz." *American Literary History* 4, no. 4 (1992): 607–28.

Culver, Stuart. "What Mannikins Want: *The Wonderful Wizard of Oz* and The Art of Decorating Dry Goods Windows." *Representations* 21 (1998): 97–116.

Daniel, Carolyn. *Voracious Children: Who Eats Whom in Children's Literature*. New York: Routledge, 2006.

Dayal, Samir. "By Way of an Afterword." *Post-Colonial, Queer: Theoretical Intersections*. Edited by John Hawley, 305–25. Albany: State University of New York Press, 2001.

Deane, Paul. *Mirrors of American Culture: Children's Fiction Series in the Twentieth Century*. Lanham, MD: Scarecrow, 1991.

Deleuze, Gilles. *Masochism: Coldness and Cruelty*. Brooklyn, NY: Zone, 1991.

Devroe, Teresa. "Follow the Yellow Brick Road to Nirvana." *Wittenberg University East Asian Studies Journal* 16 (1991): 1–20.

Dietze, Gabriele, Elahe Haschemi Yekani, and Beatrice Michaelis. "Modes of Being vs. Categories: Queering the Tools of Intersectionality." In *Beyond Gender: An Advanced Introduction to Futures of Feminist and Sexuality Studies*, edited by Greta Olson, Mirjam Horn-Schott, Daniel Hartley, and Regina Leonie, 117–36. New York: Routledge, 2018.

Doolen, Andy. *Fugitive Empire: Locating Early American Imperialism*. Minneapolis: University of Minnesota Press, 2005.

Doty, Alexander. *Making Things Perfectly Queer: Interpreting Mass Culture*. Minneapolis: University of Minnesota Press, 1993.

Dove, George. *The Reader and the Detective Story*. Bowling Green, KY: Bowling Green State University Popular Press, 1997.

Doyle, Arthur Conan. *The Sign of the Four*. Edited by Christopher Roden. 1890. Oxford: Oxford University Press, 1993.

Drummond, Kent, Susan Aronstein, and Terri Rittenburg. *The Road to Wicked: The Marketing and Consumption of Oz from L. Frank Baum to Broadway*. New York: Palgrave Macmillan, 2018.

Duffley, Sean P. "Baum under Scrutiny: Early Reviews of *John Dough and the Cherub*." *Baum Bugle* 50, no. 3 (2006): 14–17.

Eco, Umberto. "The Frames of Comic Freedom." In *Carnival!*, edited by Thomas A. Sebeok, 1–9. Berlin: Mouton de Gruyter, 1984.

Edelman, Lee. *No Future: Queer Theory and the Death Drive*. Durham, NC: Duke University Press, 2004.

Elder, George R. *An Encyclopedia of Archetypal Symbolism*. 2 vols. Boulder, CO: Shambhala, 1996.

Fletcher, Horace. *Fletcherism: What It Is, or How I Became Young at Sixty*. Brooklyn, NY: Frederick A. Stokes, 1913.

Fletcher, Horace. *The New Glutton or Epicure*. Brooklyn, NY: Frederick A. Stokes, 1917.

Freud, Sigmund. "Family Romances" (1909). In *The Standard Edition of the Complete Psychological Works of Sigmund Freud*, edited by James Strachey, 9: 235–41. 24 vols. London: Hogarth Press, 1953–1974.

Gates, Henry Louis Jr. *Loose Canons: Notes on the Culture Wars*. Oxford: Oxford University Press, 1992.

Gessel, Michael. "Tale of a Parable." *Baum Bugle* 36, no. 1 (1992): 19–23.

Gessel, Michael, Nancy Tystad Koupal, and Fred Erisman. "The Politics of Oz: A Symposium." *South Dakota History* 31, no. 2 (2001): 146–68.

Gill, R. B. "*The Wind in the Willows* and the Style of Romance." *Children's Literature in Education* 43 (2012): 158–69.
Gill-Peterson, Julian. *Histories of the Transgender Child*. Minneapolis: University of Minnesota Press, 2018.
Giovanelli, Dina, and Natalie Peluso. "Feederism: A New Sexual Pleasure and Subculture." In *Handbook of the New Sexuality Studies*, edited by Steven Seidman, Nancy Fischer, and Chet Meeks, 331–36. New York: Routledge, 2006.
Girard, René. *Deceit, Desire, and the Novel: Self and Other in Literary Structure*. Translated by Yvonne Freccero. Baltimore: Johns Hopkins University Press, 1965.
Gray, Paige. *Cub Reporters: American Children's Literature and Journalism in the Golden Age*. Albany: SUNY Press, 2019.
Green, Jonathon. *Green's Dictionary of Slang*. Edinburgh: Chambers, 2010. Online.
Greene, Douglas G., and Peter E. Hanff. *Bibliographia Oziana: A Concise Bibliographical Checklist of the Oz Books by L. Frank Baum and His Successors*. Rev. ed. 1976. N.p.: International Wizard of Oz Club, 1988.
Gubar, Marah. "Risky Business: Talking about Children in Children's Literature Criticism." *Children's Literature Association Quarterly* 38, no. 4 (2013): 450–57.
Guglielmo, Jennifer, and Salvatore Salerno, eds. *Are Italians White? How Race Is Made in America*. New York: Routledge, 2003.
Halberstam, J. *The Queer Art of Failure*. Durham, NC: Duke University Press, 2011.
Hall, G. Stanley. *Adolescence*. 2 vols. New York: Appleton, 1915.
Hamby, Alonzo. "Progressivism: A Century of Change and Rebirth." In *Progressivism and the New Democracy*, edited by Sidney Milkis and Jerome Mileur, 40–80. Amherst: University of Massachusetts Press, 1999.
Hearn, Michael Patrick. "Introduction to *The Annotated Wizard of Oz*." In *The Annotated Wizard of Oz: Centennial Edition* by L. Frank Baum. Edited by Michael Patrick Hearn, xiii–cii. Norton, 2000.
Hearn, Michael Patrick. "John R. Neill: The Royal Illustrator of Oz and More!" *Illustration* 5, no. 17 (2006): 6–33.
Hearn, Michael Patrick. *W. W. Denslow: The Other Wizard of Oz*. Chadds Ford, PA: Brandywine Conservancy, 1996.
Herring, Scott, ed. *Autobiography of an Androgyne* by Ralph Werther. New Brunswick, NJ: Rutgers University Press, 2008.
Hudlin, Edward W. "The Mythology of Oz: An Interpretation." *Papers on Language and Literature* 25, no. 4 (1989): 443–62.
Huhndorf, Shari. *Going Native: Indians in the American Cultural Imagination*. Ithaca: Cornell University Press, 2001.
Impelluso, Lucia. *Nature and Its Symbols*. Translated by Stephen Sartarelli. Los Angeles: J. Paul Getty Museum, 2004.
Janes, Dominic. *Oscar Wilde Prefigured: Queer Fashioning and British Caricature, 1750–1900*. Chicago: University of Chicago Press, 2016.
Jiménez, Laura. "My Gay Agenda: Embodying Intersectionality in Children's Literature Scholarship." *Lion and the Unicorn* 41, no. 1 (2017): 104–12.

Junko, Yoshido. "Uneasy Men in the Land of Oz." In *Children's Literature and the Fin de Siècle*, edited by Roderick McGillis, 157–68. Westport, CT: Praeger, 2003.

Karp, Andrew. "Utopian Tension in L. Frank Baum's Oz." *Utopian Studies* 9, no. 2 (1998): 103–21.

Keeling, Kara, and Scott Pollard. *Table Lands: Food in Children's Literature*. Jackson: University Press of Mississippi, 2020.

Kidd, Kenneth. *Freud in Oz: At the Intersections of Psychoanalysis and Children's Literature*. Minneapolis: University of Minnesota Press, 2011.

Kidd, Kenneth. "Introduction: Lesbian/Gay Literature for Children and Young Adults." *Children's Literature Association Quarterly* 23, no. 3 (1998): 114–19.

Kidd, Kenneth. *Making American Boys: Boyology and the Feral Tale*. Minneapolis: University of Minnesota Press, 2004.

Kidd, Kenneth. "Queer Theory's Child and Children's Literature Studies." *PMLA* 126, no. 1 (2011): 182–88.

King, Thomas. "Performing 'Akimbo': Queer Pride and Epistemological Prejudice." In *The Politics and Poetics of Camp*, edited by Moe Meyer, 23–50. New York: Routledge, 1994.

Lacan, Jacques. *The Seminar of Jacques Lacan, Book VII: The Ethics of Psychoanalysis, 1959–1960*. Edited by Jacques-Alain Miller. Translated by Dennis Porter. New York: Norton, 1997.

Lady Gaga. "Born This Way." Streamline, 2010.

Lesnik-Oberstein, Karin. *Children's Literature: Criticism and the Fictional Child*. Oxford: Clarendon, 1994.

Lévi-Strauss, Claude. *The Origin of Table Manners*. Vol. 3 of *Mythologiques*. Translated by John and Doreen Weightman. New York: Harper & Row, 1978.

Littlefield, Henry M. "The Wizard of Oz: Parable on Populism." *American Quarterly* 16 (1964): 47–58.

Loncraine, Rebecca. *The Real Wizard of Oz: The Life and Times of L. Frank Baum*. New York: Gotham, 2009.

Love, Heather. "Queer." *Transgender Studies Quarterly* 1, no. 1–2 (2014): 172–76.

Lucchesi, Joe. "'The Dandy in Me': Romaine Brooks's 1923 Portraits." In *Dandies: Fashion and Finesse in Art and Culture*, edited by Susan Fillin-Yeh, 153–84. New York: New York University Press, 2001.

Lurie, Alison. *Boys and Girls Forever: Children's Classics from Cinderella to Harry Potter*. New York: Penguin, 2003.

Lurie, Alison. *Don't Tell the Grown-Ups: The Subversive Power of Children's Literature*. Boston: Back Bay, 1990.

MacDonnell, Francis. "'The Emerald City Was the New Deal': E. Y. Harburg and *The Wonderful Wizard of Oz*." *Journal of American Culture* 13, no .4 (1990): 71–75.

Mangan, J. A. "Noble Specimens of Manhood: Schoolboy Literature and the Creation of a Colonial Chivalric Code." In *Imperialism and Juvenile Literature*, edited by Jeffrey Richards, 173–94. Manchester: Manchester University Press, 1989.

Martínez-San Miguel, Yolanda, and Sarah Tobias. "Trans Fantasizing: From Social Media to Collective Imagination." In *Trans Studies: The Challenge to Hetero/Homo Normativities*, edited by Yolanda Martínez-San Miguel and Sarah Tobias, 230–42. New Brunswick, NJ: Rutgers University Press, 2016.

Mason, Derritt. *Queer Anxieties of Young Adult Literature and Culture*. Jackson: University Press of Mississippi, 2021.

Mason, Derritt. "Trans." In *Keywords for Children's Literature*, edited by Philip Nel, Lissa Paul, and Nina Christensen, 181–84. New York: New York University Press, 2021.

May, Ernest. *American Imperialism: A Speculative Essay*. Boston: Atheneum, 1968.

McGerr, Michael. *A Fierce Discontent: The Rise and Fall of the Progressive Movement in America, 1870–1920*. New York: Free Press, 2003.

McInally, Kathryn. "Not Quite White (Enough): Intersecting Ethnic and Gendered Identities in *Looking for Alibrandi*." *Papers: Explorations into Children's Literature* 17, no. 2 (2007): 59–66.

Michel, Dee. *Friends of Dorothy: Why Gay Boys and Gay Men Love The Wizard of Oz*. N.p.: Dark Ink Press, 2018.

Mills, Robert. "'Whatever You Do Is a Delight to Me!' Masculinity, Masochism, and Queer Play in Representations of Male Martyrdom." *Exemplaria* 13, no. 1 (2001): 1–37.

Montaigne, Michel de. "Of Cannibals." In *The Complete Works: Essays, Travel Journal, Letters*, edited and translated by Donald M. Frame, 182–93. New York: Everyman's Library, 2003.

Moore, Colin. *American Imperialism and the State, 1893–1921*. Cambridge: Cambridge University Press, 2017.

Moore, Raylyn. *Wonderful Wizard, Marvelous Land*. Bowling Green, KY: Bowling Green University Press, 1974.

Morrison, Toni. *Playing in the Dark: Whiteness and the Literary Imagination*. Cambridge: Harvard University Press, 1992.

Neill, John R. *Lucky Bucky in Oz*. Chicago: Reilly & Lee, 1942.

Neill, John R. *The Runaway in Oz*. Illus. Eric Shanower. New York: Books of Wonder, 1995.

Neill, John R. *The Scalawagons of Oz*. Chicago: Reilly & Lee, 1941.

Neill, John R. *The Wonder City of Oz*. Chicago: Reilly & Lee, 1940.

Nel, Philip. *Was the Cat in the Hat Black? The Hidden Racism of Children's Literature and the Need for Diverse Books*. Oxford: Oxford University Press, 2017.

Nel, Philip, Lissa Paul, and Nina Christensen, eds. *Keywords for Children's Literature*. New York: New York University Press, 2021.

Nodelman, Perry. *The Hidden Adult: Defining Children's Literature*. Baltimore: Johns Hopkins University Press, 2008.

Norton, Jody. "Transchildren and the Discipline of Children's Literature." In *Over the Rainbow: Queer Children's and Young Adult Literature*, edited by Michelle Ann Abate and Kenneth Kidd, 293–313. Ann Arbor: University of Michigan Press, 2011.

Obeyesekere, Gananath. *Cannibal Talk: The Man-Eating Myth and Human Sacrifice in the South Seas*. Berkeley: University of California Press, 2005.

Oxford English Dictionary. oed.com.

Pattison, Stephen. *Shame: Theory, Therapy, Theology*. Cambridge: Cambridge University Press, 2000.

Pearsall, Derek. *Arthurian Romance: A Short Introduction*. London: Blackwell, 2003.

Pickrell, H. Alan. "L. Frank Baum's *Aunt Jane's Nieces*: Pseudonyms Can Pay Off." *Dime Novel Round-Up* 74 (October 2005): 163–75.

Pickrell, H. Alan. "Recycled Steele: L. Frank Baum's Boys' Series Books." *Baum Bugle* 51, no. 1 (2007): 21–27.

Plato. *The Symposium.* Translated by Christopher Gill. New York: Penguin, 1999.
Poe, Edgar Allan. *The Portable Edgar Allan Poe.* Edited by Gerald Kennedy. New York: Penguin, 2006.
Ponce, Martin Joseph. "Queers Read What Now?" *GLQ* 24, no. 2–3 (2018): 315–41.
Prime-Stevenson, Edward. *Left to Themselves: Being the Ordeal of Philip and Gerald.* Edited by Eric Tribunella. 1891. Richmond, VA: Valancourt, 2016.
Rahn, Suzanne. "Analyzing Oz: The First One Hundred Years." In *L. Frank Baum's World of Oz: A Classic Series at 100*, edited by Suzanne Rahn, ix–xxxviii. Atlanta/Lanham, MD: Children's Literature Association/Scarecrow Press, 2003.
Rahn, Suzanne. *The Wizard of Oz: Shaping an Imaginary World.* New York: Twayne, 1998.
Reneau, Reneau H. *Misanthropology: A Florilegium of Bahumbuggery.* Inglewood, CA: Donlazaro Translations, 2003.
Revzin, Rebekah. "American Girlhood in the Early Twentieth Century: The Ideology of Girl Scout Literature, 1913–1930." *Library Quarterly* 68, no. 3 (1998): 261–75.
Reynolds, Kimberley. *Girls Only? Gender and Popular Children's Fiction in Britain, 1880–1910.* Philadelphia: Temple University Press, 1990.
Reynolds, Kimberley, ed. *Modern Children's Literature: An Introduction.* New York: Palgrave Macmillan, 2005.
Rich, Adrienne. "Compulsory Heterosexuality and Lesbian Existence." *Signs* 5, no. 4 (1980): 631–60.
Rich, Adrienne. "Reflections on 'Compulsory Heterosexuality.'" *Journal of Women's History* 16, no. 1 (2004): 8–11.
Riley, Michael. *Oz and Beyond: The Fantasy World of L. Frank Baum.* Lawrence: University of Kansas Press, 1997.
Ritter, Gretchen. "Silver Slippers and a Golden Cap: L. Frank Baum's *The Wonderful Wizard of Oz* and Historical Memory in American Politics." *Journal of American Studies* 31, no. 2 (1997): 171–202.
Rogers, Katharine. *L. Frank Baum: Creator of Oz.* New York: St. Martin's, 2002.
Rose, Jacqueline. *The Case of Peter Pan, or the Impossibility of Children's Fiction.* Philadelphia: University of Pennsylvania Press, 1984.
Rutter, Richard. "Cyclic Mysteries: Parallel Tracks in the Detective Fiction of L. Frank Baum and Arthur Conan Doyle." *Baum Bugle* 35, no. 3 (1991): 2–3.
Rzepka, Charles. "'If I Can Make It There': Oz's Emerald City and the New Woman." *Studies in Popular Culture* 10, no. 2 (1987): 54–66.
Sackett, S. J. "The Utopia of Oz." *Georgia Review* 14 (1960): 275–91.
Said, Edward. *Orientalism.* New York: Vintage, 1979.
Sampson, Emma Speed. *Josie O'Gorman.* Chicago: Reilly & Lee, 1923.
Sampson, Emma Speed. *Josie O'Gorman and the Meddlesome Major.* Chicago: Reilly & Lee, 1924.
Sampson, Emma Speed. *Mary Louise and Josie O'Gorman.* Chicago: Reilly & Lee, 1922.
Sampson, Emma Speed. *Mary Louise at Dorfield.* Chicago: Reilly & Lee, 1920.
Sampson, Emma Speed. *Mary Louise Stands the Test.* Chicago: Reilly & Lee, 1921.
Sanday, Peggy R. *Divine Hunger: Cannibalism as a Cultural System.* Cambridge: Cambridge University Press, 1986.

Sanders, Joe Sutliff. "Spinning Sympathy: Orphan Girl Novels and the Sentimental Tradition." *Children's Literature Association Quarterly* 33, no. 1 (2008): 41–61.
Schwartz, Evan. *Finding Oz: How L. Frank Baum Discovered the Great American Story*. New York: Houghton Mifflin, 2009.
Sedgwick, Eve Kosofsky. *Between Men: English Literature and Male Homosocial Desire*. New York: Columbia University Press, 1985.
Singleton, Ellen. "Grace and Dorothy: Collisions of Femininity and Physical Activity in Two Early Twentieth-Century Book Series for Girls." *Children's Literature in Education* 35, no. 2 (2004): 113–34.
Skubal, Susanne. *Word of Mouth: Food and Fiction after Freud*. New York: Routledge, 2002.
Smith, Victoria Ford. "Adult." In *Keywords for Children's Literature*, edited by Philip Nel, Lissa Paul, and Nina Christensen, 1–3. New York: New York University Press, 2021.
Snow, Jack. *Who's Who in Oz*. Chicago: Reilly & Lee, 1954.
Somerville, Siobhan. *Queering the Color Line: Race and the Invention of Homosexuality in American Culture*. Durham, NC: Duke University Press, 2000.
Spears, Richard. *Slang and Euphemism*. New York: Jonathan David, 1981.
Steinberg, Leo. *The Sexuality of Christ in Renaissance Art and in Modern Oblivion*. London: Faber & Faber, 1984.
Stockton, Kathryn Bond. "Eve's Queer Child." In *Regarding Sedgwick: Essays on Queer Culture and Critical Theory*, edited by Stephen M. Barber and David L. Clark, 181–99. New York: Routledge, 2002
Stockton, Kathryn Bond. *The Queer Child, or Growing Sideways in the Twentieth Century*. Durham, NC: Duke University Press, 2009.
Stryker, Susan, and Paisley Currah. "Introduction." *Transgender Studies Quarterly* 1, no. 1–2 (2014): 1–18.
Stryker, Susan, and Jim van Buskirk. *Gay by the Bay: A History of Queer Culture in the San Francisco Bay Area*. San Francisco: Chronicle Books, 1996.
Suited. Directed by Jason Benjamin. Casual Romance Productions, 2016.
Tangney, June Price, and Ronda L. Dearing. *Shame and Guilt*. New York: Guilford, 2002.
Tatar, Maria. "From Rags to Riches: Fairy Tales and the Family Romance." *Children's Literature Association Quarterly* 7, no. 2 (1982): 31–34.
Tatar, Maria. *The Heroine with 1001 Faces*. New York: Liveright, 2021.
Teverson, Andrew. *Fairy Tale*. Abingdon: Routledge, 2013.
Thomas, Ebony Elizabeth. *The Dark Fantastic: Race and the Imagination from Harry Potter to the Hunger Games*. New York: New York University Press, 2019.
Thompson, Bill. "Bibliographia Pseudonymiana. Capt. Hugh Fitzgerald: *Sam Steele's Adventures on Land and Sea* and Floyd Aker's: *The Boy Fortune Hunters in Alaska*." *Baum Bugle* 51, no. 1 (2007): 28–31.
Thurber, James. "The Wizard of Chitenango." *New Republic* 12 (December 1934): 141–42.
Tosenberger, Catherine. "The True (False) Bride and the False (True) Bridegroom." In *Transgressive Tales: Queering the Grimms*, edited by Kay Turner and Pauline Greenhill, 207–21. Detroit: Wayne State University Press, 2012.
Tribunella, Eric. "Childhood Studies: Children's and Young Adult Literatures." *The Cambridge History of Gay and Lesbian Literature*, edited by E. L. McCallum and Mikko Tuhkanen, 695–711. Cambridge: Cambridge University Press, 2014.

Trites, Roberta Seelinger. "Queer Discourse and the Young Adult Novel: Repression and Power in Gay Male Adolescent Literature." *Children's Literature Association Quarterly* 23, no. 3 (1998): 143–51.

Trites, Roberta Seelinger. *Waking Sleeping Beauty: Feminist Voices in Children's Novels.* Iowa City: University of Iowa Press, 1997.

Tuerk, Richard. "Dorothy's Timeless Quest." *Mythlore* 17, no. 1 (1990): 20–24.

Tuerk, Richard. *Oz in Perspective: Magic and Myth in the L. Frank Baum Books.* Jefferson, NC: McFarland, 2007.

Venables, Robert W. "Looking Back at Wounded Knee." *Northeast Indian Quarterly* 7, no. 1 (1990): 36–37.

Wagenknecht, Edward. *Utopia Americana.* Seattle: University of Washington Book Store, 1929.

Walters, Karla. "Seeking Home: Secularizing the Quest for the Celestial City in *Little Women* and *The Wonderful Wizard of Oz.*" In *Reform and Counterreform: Dialectics of the Word in Western Christianity since Luther*, edited by John C. Hawley, 153–71. Berlin: Mouton de Gruyter, 1994.

Warner, Marina. "Fee Fie Fo Fum: The Child in the Jaws of the Story." *Cannibalism and the Colonial World*, edited by Francis Barker, Peter Hulme, and Margaret Iversen, 158–82. Cambridge: Cambridge University Press, 1998.

The Wizard of Oz. Directed by Victor Fleming. MGM, 1939.

Wood, Roy C. *The Sociology of the Meal.* Edinburgh: Edinburgh University Press, 1995.

Yellin, Eric. *Racism in the Nation's Service: Government Workers and the Color Line in Woodrow Wilson's America.* Chapel Hill: University of North Carolina Press, 2013.

Zipes, Jack. *Fairy Tale as Myth, Myth as Fairy Tale.* Lexington: University Press of Kentucky, 1994.

INDEX

Abate, Michele Ann, 9, 31, 63
Aberdeen Saturday Pioneer, 18, 23, 117
adolescence, 30, 138–39
Alcott, Louisa May, 175
Akers, Floyd (L. Frank Baum), 4, 18, 133; cultural projection in Boy Fortune Hunters series, 136–46; depictions of homosocial attraction in, 146–53; queer character names in, 6; queer desire and narrative closure in, 153–58
Andersen, Hans Christian, 163–64
Anzaldúa, Gloria, 191
Aunt Jane's Nieces series, 4; antisemitic depictions in, 25; as detective fiction, 19, 168–74; as fairy tale, 162–67; queer and trans-ish characters in, 42, 61–65, 68–70; as queer family romance, 182–85; racist language in, 28; as romance, 175–82; and women's pseudonymous publishing, 18

Bakhtin, Mikhail, 195n31
Bancroft, Laura (L. Frank Baum), 4, 18, 19; *Policeman Bluejay*, 4, 18, 19, 111, 188; *Twinkle and Chubbins: Their Astonishing Adventures in Nature Fairyland*, 4; *The Twinkle Tales*, 4, 29
Baum, Frank Joslyn, 18, 53, 197n22
Baum, L. Frank: anti-Arabic depictions by, 28, 108–9, 190, 200n22; anti-Asian depictions by, 28–29, 85, 143, 156, 190; anti-Black and racist depictions by, 15, 26–29, 85, 190; anti-Hispanic depictions by, 63–64, 142–43, 190, 202n13; anti-Italian depictions by, 64, 190; anti-Native American depictions and literary treatment of genocide by, 23–24, 165, 190; antisemitic depictions by, 24–25, 190; brief biography of, 17–18; dedication pages of his books, 118, 131; depictions of heterosocial couples, 88–89; depictions of homosocial couples, 71–83, 148–53; depictions of queer male identities, 67–71; depictions of whiteness, 15, 25–26, 64, 139–41, 146, 165, 190; and fairy tales, 20; female personas of, 18–19; inconsistencies in his plotlines, 187–88; potential queerness of, 3–4; progressive politics of, 21–29; pseudonyms of, 4, 18–19; puns and wordplay of, 4–5, 187; queer lexicon of, 4–12; and series fiction, 28–30; views of women's rights, 22–23; views on monopolies, 21

Works by: *American Fairy Tales*, 4, 20, 24, 27, 42, 43, 111, 186; *The Army Alphabet*, 18; *The Art of Decorating Dry Goods Windows and Interiors*, 18, 84, 197n13; *By the Candelabra's Glare*, 18, 203n19; *The Daring Twins*, 4, 19, 21, 71, 111, 137, 168, 173, 188; *Dot and Tot of Merryland*, 82, 86, 97, 186, 187; *The Enchanted Island of Yew*, 5, 8–9, 34, 36, 42, 44–47, 51, 82, 86–88, 186; *John

Dough and the Cherub, 4, 5, 34, 51–54, 66, 86, 108–9, 111, 126–28; *The Last Egyptian: A Romance of the Nile*, 4, 8, 42, 149, 175; *The Life and Adventures of Santa Claus*, 4–5, 190; *The Master Key: An Electrical Fairy Tale*, 4, 20, 24, 103, 141, 149, 203n5; *Mother Goose in Prose*, 18, 24, 111, 187; *The Navy Alphabet*, 18; *Our Landlady* columns, 18, 22, 24, 117, 197n15; *Phoebe Daring*, 4, 23, 27, 70–71, 168, 170, 174, 188, 203n15; *Queen Zixi of Ix, or the Story of the Magic Cloak*, 4, 12, 47–52, 67; *Rose Lawn Home Journal*, 17; *The Sea Fairies*, 5, 21, 41, 114; *Sky Island*, 22, 68, 82–83, 186, 198n17; *The Songs of Father Goose*, 5; *The Surprising Adventures of the Magical Monarch of Mo*, 4, 27, 69, 109, 187; *The Woggle-Bug Book*, 84–85, 187, 190. *See also* Oz series
Baum, L. Frank pseudonyms and publications. *See* Akers, Floyd; Bancroft, Laura; Cook, John Estes; Metcalf, Suzanne; Staunton, Schuyler; Van Dyne, Edith
Baum, Maud Gage, 18, 110, 203n12
Bell, J. L., 37, 52
Bernstein, Robin, 26, 32
Butler, Judith, 12–13, 135

camel tramplings, 188, 204n1
Campbell, Joseph, 37, 197n11
canons, literary and queer, 188–92
carnivalesque, 10, 12, 17, 30–33, 37, 86, 110
Carroll, Lewis, 10, 164
castration, 79
Cervantes, Miguel de, 174
Chaston, Joel, 118
children's literature: books with queer titles, 9; carnivalesque nature of, 30–33, 110; constructions of children and childhood in, 31–32; defined fiction series, 19; depictions of gender, 32; queerness of, 29–33, 67, 73–83; readers of, 31–32; trans possibilities in, 36

Clark, Beverly Lyon, 32
Clueless (film), 3
Cook, John Estes (L. Frank Baum), 4, 18; *Tamawaca Folks: A Summer Comedy*, 4, 8, 42, 64, 88, 184, 188
Crenshaw, Kimberlé, 191

dandies and dandyism, 68–71, 75, 148
Daniel, Carolyn, 93, 99
Denslow, W. W., 76, 110–12, 120–23
deus ex machina conclusions, 172–73
"dick" (word), 6–7
Doyle, Arthur Conan, 19, 168–70

Eco, Umberto, 31
Edelman, Lee, 73
Edison, Thomas, 5
Ellis, Havelock, 30
erotic triangles, 57, 75, 77–78, 81

"faggot" (word), 5, 7
fairy tales, 20, 66, 85, 161–67, 180
fat festishism/feederism, 85–86
feminist theories, 35
fetishes and fetishism, 30, 83–86, 158
Fleming, Victor, 11
Fletcher, Horace, and Fletcherism, 103, 200n20
Flower, Jessie Graham, 162
Freud, Sigmund, 30, 180
"friends of Dorothy" (phrase), 11–12, 194n19

Garland, Judy, 11
Gates, Henry Louis, Jr., 189
"gay" (word), 7–8, 111–12
gender studies, 189
Gilbert and Sullivan, 11
Girard, René, 75, 78
"going native," 140–41

Hall, G. Stanley, 138
Haggard, H. Rider, 133–34
Hawthorne, Nathaniel, 174
Hearn, Michael Patrick, 123, 128

imperialism and imperialist fictions, 134–35, 139

Jesus, depictions of, 114

Kidd, Kenneth, 9, 30, 32–33
"kiki" (word) and Baum's "Ki-Ki," 8–10, 193n13
Koupal, Nancy Tystad, 117, 197n14–15

Lacan, Jacques, 80
lace smuggling, 188, 204n1
"lesbian" (word) and lesbianism, 5–6, 57, 60, 129
Lévi-Strauss, Claude, 91, 99
Littlefield, Henry, 21
Low, Juliette Gordon, 162
Lurie, Alison, 31, 93

Mary Louise series, 4, 22, 25; and detective fiction, 168–69, 173–74; illustrations in, 111; masochism, 30, 83, 86–88; queer and trans-ish characters in, 5–7, 10, 41, 59, 68; racist tropes in, 27, 165; romance in, 89; violence against women in, 185; wholesomeness of, 28
Mason, Derritt, 30, 36
Metcalf, Suzanne (L. Frank Baum), 4, 18, 89; *Annabel: A Novel for Young Folks*, 4, 22, 89, 186
monomyth, 37, 197n11
Montaigne, Michel de, 95
Morrison, Toni, 25–26

Neill, John R., 14; queer illustrations of Baum's books, 112–28; queer illustrations of his own Oz books, 128–31; and the Golden Age of Illustration, 111
Nel, Philip, 26
Norton, Jody, 36–37

Orientalism, 149, 199n21
Oz series, 4; as American and modernized fairy tales, 20, 66; antinormative themes, 16; Baum's attempt to end, 19–20; depictions of cannibalism, 90–109; female armies in, 38–40; gender roles in, 38–43; as modernized fairy tales, 20; queer allusions in, 6–7; queer readers' reception of, 15–16; queerness of, 72–83; trans characters in, 44–45, 53–54; utopian themes, 37–38, 90

Parrish, Maxfield, 111
Plato, 81–82
Poe, Edgar Allan, 168
Ponce, Martin Joseph, 189–90
Prime-Stevenson, Edward, 30
Progressivism, 20–29

"queer" (word), 9–10
queer theories, 35
queers and queerness: Baum's homosocial couples, 71–83; Baum's queer male identities, 67–71, 77; cannibalism as queer theme, 90–91; and children, 32; and children's literature, 29–33; and ethics, 186–92; meaning of in Baum's fiction, 9–11; slang, 5–11

realism and "gentle realism," 163
Rogers, Katharine M., 21, 120
Rose, Jacqueline, 31

Said, Edward, 149
Sampson, Emma Speed, 89, 199n22
Scott, Walter, 133
Sedgwick, Eve, 75, 78
series fiction, 18–20
sexology, 29–30
Shakespeare, William, 3, 55
Sherlock Holmes, 19, 168–70
Snow, Jack, 112, 194n6
Staunton, Schuyler (L. Frank Baum), 4, 5, 12, 18, 25, 34, 41, 55, 88; *Daughters of Destiny*, 4, 25, 41, 89, 199n21; *The Fate of a Crown*, 4, 12, 55–61, 64–65; queer characters in *The Fate of a Crown*, 5–7
Steinberg, Leo, 114

Stevenson, Robert Louis, 133
Stockton, Kathryn Bond, 32
Swift, Jonathan, 24

Tatar, Maria, 180, 197n11
Thomas, Ebony Elizabeth, 26
Thompson, Ruth Plumly, 111, 128, 194n6
Thurber, James, 112
tomboys, 63, 169, 185, 200n22
transness, transgenderness, and "trans touches": in Baum's adventures tales, 55–65; Baum's characters with "trans touches," 37–65; in Baum's fantasy tales, 43–54; in children's literature, 36; trans theories, 35–36
Tribunella, Eric, 30
Trite, Roberta Seelinger, 31, 32

utopias and utopianism, 14, 21, 37, 44–45, 72–76, 90, 105–8, 187

Van Dyne, Edith (L. Frank Baum), 4, 5, 11, 18, 23, 28, 55, 89, 158; Flying Girl series, 4, 19, 23, 42, 70, 170, 184–85, 202n13. *See also* Aunt Jane's Nieces series; Mary Louise series
Venables, Robert W., 24
Verne, Jules, 134
von Sacher-Masoch, Leopold, 86

Wagenknecht, Edward, 188
Wells, H. G., 134
Wilde, Oscar, 3, 10–11, 68–69
Wilson, Woodrow, 23
Wizard of Oz, The (film), 11, 194n18

ABOUT THE AUTHOR

Tison Pugh, Pegasus Professor of English at the University of Central Florida, is author or editor of over twenty books. His work in the field of children's culture includes *Harry Potter and Beyond: On J. K. Rowling's Fantasies and Other Fictions*, *The Queer Fantasies of the American Family Sitcom*, and *Innocence, Heterosexuality, and the Queerness of Children's Literature*.

www.ingramcontent.com/pod-product-compliance
Lightning Source LLC
Chambersburg PA
CBHW020539200725
29784CB00006B/31